GOD'S JOYFUL SURPRISE

GOD'S JOYFUL SURPRISE

FINDING YOURSELF LOVED

Sue Monk Kidd

1817

Harper & Row, Publishers, San Francisco

Cambridge, Hagerstown, New York, Philadelphia, Washington
London, Mexico City, São Paulo, Singapore, Sydney·

Library of Congress Cataloging-in-Publication Data

Kidd, Sue Monk.
  God's joyful surprise.

  Bibliography: p.
  1. God—Love. 2. Spiritual life. 3. Kidd, Sue Monk. I. Title.
BT140.K53 1987   248.4   87- 45182
ISBN 0-06-064579-2

87 88 89 90 91 RRD 10 9 8 7 6 5 4 3 2 1

*To my
mother and father
with
love and gratitude*

Contents

Acknowledgments

God's Joyful Surprise could not have been published without the help of many people. Among them is Arthur Gordon, who believed in me when I was an inexperienced and tentative beginner. It was he who first suggested that I write it, and his early nurture that gave me the audacity to begin.

I am deeply grateful to the book editors at Guideposts for their kindness and great patience with me as I embarked on my first book. To Terri Castillo for her insightful suggestions and creative collaboration throughout the writing. To Mary Ruth Howes for her long labor and sensitive editing, which had a transforming effect on this work. And to Harold Van't Hof and Betty Gold for their expert help and guidance.

I also feel appreciation for the magazine editors at Guideposts who have offered me their friendship and encouragement as I worked.

I owe a debt of gratitude to Rev. Robert Burgreen and Betty Blackerby, who prayed with me over the writing of the manuscript for more than two years, and Dr. Frances Mims, whose earlier classes opened me to the world of writing.

And certainly I thank my two children for their long-suffering during the intensive periods of writing this book. But my deepest thank you goes to my husband Sandy, who has been there through it all with his remarkable understanding and insistence that I *could* write this book . . . I really could. For every meal he has helped cook, for every minute he has cared for the children so I could concentrate on this work, I will love him always.

And finally, I am grateful to the Father of us all, to whom I owe everything.

GOD'S JOYFUL SURPRISE

Introduction

WHEN I WAS small and my father arrived home from work, I would race to the door to greet him. Now and then I would find him standing there with his hands behind his back. "Pick a hand," he would say. Those words touched me like an electric current. For I knew, hidden behind my father, buried in the fold of one of his hands, there was a surprise meant for me.

"This one!" I would shout, pointing wildly. And he would whisk out his hand and slowly, too slowly, uncurl his fingers. And finally there it would be, shining in his palm, a gift I could not have imagined. A golden paper ring from one of my grandaddy's cigars to wear on my finger, a cardinal feather for my hair or sometimes a silver nickel.

I have not thought of it until now, but it seems my father's surprises had a curious way of coming on the days I needed them most. The days I fell off my bicycle or went to the doctor with a sore throat or broke something irreplaceable in the house. I suppose Mother told him. Somehow he knew that I needed to be surprised with a gift of love that would help bind up my broken day.

Now I like to think of myself as grown up. Yet I cannot seem to get rid of the longing to search my father's hands. Perhaps that's why I have found such joy in discovering that God is a Father of infinite surprises. And sure enough, they always seem to come at one of those broken or special times in life when you need them most.

We seem to have lost touch with the God of surprises. We forget that He is always up to something wondrous and unexpected where you and I are concerned. He taps on our heart's door, waiting for us to open up and discover what He holds for us. If we manage to hear His knock, sometimes what we find is almost unbearably precious. It turns out to be the one thing we need most in our life, or as my daughter Ann used to say, "the onliest thing," meaning there is nothing more splendid in the universe.

This book is about the adventure of opening up one of God's surprises, the most joyful one of all—His love. I want to share the ups and downs, ins and outs, whys and hows of finding yourself loved by God. I don't mean a simple Sunday school awareness that God loves us. I'm talking about *experiencing* in the depths of our soul, the breathtaking intimacy with God's presence that is available to each of us. I'm talking about discovering God's love as a transfiguring source of wholeness for whatever brokenness we have in our life.

This surprise of God's is more than anything we have imagined. The one echo in the universe is God's great confession, "I love you." Yet I'm convinced most of us have never heard it, not in the sense that we leave everything and follow after it. Not in the sense that our lives are transformed by it. God's love is so immense and powerful, so tender and dazzling with joy that most of us have only felt the hem of it. We have underestimated its power, its availability, its passion. Likewise we have underestimated our ability to tap into it.

Many of us have become so busy and hurried, so sunk in our troubles and trivialities, that we lose the heart-to-heart intimacy with God's presence that He intends. We miss the core of joy his love can create in our lives, the way it heals our broken places and pulls us toward wholeness. Instead our lives fill up with quiet hungers and empty pockets.

The deepest need of the human heart is to be loved. To be loved utterly and completely just as we are, no matter what. We respond to this need in a lot of different ways. Sometimes we try to be perfect in order to earn love. Or we repress our need until all that remains of it is a vague sense of restlessness and yearning. And meanwhile, inside that secret place which God fashioned for us to dwell with Him, we grow hungrier, emptier. The experience of God as a loving, encompassing reality in the midst of our days can be the most elusive one of our lives.

Yet it is the very surprise God lifts out to us. How then, can we discover it? How can we find ourselves so profoundly loved by God? How do we embark upon this inner and outer journey of intimacy that makes all things new? And how will we be able to sustain it?

That is why I am writing this book. To try and shed a bit of light on these questions. The truth is we need help learning how to hear the knock of God's love upon our life. We need help learning how to open the door and receive His love as fully and deeply as possible. And probably most of all we need assistance to make a new home for God within our inner life. A home that lasts. One that sends us out into the world braver, stronger and more loving.

I'm not speaking impersonally here, but with the conviction of experience. I know firsthand about the desperate need to be loved by God just as I am. For years there was an awful hole in my heart that I tried to fill in an odd assortment of ways, ways typical to lots of Christians, I'm afraid, though at the time I had no idea that's what I was doing.

It was during a difficult and broken time in my life that I caught the faint sound of God's knocking on my door. He came with a breathtaking surprise, with the one thing I needed most in all the world—the words, "I love you." And gradually, sometimes with much struggle and vacillation, I stepped out into what was for me an immense and extraordinary pilgrimage into God's love and presence.

I want to share this journey with you as honestly and personally as I can, knowing that as we listen to the stories of others, we somehow hear our own story more clearly. Our stories are the bread we have to offer one another. So I share my bread, as well as the bread others have passed along to me, with the hope we will be not only companions through the pages ahead, but friends on a kindred journey deep into the heart of God.

As we begin, I confess that inside I have the same electric feeling I used to have as a child when I searched my father's hands. Only now it has grown sharper still. For God's hands are full. The surprise of His love awaits.

SUE MONK KIDD
ANDERSON, SOUTH CAROLINA

Behold, I have set before thee an open door.
REVELATION 3:8

1

A Sound at the Door

DECEMBER SUNLIGHT streamed through the window, creeping across the kitchen table where I huddled over one of my things-to-do list. The list was long and ragged. The week before I had dived into Christmas, and today I noticed I was to begin decorating the house. I pushed the list aside, washed the breakfast dishes, then dragged the paint-splotched ladder to the fireplace, intending to drape the mantle with cedar. But as I started up the ladder, the most astonishing thing happened. A sudden pain sliced across my chest—gripping, searing, frightening pain.

It vanished, and I took a deep breath, blinking at the room. Then without warning it came again, all across my chest. My heart meanwhile seemed to leap in my ears and beat against my eardrums.

Instinctively I reached for my pulse, as I had been taught to do in nurse's training, glancing at the second hand sweeping around the clock—160 beats a minute. That couldn't be right. It should be half that! I slowed my breathing and counted again ... 162! My heart thundered, blocking every other sound from the room. The pain swelled, faded, returned. A thread of panic threatened to unravel in me as I walked to the phone and called the doctor.

"Come to the office immediately," I was instructed.

I hung up and dialed my husband at the college where he works as chaplain and religion teacher. I hesitated to drive myself to the doctor—what if the pain came back . . . only worse? The phone in his office rang and rang. *Please, Sandy, answer.* Once again I could feel the odd sensation rising in my chest, could hear my pulse beginning to hammer in my ears faster and faster. *Dear God* . . . I gave up and grabbed my car keys.

Minutes later I was lying on the table in the doctor's office attached to an electrocardiograph, wondering how such an incomprehensible thing could happen to a healthy young woman. I'd never been sick, not really. As the doctor squinted at the squiggly lines on the EKG, all the sights and sounds swirling around me seemed strange and ominous—the cold metal stethoscope on my skin, the syringe drawing blood from my arm, the network of wires attached to my chest and ankles, the rustle of EKG paper scrolling onto the floor. Never mind that I was myself a registered nurse. None of that prepared me in the least for being on the table myself. None of it made any difference now as the fear rose in me.

I tried to think of other things. Sandy, my husband. Our two children. I could see Bob, the oldest at eight with his straight, penny-brown hair and easy grin. Ann at four with curling hair and darkly fringed blue eyes. Suddenly I tried to sit up. Who was going to pick up Ann at play school at noon? And what about the Christmas cookies I was supposed to bake for Bob's school party tomorrow? *Oh Lord, what am I doing here?*

I simply didn't have time to get sick.

Somewhere in my head I harbored an image of myself holding up a big round sphere of family, career, home, church, community and self—like a smaller version of Atlas, the Titan who bore the earth on his shoulders. Unfortunately, the world

I carried around had gotten bigger and heavier, and I'd been spinning it as fast as I could to keep everything going the way I envisioned it should. I seemed to think if I stopped, if I let go, everything would tumble down and break into pieces, or at the very least develop a few cracks.

I wanted to be supermom, superwife, successful career woman, church pillar, community helper and fulfilled person, all at once. The past couple of years especially had been spent trying to accomplish all that. If I'd been inclined, perhaps I could have looked back over those months and seen how I was defining my life around those herculean expectations. But I was too busy, too lost in all my doings.

I Will Be a Writer . . .

A typical glimpse into that period of my life might be the morning a couple of years earlier when I had made an announcement at the breakfast table: "I've decided to become a writer." Sandy's eyebrows lifted slightly. No one said a word. Only the cereal popped in the bowl. "But Mama, you're already a nurse," Bob finally said.

"I know. But I'm going to be a writer, too," I replied, trying to convince myself as much as him. Even as a child I had always wanted to be two or three things when I grew up. I had no idea how I would manage it. I was working three evenings a week at the hospital, caring for the house and children during the day and trying to carry on an array of other activities. But writing was something I *had* to do.

I poked a spoon of oatmeal in Ann's mouth and hurried Bob toward the bathroom to brush his teeth. "When will you have time?" Sandy asked. "You're already carrying on two jobs." I hated it when he sounded so sensible.

"Organization," I proclaimed. "If you're organized, you can do just about anything."

He grinned a little.

After breakfast I phoned and signed up for a weekly night

class in writing. Then I made out an organization chart. I drew a circle on a sheet of paper and divided it into five parts labeled family/household, career, church, social and self. For me life always fell into categories. My only control over the influx of demands seemed to be sorting and organizing it into form and order. Next I penciled inside each section my responsibilities in that area and a time schedule for activity. By the time I was through, I had written over the sides of the circle and up and down the page, listing a bewildering array of things I had to do.

Robert Johnson wrote in his book *She* that the ego is like a goblet that we dip into the full, thundering river of life. A woman is "flooded by the rich vastness of possibilities of life and is drawn to all of them, usually all at once."[1] We need to develop he said, the capacity to view the river from above with eagle vision, then dip the goblet in at one meaningful place. Without this ability we tend to wade out into the river from the banks and become overwhelmed.

That was me. I was splashing about from one part of the river to the other, scattering myself in countless endeavors. Focus. What a fragile and elusive thing it was for me! I had not caught onto the power contained in focusing at all.

Despite my organization chart, I couldn't find a spare block of time in which to write, so I made a pact with myself to write two hours every day in snatches of time—fifteen minutes here, twenty there. It was an up-and-down experience in more ways than one. That first morning I sat down with pen and paper, wrote two sentences, got up and poured grape juice for Ann, sat down and wrote one more, then got up to mop the juice she had spilled. Two years old at the time, Ann's demands were constant. Absorbed momentarily in my writing, my mind drifted away. When I "came to," Ann had squeezed the toothpaste onto the bath mat and dunked the toilet paper roll in the toilet. By bedtime I had seven sentences.

At mid-morning Ann and I walked the neighborhood collecting for the heart fund. Her legs got tired at the second house and I carried her the rest of the way, writing receipts and making change with her in my arms. *Please God, let this be over soon*, I kept repeating.

As we trudged back home, she fretted, late for her nap. When I laid her down on the bed, I felt an overwhelming need to lie down, too. I stared at the pillow, then turned abruptly and left. Merely thinking about lying down in the middle of the day, when I wasn't even sick, made me feel guilty. There was too much to do.

While she napped, I hurriedly put together a slide presentation for a church group about our year in Africa, jotted a few notes for the devotional I was to give at the faculty wives club, and mixed a batch of cookie dough for Bob's after-school snack. I didn't buy cookies—good mothers "made" cookies.

Then as Ann and I ate lunch, I quickly pushed a needle and thread through a piece of cross stitching for a hobbies display at church. It seemed unlikely I would complete it on time, though I'd set aside lunch times for getting it done—it was even penciled on my calendar.

I lived by the lists and scribbles jotted there. I may have had a lot of clutter in my life. But it was organized clutter! Glancing over the day's page as I tried to sew and eat, I noticed a 1:30 appointment for the spaniel's rabies shot. How had I overlooked that? It was 1:20. I tossed the dishes in the sink, grabbed Captain and raced out the door. I lived with a chronic sense of being behind, trying to catch up.

In fact, the vet took longer than expected and I was ten minutes late picking up Bob at school. There he was standing all alone in the school yard, holding his Luke Skywalker lunch box. "Where were you, Mama?" he asked with the slightest tremble in his throat.

Throughout the afternoon we sped from one errand to another as I followed my list—groceries, the cleaners, Bob's soccer shoes, a quick visit to the Home for Abused Children where I was helping remodel the nursery. Finally the three of us hurried home, so I could cook dinner, get to exercise class and still make my first writing class. I fell into bed exhausted, feeling vaguely unraveled inside. "There has to be a better way," I muttered to Sandy from my pillow.

"What are you referring to?" he asked in a puzzled voice.

"Life," I answered and fell fast asleep.

. . . and Supermom

The next morning I was more determined than ever to deal smoothly with the day's activities. Bob woke complaining with an earache. I sat beside him on the bed, feeling torn, knowing I had to work the afternoon shift at the hospital, yet needing to stay with him, too. Sandy offered to come home early so I could go to work. I agreed, but that did not stop the irrational guilt.

Now, looking back, I see the convergence of so many harmful patterns. Not only role-overload and role-conflict, but a perfectionist attitude that set up rigid requirements for all my roles and left me plowed with guilt when I didn't measure up. Which was most of the time. But I never let myself stop to examine my life.

After an hour with Bob at the doctor's office, I came home to prepare an evening meal before going to work. Sandy was more than willing to cook, or do most anything else. But doing it myself, was, I figured, part of being a superwife. I had a little chart of yellow and green vegetables on the refrigerator just to make sure they got a variety. I clipped articles on nutrition and spent hours working out menus. They got brownies made with carob powder instead of chocolate and I squeezed all the juice fresh. Practically every slice of whole wheat bread I ever put in Bob's lunch box was cut with cookie cutters into some appealing shape. I'd gotten that idea from an article called "Supermom Tips." I had a file of them.

When I arrived home from the hospital shift at 11:30 P.M. I tiptoed into Bob's room and touched his forehead. Cool, thank goodness. Then, because I was so keyed up from nearly nine hours on a hectic pediatric ward and could never fall asleep right away, I washed clothes and folded laundry. It was quiet and there was only me in the late-night silence of the house.

As the months went by, I gradually squeezed out more time to pursue a writing career, pounding away at odd times on a little portable typewriter, which I set up on the ironing board in a corner of the den. I began getting assignments, deadlines. Sometimes I crawled out of bed in the middle of the night to finish articles. I lugged the typewriter outside while Ann played, and sat in the parking lot at the dentist's office, furiously trying to type while Bob got his teeth cleaned.

As the pace grew more relentless, the need to spend time with the children increased, too. I was forever thinking up activities like trips to the zoo, building a bird feeder, planting avocado seeds, visits to the library. I actually penciled them on my calendar. One day I bought C. S. Lewis' Narnia Chronicles and at bedtime we curled up together in Bob's bed to read *The Lion, the Witch and the Wardrobe*. I fell asleep in the first chapter and they went and got their daddy, who put me to bed.

I was a PTA grade mother that year and had planned the Christmas party for Bob's schoolroom. It hadn't seemed enough to simply make sugar cookies. I did that every ordinary week. For several nights I stayed up past midnight icing and decorating an array of Santas, reindeers and snowmen with green scarves and top hats. Then I hung them on a cookie tree. The next day the children ripped them off and gobbled them down without noticing a thing. "Did you see Santa's hand-painted eyelashes?" I asked one little boy. He shook his head and I got that same futile feeling I had the time I worked six hours on Ann's Raggedy Ann birthday cake and it was demolished in six minutes.

Would I be team mother for Bob's soccer team? Would I work the bake sale for the school carnival? Would I make posters for a cub scout activity? Yes. Yes. Yes. The requests flowed in an endless stream. I accepted those three all in the same day.

Basically, whatever I was asked to do, I did. How desperately I wanted to please everyone! I could not say the word *no*. I nearly did once. The principal of a local elementary school called and asked me to serve as judge of their writing contest. I would have to read about fifty compositions during the week. It was the same week I was entertaining fourteen college students for a cookout. "I'm so sorry," I said. "Could you possibly find someone else?" Later I felt so badly about it, I called back and accepted. I was reading themes while I bathed and walked to the mailbox.

Maybe it would have been a bit easier if I hadn't been one of those meticulous housekeepers, a "neat-freak," as Bob termed it. There was a joke in our house that if you were drinking a glass of water, you should never set it down till you were completely finished, because I would scoop it up, wash and dry it between swallows. I was like a human vacuum cleaner walking the house, picking up toys, socks, books and cups, putting everything away. I suppose I wanted "house beautiful." In fact that spring I launched a redecorating project that had me agonizing for weeks over wallpaper swatches and how many walls to knock out.

. . . and Community-Minded

But house, family and career were not the only parts of my life that had become rushed and busy and cluttered. I had a list of things on my organization chart under the categories "social" and "self." There were frequently college teas where I poured punch as the chaplain's wife, or meetings of one sort or another.

We had also joined a country club and tried to keep up our membership by frequenting the pool in the summer and dropping in for dinner. It was never very relaxing, however, since arranging to leave the children with a baby sitter was generally a monumental task. Plus I seemed to have an overwhelming concern about what I should wear, and whether I'd worn it the last time and who would see me.

"We really ought to put in an appearance," I would say to Sandy from time to time, referring to some fundraiser or an art exhibit. When we attended, I was usually smiling grandly, wishing I were home.

As program chairman of the city writers' guild, along with PTA and church committees, I stayed on the phone a lot. But I discovered that with a long cord, I could talk and prepare a meal in the kitchen at the same time. My aim was to do two or three things at once. I could not simply sit down and watch the television news. I hemmed blue jeans, checked Bob's homework *and* watched the news.

Psychologists have named people like me "type A." We are the impatient, perfectionist bunch, who hurry up to stop at red lights, then rev our motors till the lights turn green. Type As run higher risks of harmful stress. But I'd never heard of type A folks. I only knew it seemed urgent to accomplish the most I could in each moment. I carried various projects in the front seat of the car, so I could pick them up when caught at train crossings or while waiting for the school bell to ring. Half the time I went from task to task as though propelled from a sling shot, sped by an immense hungry push inside to do a lot, do it perfect, and do it fast. Doing was everything. I measured myself by how much I accomplished. I mean, nobody ever said, "What did you *become* today?" They asked, "What did you *do*?"

"Take time for yourself" was a theme that was coming into vogue about that time. I was hearing how I needed to do some things just for me. I needed to be fit, have a hobby, go back to school, read, travel. . . . I'd ruled out going back to school, remembering the graduate course in nursing I'd attempted the year before. The vast amount of required reading while tending two pre-schoolers had been impossible. I was sticking to things like aerobics classes, cross-stitching and a reading group which met monthly. But ironically, this "time just for myself" turned into a burden, putting more strain on an already thinned-out schedule.

. . . and Perfect Christian

But perhaps the most driven part of my existence was none of the things I've already mentioned. It was most likely my category labeled "church and religion." I'd grown up in church on something called the "six and eight point record system." As a child, every Sunday morning I filled out a little slip of paper listing six items to be checked off: Present, On Time, Bible Brought, Giving, Worship Attendance and Prepared Lesson. Then when I returned to church on Sunday evening for what we called "Training Union," I got another slip of paper with eight boxes to check. Added were boxes for Daily Bible Reading and Being on the Program.

Among us kids, there was a flurry of competition about who had the most checks. "How many got all eight checks?" my teacher usually asked. In my small eyes an eight-check person was as good as you could get. They got their names written on the blackboard and were asked to hand out hymnbooks or pass the offering basket. This slowly became one of the most important things about religion to me . . . filling up my slip of paper with checks.

As I grew older I became wrapped up in fulfilling the "oughts" of religion. My experience of Christianity evolved into doing things. I took it further than the eight-point slip of paper. I taught Sunday school, planned fellowships, worked in the nursery now and then, served on church committees, and turned up practically every time the church doors opened. In addition to Sunday I went each Wednesday for church supper, prayer service and choir practice. I couldn't sing, so I served as a worker for a children's choir, keeping records and insisting the boys in the back row stand up straight and remove their gum.

Many Sundays, I picked up a prospect card of unchurched people to visit. But the truth was I rarely got to their houses and ended up calling my "prospects" on the phone. My Bible was full of cards I'd never followed up on. Practically every time I opened it, I was reminded what a failure I was at witnessing. But I kept taking the cards, vowing to make more time for them. What was driving me? Why was I constantly "doing"? Why did it never fill the insatiable spaces within? Such questions I never thought to ask.

The pace of my religious activities left little time to get to know God personally, let alone enter the depths and mysteries of God. Unknown even to myself, the spiritual places inside of me, places that should have been nurtured by loving encounters with the Divine and a learning to "be" intimately in God's presence, grew dry and cracked . . . swept with guilt and emptiness.

Despite years of working for God through my organized chaos, I was quietly withering inside . . . hungry to taste God's love. But I never let such pain surface. If it bubbled up, I promptly pushed it down again so that I could walk about in a general state of satisfaction.

The summer before the EKG my church involvement had reached a fevered intensity. As director of the sixth grade Vacation Bible School I'd spent a harried week with over thirty eleven-year-olds, rushing through activities, games and field trips that had taken nearly a month of planning and meetings. On the last day, with all the children gone, I crawled about the room on my hands and knees, scraping papier-mâché off the floor with a kitchen knife, my head throbbing with the confusion of the week. A co-worker stuck her head in the door. "Do you do windows, too?" she joked.

I managed a laugh. "Boy, I hope God appreciates this," I muttered when she'd gone. For that was the whole point. Doing in order to be totally committed. Of course I knew salvation had nothing to do with works, but didn't every "good" Christian get eight checks? Didn't she do all she could for God? Wasn't that the yardstick for a life "laid on the altar"? It was all I seemed to know anyway.

Late one Sunday afternoon in August while the children were lying on the grass catching "roly poly" beetles and dropping them in a jar, I stuck my head through the door and called them inside. "Time for church," I said. It was four thirty. "But Mama, I got eleven roly polies, and I only have to get nine more to have twenty. I've got to get twenty."

"Hurry. We'll be late!" I said.

"But Mama—"

"Hurry up! Church supper begins at five."

Bob set his jar on the patio and shuffled inside. "I don't want to go," he said. "I need to catch nine more." Tears wound through the smudges of dirt on his face.

Ann balked, too. "I'm tired," she cried. "Let's read."

I scrubbed their faces and pulled a Sunday shirt over Bob's head. "I just took it off," he said. It was true. I'd wakened everyone at eight that morning so we could be on time for Sunday school. Then there was "big church," as they called it. We'd arrived home at twelve thirty. I'd cooked, cleaned up the kitchen, turned around twice and it was four. Time to go back for a snack supper, Church Training meeting and finally the evening worship service. Tonight there would be a watermelon cutting after that.

"Don't you want some watermelon?" I asked, trying to assuage the tears.

"No, I just want to catch nine more," Bob insisted. Wails broke out and I rubbed my forehead, realizing I had another awful headache.

But we were *going* to church. It never occurred to me that catching bugs could be very holy business, or that my tenseness was catching—that we needed time to relax. I dragged everyone there, tears and all.

I shall never forget the Scripture we read in Church Training that night. "Be ye therefore perfect, even as your Father which is in heaven is perfect" (Matthew 5:48). I certainly wasn't perfect. If I could just keep showing up and supporting every service and program; if I could just keep doing everything possible for God's kingdom—witnessing, studying the Bible, teaching—maybe . . . I did not know that the word *perfect* in this verse means "whole." That I would figure out the hard way, many struggles later.

Me, Stressed?

By early fall the last twenty months of unrelenting involvement and constant busyness were beginning to wear away the last layer of strength I had. I'd resigned my job at the hospital as the tension grew, but immediately filled the time with writing projects. Those fall mornings I woke feeling tired and overloaded before I even began. But I ignored every warning sign—the increasing sense of frustration, the headaches. Even that December morning, attached to an EKG in the doctor's office, pain coming and going in my chest like a flashing light, denial was still my first response.

When the EKG and other tests proved normal, my doctor sent me right over to the hospital for a more sophisticated echo-cardiogram, promising we would get to the bottom of this, whatever it was. Before I drove to the hospital, I left a message at Sandy's office for him to pick up Ann.

At the hospital I watched the dips and waves on the monitor for nearly two hours. Finally a pleasant cardiologist sauntered into the room. "We've discovered nothing wrong with your heart," he said. "Physically things seem to be fine." He smiled at me, assisting me down from the table. But there was something about his last comment that marred my great relief. What did he mean, *physically* there was nothing wrong? What was this all about?

When I returned home, Sandy was waiting. I poured out the improbable events of the morning, emphasizing that the tests were normal. But he saw the hint of fear in my eyes and held me, stroking the back of my hair. I thought I could feel a tremble in his hands, too.

Inexplicably the episodes of pain came and went the next few days, coupled with the racing pulse. When I returned to my doctor for the follow-up visit, I halfway expected more tests, some news about something they had overlooked. But he glanced over the hospital results and startled me with a question.

"Sue, are you under a lot of pressure?"

For a moment I only looked at him. The rush and clutter of activities that filled my life swirled suddenly through my head . . . the vague restlessness . . . the sense of being unfocused. No, I was simply an active, busy person, doing what practically everyone else was doing. I was involved, that's all. Wasn't that what I was supposed to be?

"Nothing out of the ordinary," I answered him.

"Stress is more ordinary than you might think. And it can have very potent effects," he said, pushing back and looking as if he'd given the talk before. "It creeps up on you."

The rest of it was benign warnings about "learning to relax." I listened in disbelief. He was telling me I was a stress victim! He prescribed tranquilizers, a heart medication, and sent me home thoroughly shaken.

All that evening the pains continued. Sandy cooked dinner, took care of the children's baths and patted my shoulder every time he walked by. He was as bewildered as I was. I sat on the sofa tight as a clenched fist and counted the beats in my wrist like the years of my life. The doctor couldn't be right about the stress . . . could he? It seemed more plausible to me that I was having a heart attack. I just knew I'd end up like the woman who wrote on her tombstone, "See, I told you I was sick"!

Stress . . . did this kind of thing happen to Christians?

It made no sense. Didn't people tell me how "together" I was, meaning I suppose that I seemed to have things under control and get lots done? That part was true. In addition to working for a living and never missing church, I chaired committees, swam for my health (which now seemed ironic), smiled pleasantly and had clean socks in everyone's drawer. But underneath all that, on levels not vividly conscious to me, wasn't it true I was often scrambled and distracted . . . without peace? Even hungry for . . . for *what?*

No, this is ridiculous, I thought, sitting in my den that evening. I didn't want to hear all the "noise" buried inside myself. I didn't want to know what might lie at the depths of my spirit or even guess at what I might come across there.

The doctor said slow down. I would slow down. I wouldn't ask a lot of questions.

I called Ann and Bob over and explained that Mama was going to try and take it a bit easier. "But you are gonna make the gingerbread house, aren't you?" asked Bob.

I looked at him. "Of course, I am." Sandy shot me a sharp frown across the room. He was worrying about practically everything I did. But I felt guilty letting so much go. I sighed. My chest was hurting.

Throughout the holidays I cut out a few of the parties on our calendar and abandoned decorations. I never did hang the cedar on the mantle. But these were mostly token gestures. For despite Sandy's reminders, I carried on much as before. It was as if I didn't know how to "do" life any other way. Besides there was so much around to contend with . . . like Bob and the pink flamingo costume for the Christmas play. His church choir was performing a musical and to Bob's horror he was to wear pink slacks, pink shirt and a vest of pink feathers. He refused to wear "girl stuff" and we went round and round about it for days. Finally I dragged him through store after store in search of pink pants which, as it turned out, could only be found in the girls' departments. Before it was over I wondered if I would need another EKG.

Despite all my activity the chest pains and racing pulse faded completely away as I swallowed the little blue tranquilizers. If I stopped taking them, the episodes returned. That absolutely amazed me. I began to accept that the doctor was right. The problem *was* stress.

I'd had lots of experiences in my life, but none which had had the impact of this encounter with stress. On one level I felt exposed, vulnerable, helpless and angry. How dare something so dumb happen to me! Embarrassment rang through the whole affair. Couldn't I manage my own life any better than this? How in the world had this happened?

But on another level, I felt drawn, touched and compelled,

as if something about the episode reached in and stirred the deep waters of my soul. Perhaps that sounds . . . well, peculiar. It even seemed so to me at the time. But a small whispering voice began to filter out of those days, saying, "You have come upon a time when you must pause and discover and change. This is an opportunity to reshape your life. It is the fullness of time." The resolve not to ask a lot of questions became increasingly impossible. My whole life turned into a question. In the end I couldn't help but wonder what was back of it all.

Is There Anything More?

Do you remember that curious verse in the Bible that tells of a pool in Jerusalem called Bethesda, where the sick, blind and lame gathered? It goes like this: "For an angel went down *at a certain season* into the pool, and troubled the water: whosoever then first after the troubling of the water stepped in was made whole of whatsoever disease he had" (John 5:4, italics mine). The year before the chest pains began, I'd traveled to Israel and stood over the archeological remains of the Bethesda pool in Jerusalem, gazing into its water, puzzling over that verse.

Perhaps the mystery of the waters of Bethesda is also a mystery that happens *inside* us. "At certain seasons," if we are attentive to what's happening in our own soul, in the hidden recesses of our lives, we will see the inner waters of Bethesda troubled by wind and angels . . . readied for something wondrous and healing. The time is ripe. And if we do not ignore our "troubling" event, but listen to it . . . if we step down into our experience like the trusting ones who waded into Bethesda, who knows what can happen. For we do not find wholeness until we are willing to enter the broken, empty places in our lives and confront them honestly. We do not find God's presence without first wading through His absence.

Wholeness comes to those who are willing to risk entering deep into their own experience. If the experience is a painful one—some loss, illness, hunger, restlessness or loneliness—it may be difficult to face. We are conditioned to deny, run from, smooth over or banish what causes us pain. But to grow toward deeper places we must pay attention to our pain and its causes and be willing to let them lead us somewhere.

So it was good I didn't wave the episode away and swallow pills as if nothing had happened. I thought more and more both about the water-stirring event which had disrupted my life, and about how I should respond to it. Gradually I began to "step down" into the experience even though I was still afraid of it and sometimes felt as though I was turning my whole life inside out like a pocket.

Just before Christmas Eve I drove along Main Street on my way shopping. Because what had happened was so much on my mind and heart, because it pricked and pulled and would not go away, I suddenly started praying. It was the first time I'd invited God's attention to the matter, and it's a miracle I didn't run over somebody, for quite suddenly tears blurred my eyes and my shoulders shook as I drove along. "O God, I don't understand any of this," I cried.

I went over the whole thing as if this were the first time He'd heard of it. Finally my tears dried into a tight little knot in my throat. "What is going on in me that could allow this to happen? I can't go on swallowing tranquilizers the rest of my life. Show me what I must do," I prayed.

I don't know what I expected, but clearly nothing happened. I kept driving. Yet it felt good at least to have shared the whole experience with Someone. I let out a long breath and felt the ache and confusion inside me wane a bit.

When I pulled in my driveway after finishing the shopping, it was nearly five. Time for my next tranquilizer. I paused at the steering wheel. Stress. Chest pains. Little blue pills to get through the day. I still could hardly believe it had come to this. Then once again I had the odd, penetrating feeling that I had come upon an opportunity . . . some holy moment in which to change the direction of my life.

21

Longing rose in me like a quickening. Could God be somewhere inside this experience beckoning me to wholeness and new meaning? Somehow that thought—simple, almost casual—flashed into my consciousness like a beam of light. I cannot tell you how I knew it was true—that this event was somehow the beginning of an unfolding advent. I simply knew it . . . deeply, and intuitively.

As I climbed out of the car and stepped through the thinning light, I was still very bewildered and fearful. But I sensed that I was not alone in the chaos any longer. That something would come of it. And in those moments, those small unlikely moments, I think I heard the first, faint sound of God knocking.

I had been asleep, lying by Bethesda year after year, and not known it. Maybe we all spend time on the porticoes of Bethesda, some of us asleep in the complexities and busyness of our lives, others locked in by loneliness or boredom or depression. We wait for the moment when the water stirs and we are roused, awakened, touched and beckoned to wholeness and a new journey in the spiritual life.

The continuum of our Christian experience is often a rhythm of sleeping and waking to God. It's not falling asleep that's so deadly as much as it is staying asleep. Jesus was always going about the hills of Judea and the slopes of Galilee telling folks, "Rise up . . . Wake up! . . . Why do you sleep?" The Gospels give us numerous accounts of people waking up, I mean literally waking up from death and sleep: Lazarus, the little daughter of Jairus, the widow's son from Nain, the disciples dozing in Gethsemane. The Apostle Paul echoed Jesus' call when he wrote to the Ephesian Christians, "Awake, O sleeper . . . and Christ shall give you light" (Ephesians 5:14 RSV). But mostly the Gospels are an unfolding chronicle of persons who heard Christ's knock and began to wake in a far deeper way . . . in the inner labyrinths of their spirits.

I think I knew in the most rudimentary way that an awakening experience was beginning like a small current in the deep places of my spirit, though I'm not sure I would have put that label on it at the time. I only knew that I was full of longings, desires and stirrings.

Longing for Love

Though I had no words for it then, I believe with all my heart that what I was seeking—what we all may be seeking in this age of frantic paces, overloaded schedules and religious "doing" was the experience of being loved. Loved by God.

Is it possible? When it comes to being loved, what do people grow up learning and later incorporating into our lives? *To be loved, you must be lovable.* In other words, love comes as a result of what you do and accomplish. You are liked best if you look and behave a certain way. You are valued more if you are a good little boy or girl. You are applauded loudest if you make a success of things. You know the unwritten rule. Everybody loves a winner. Conditional love is the common rule of thumb. It sifts so deeply into our reality that it becomes hard to experience or even accept the idea of unconditional love, of being loved without doing something to deserve it.

"How difficult it is to receive, and to go on receiving . . . a love that does not depend on our own attraction," wrote C. S. Lewis. "We want to be loved for our cleverness, beauty, generosity, fairness, usefulness. The first hint that anyone is offering us the highest love of all is a terrible shock."[2] It is a vast, unthinkable surprise.

Though I was loved thoroughly and probably as unconditionally as a child could be, I still seemed to pick up very early that if I truly wanted to feel valued "out there" in the eyes of the world and other people, I must *make* myself lovable. I would have to acquire love by my own efforts. I was always aware of a nagging need to *do* lots of exceptional things in order to win pleasing nods. As a consequence I became extremely competitive. I didn't just swim as a child, I swam competively, filling my room with blue ribbons. I lined them up beside my 4-H ribbons and cheerleading trophies, all of them little badges that I imagined saying, "You are loved, Sue." I insisted on making A's on my report card, not because my parents demanded it, but because *I* did. Whatever I did, it had to be the best. For that assured being liked, being popular. Being loved.

A number of years ago Dr. Darold Treffert, director of a mental health institute, wrote about the "dangerous ideas our children have about life." One of them was the pervading idea that happiness—feeling special and valued—comes from what you do. Calling it a theme of "The American Fairy Tale," he wrote:

> We are preoccupied with doing and producing, instead of being. We measure our country in terms of our gross national product while we overlook our gross national neurosis, which is our preoccupation with the gross national product.[3]

Doing things in order to win love and approval is like eating one potato chip. You can't stop with just one. No matter how many "badges of love" you collect, they are never enough, because they are empty of real nourishment and cannot seem to feed the hunger gnawing deep inside. So you keep doing more, working a little harder, hoping this time it will take the awful emptiness away.

When one's culture and existence is shaped to a large extent by doing and accomplishing in order to experience love, it usually spills over into religion, too. Despite our "head-knowledge" that God loves us just as we are, there is usually some sneaking notion curdling way down inside that we will be loved best by God when we are doing the right things and achieving for His kingdom.

In 1979 John Claypool, while delivering the Beecher Lectures at Yale Divinity School, said:

> It is so hard for us to hear that God's love is uncondi-

tional. We have been raised, most of us, to think that if we do right, then we will be liked and approved. Therefore love is out there as the effect and our performance and obedience is the cause . . . . How can [we] . . . somehow help people unlearn, relearn that the love of God is not the effect that awaits us out at the end?[4]

As Claypool says, secretly instilled at my core was a certain unspoken understanding that said, "You must perfect yourself and *then* God will love you." I would never have said it out loud. I would have denied it vehemently if accused. I knew by heart every single verse of "Just As I Am"—"Just as I am, without one plea . . . poor, wretched, blind . . . O Lamb of God, I come."[5] But without even knowing it, I was going about my life trying to earn God's love and appease the nagging sense of not living up to His standards. Trying to be perfect in every area of my life, especially church. And all the while, longing inside, yearning to be loved just for me.

How desperately I needed to stop, and let Him love me . . . to taste the intimacy He was so ready to give. But I was too busy working and doing, too ingrained in earning His love to notice any other way. I was fast asleep in my busyness. And so it was, that December, though I did not know it was He, God came knocking . . . stirring me awake.

A heightened expectant feeling invaded me, not unlike spring fever when the urge to participate in the renewing of creation pulses inside of us. It was the beginning of winter, but the throb for renewal beat inside of me with intensity, and with gentleness, too.

When I was maybe ten, I saw a chick peck through an eggshell where he had been growing, curled in his dark little cocoon. I stood there mesmerized with anticipation while a faint tick, tick, ticking vibrated inside the shell and the egg began to crack. What I remember as much as the unfurling of the chick from the shell was the sound of its birth, those small vibrations that preceded the hatching. They happen to us, too—faint, inimitable vibrations of awakening. That's what I was sensing. A tick, tick, ticking, quiet and subtle, coming from the core of me.

So there I was—an active Christian, a woman with a husband, two children, a career, an ordinary, busy life . . . and stress, stress that seemed to crack open the whole neat thing. But at least I was beginning to catch the sounds of awakening. At this point I wasn't sure in what sense I'd been asleep, and certainly I didn't know what I was waking up to. But it would be the most wondrous surprise of my life.

Keep silence before me.
Isaiah 41:1

2

Who's That Knocking?

ONE AFTERNOON during December as I iced the roof of the gingerbread house, I heard Ann singing the same line over and over. "Who's that knocking at my door? Who's that knocking at my door?" Actually she'd sung the words lots of times before, but this afternoon I paused to listen. I have no idea where she learned the song—perhaps at playschool—but we both liked the little tune.

The best part of the song, however, was the game she played with it. Ann often acted out her songs. This day she popped about, swinging open the doors in the house as she sang, greeting some invisible someone. Of course there was nothing there but the wind.

The words continued to echo in my ears—and my heart—calling forth the question that was haunting me. Who was knocking on my door? Was it God? Or was I just imagining things? How could I know for sure?

I had not yet learned what I know now—that God is continually calling us in order to waken us to the sublime experience of loving and being loved by Him. It is the most fundamental call of our faith. Yet when we discover it resonating through our lives, it is nearly always a surprise.

Somehow we tend to miss the part about communing throughout our days with God, being His intimate friend, a "sharer of his very life and being."[1] Many of us bypass the call to intimacy in pursuit of religious "doing," keeping the rules, learning doctrines and correct "answers," and trying hard to live up to the demands of an active Christian life. We seem to forget that God desires more than our works, our sacrifices or our constant busyness in His behalf. What He wants is the deep and secret space in our heart where we abide in Him and He in us. The God of the universe, the mighty One who made us and saves us, wants us to live in loving communion with His presence! Maybe this is why the call to intimacy becomes such an astonishment.

And the call is for every Christian. "Behold, I stand at the door, and knock; if any . . . hear my voice, and open the door, I will come in to him, and will sup with him, and he with me" (Revelation 3:20). The word *sup* is a curious word. It symbolizes the intimate communion and fellowship with God that can characterize our days. Every ordinary moment carries the possibility of awareness and encounter so deep and close it is like sitting down to share an intimate meal with God.

So God knocks, wanting not just our salvation and our good works, but rather to awaken us to journey further and deeper into the spiritual life . . . into the depths of His presence. But how do we wake if we've been asleep? How does God's call to intimacy come?

Awakening Events

It seems to me that Christ continually calls us through the daily events in our lives—pain on a ladder, fire in a mountain bush, a potter at his wheel. In moments like these God stirs the waters of our lives and beckons us beyond where we are to a new dimension of closeness with Him. I don't necessarily mean that He "causes" the experiences, but rather that He "uses" them as a door upon which to knock.

God desires to transform certain experiences of ours into awakening events. These may be our most common moments, but if we let them they can become doorways to a deeper encounter with Him. Who knows at what moment we may begin to wake up to the astonishing fact that Emmanuel (God with us) is still God's name, that every moment the Word of God, Jesus Christ, is coming to us.

Every event, I believe, carries the hidden possibility of a word coming from God. Is there any moment, any event through which God does not speak? One autumn you see a flock of geese migrate over your house. You wake up to rain spattering on dark bedroom windows. You read a poem. A child reaches for your hand. You see someone on the street. You meet a friend in a shopping mall. And in the midst of them you recognize the sound and touch of God . . . or you do not. That is His gentle, noncoercive way of coming to us—always coming.

Yet it is important to say that there are *distinct* experiences that seem to evolve into real, life-changing spiritual awakenings. Advent-moments when God comes and knocks and the event gives rise to a new way of being, to a new journey of love and intimacy with Him.

Often, to some degree, these events are painful ones. Such was my episode with stress, though I hardly knew at the time what a pivotal experience it would become. In a sense I climbed up a ladder, and when I climbed down, it was into a brand new pilgrimage. The ladder was a hinge in more ways than one.

We all have hinges in our lives—precipitating events that launch us into a wholly unforeseen newness. Church history is punctuated with such events. For instance, Francis of Assisi was galloping along a dusty road to do battle as a wealthy, self-indulgent knight. Along the way he happened to glimpse a leper, nauseating with untouchable sores. Normally, Francis would have spurred his horse and left only a puff of dust. But in that ordinary event, one that had happened to him countless times before, he somehow began to perceive the sound of God. He was moved and summoned on deep levels. The water was stirred. Francis climbed down from his horse and kissed the leper. That act touched off an awakening and journey into love he could not possibly have imagined at the moment. It was the mysterious hinge of his life. And the rest of his days blazed with the fires of God's love. He had been awakened to intimacy.

Most hinges are not so dramatic as that. But they are no less real. God comes in an ordinary moment of time and quietly our spiritual life begins to deepen, grow and resonate anew. In ways I could not possibly foresee, my relationship to God changed. It pivoted on that ladder.

These are special moments. Gift-moments. And they are far more important than we have realized. They are the most teachable moments of our lives. If we allow them, they can set in motion a spiritual awakening, a plunge into a new journey. And whether we perceive it or not, there is a holy touch in them. A knock.

Every awakening to God begins with a knock. And what is a knock but the calling voice of God. The question is, how can we tap such moments? We cannot create these moments. We do not awaken ourselves. God awakens. But still there is something we can do. We can grow silent enough to hear what is there.

The Need for Silence

Silence. Quietness. Stillness. Is there anything twentieth-century America neglects as much?

Think about a typical day in your life. Often we wake up to the shrill ring of a radio alarm or the voice of a disc jockey. Even if we are able to manage a "quiet time" with God, we often use it to talk to Him rather than listen with a quiet mind. We spend breakfast with early morning television shows that bombard us with news. There is a constant stream of words with family members about plans for the day, lunch money, not being late.

Then, whether we rush off to work with sounds of traffic, trains, radios, or cassettes filling our ears, or remain home to work, caring for house and children or at other jobs, we are hammered all day with words, problems, demands. Our lunch hours and breaks are filled with conversations, meetings, noisy fast food restaurants or children underfoot. There is no reprieve even in the elevator where music is piped in to cover the silence. We drive to the store or home from work through a maze of billboards screaming more words at us.

All day the roar of technology around us is constant: traffic, planes, phones, dishwashers, typewriters, television, videos, electronic toys that talk, blip and beep incessantly. We are buried under a deluge of meaningless sounds, so habituated to them we hardly notice any more.

In the evening we scramble to make dinner to the sound of blenders, food processors and the evening news. Then more words, more television, more meetings or social events full of chatter. Or if we don't turn on the TV or radio, we read—a magazine, a book, the newspaper. More words. We fall into bed with the overload of sounds from the day continuing to clamor inside us, only to wake to more the next day.

The clamor inside us is just as noisy as the din outside us. There have been moments in my life when I sat in the utter quietness of a deserted room and had the noise of a fireworks show going on inside me. And there have been rare times when I stood in a crowd of noisy people and tapped into a deep inner silence. It is this interior quietness—a silence within us—that is a door through which God can come to us. But we would be missing the point if we didn't recognize that inner quietness begins in outer quietness. For the most part we cannot easily keep out all the clamor and noise that spins around us. It spills over into our lives like a river that overflows its banks. We need a measure of exterior silence in order to become silent within.

We all have our special places, I suppose, that draw us to God. The ocean is mine. I go there whenever I can because somehow it puts me in touch with a quiet place inside and nourishes the presence of God in my life. I watch the ebb and flow of the sea and listen to the undulating rhythm of the waves that pulse in time with something deep in my own spirit.

Last summer our family spent a couple of weeks at the edge of the ocean. But this time it became unusually difficult to find the re-creating power I'd experienced there in the past. Morning, afternoon and night, sunbathers, sea-gazers and those strolling along the sandy corridor blasted the beach with music from big silver radios that looked more like suitcases. There was hardly a moment that didn't remind one of being at a rock concert. At first I was angry. When it became clear that would accomplish nothing, my anger turned to curiosity. *Why do we need to bring radios to the beach?* I wondered. It wasn't just teenagers. I was amazed at the different array of people who drowned out the healing vibrations of the ocean with their battery-operated transistors. One middle-aged woman who was swimming at the water's edge called to her husband on the beach to turn up the radio: "I can't hear it over all these waves"! I was aghast.

Why must we cover the silence in our world? Why do we tote radios into every conceivable place? Why do we leave the television on even when we're not watching it? Is it because silence has become so alien to us we feel strange in its presence? Do we feel insecure in silent places because here is a part of the world we cannot control with our man-made sounds? Or do we flinch from silence because we fear what we may confront there? That was certainly true for me.

The more we grow accustomed to the roar of background noise in our world, to the constant flood of words, the more difficult it becomes to hear small healing sounds—wind rustling in a pine tree, a chirping bird, water lapping on a river bank. And, the still small voice of God whispering within.

A minister and seminary professor told me recently that he felt the number-one problem in our world was spiritual deafness. I was surprised at his comment. After all, there are some pretty dreadful problems around. But he believed that mankind's gargantuan problems would not be solved until individuals began to recover their spiritual dimensions and find again the voice of God in their lives.

"God speaks to us every day, but we do not listen," I read recently.[2] Every day? Can it possibly be true? Does God speak to us every day? All day? If it is true, the thought of what we are missing is staggering! Why don't we hear more of the voice of God in our lives?

When I brought up the question among some Christians one day, someone commented that perhaps we didn't hear God because God simply didn't communicate with us that much any more. *Now* we had the Bible. *The* book. What was left to say? But that alternative bothers me. Has God now become reticent or is it simply that human creatures have grown more deaf to His voice? Has He gone on speaking and revealing, while the sound of His voice has become submerged in our growing pollution of inner and outer noise?

I turned to the Bible, leafing through it book by book, hoping to find some light. Immediately I was struck by what an astonishingly communicative being God is. He is profoundly committed to seeking out human beings, desiring to reveal Himself to them. The Bible records that He spoke continuously in an assortment of ways. In a rainbow after a flood, in a thicket where a ram was caught, in a burning bush, a still small voice, a thick cloud, a dove, dreams, strangers, angels, prophets—and ultimately in an instrument of death, a cross. Throughout the Bible there is a recurrent theme of God speaking. God's very nature is to communicate and reveal. Why should that stop? Has He changed His nature after A.D. 100? My conclusion is that God, who is the same today as yesterday, is still speaking. It is we who have trouble hearing Him. Why?

Helmut Thielicke's account of the bombing raid's in Stuttgart during World War II offers a clue.

> Those in the German shelters would cry out through the deafening explosions around them, "Lord, save us from the bombs." Many assumed God was silent. The bombs were not. If those in Stuttgart had looked directly at God, they would have seen that his lips were moving. Had they listened, they might have heard his voice.[3]

As I ponder that description, I get an absurd image of my own life, lived in a suburban "bomb shelter" with all kinds of noise and confusion exploding around me. And right in the midst of it, God had been speaking to me. His lips were moving. But I couldn't hear a sound. There was not enough silence.

It's not like God to yell in order to make Himself heard over all the sounds in our world. Rather He calls on us to turn from our frantic lives and grow quiet. "Be still, and know that I am God," He tells us (Psalm 46:10).

Listening

The aim of silence is to create an attitude of listening to God. Without listening, silence is just a vacuum. Inside our silence we seek an encounter, a dialogue, a participation with His presence. But learning to hear His whisper is the most delicate miracle of all. "Behold, I stand at the door and knock. If anyone hears . . . " *If.* That little word says a great deal to us, doesn't it? It says God speaks, He knocks, He awakens, but . . . perhaps we will not hear Him.

Even having caught the sound of awakening we still may allow it to slip away. It could easily have happened to me. In fact it nearly did. I almost wrote my experience off as a spiritual flash in the pan. Why? For one thing, nothing tangible changed in my life for what seemed like a very long time. Not the pain, the pills, the busyness or the stress.

We are tempted to abandon the experience of awakening, to stop listening, because it is basically a slow-motion experience. I can't help but remember the day Bob planted his very first flower garden from a package of seeds that came in the mail. The next morning his flowers weren't up, so he decided that the seeds must not be there any more. "Something ate my seeds," he kept saying.

Late in the night I sometimes lay in my bed and told myself that I was probably silly to think that God was calling out to me, that anything like chest pains and stress could become the beginning of a spiritual journey. Cynicism crept in. *Maybe I'm not hearing God's knock. Maybe He doesn't knock except during altar calls. No, nothing will come of it. I am fooling myself. I don't know how my life could ever be different. I ought just to accept it as it is.*

My discontent was enormous. I remember asking God, "Are You knocking from within all this, or not?" And there was an awful stony silence. I heard nothing.

At first we may think we are wasting our time . . . listening only to a silent void. But nothing could be further from the truth.

Not long ago I stepped outside into the deep velvety darkness of an August night. Quietness swelled around me. At first it was like lying on the cool bottom of a well where no sound could reach. But as I "entered" the silence, listening to it, the night came alive with cicadas humming in the grass, birds rustling in the trees, chipmunks in the wood pile. Beneath the cloak of dark silence there was a hidden life. That is the way it is with the silence of God. As we turn from our blaring worlds and "enter" the quietness, slowly God's presence comes alive around us.

How do we enter silence? What is involved in listening to God?

Listen with Sensitivity
During a weekend retreat some time ago, I was having a casual conversation with a minister in his crowded little office.

A cascade of books ran along the shelves, spilling over onto the floor. A lone daffodil in a milk-white vase sat on a desk.

"Are you listening to God while you are here?" he asked.

There were silent periods for prayer designed into the schedule. Even our meals during this retreat were taken in silence in order to create an atmosphere of listening. But to tell the truth, I was not having much luck. "How do you listen to God?" I asked.

He had the most expressive black eyes, even though they were small as marbles, and an infectious smile. "The main thing is that you resist the desire to jump in and start talking. In other words, you suspend the notion that you must get across *your* message to God and concentrate instead on *His* message to you. Don't demand. But attend to His presence with sensitivity."

I looked past him at the daffodil. "What do you mean about sensitivity?"

"I mean you must listen with your heart," he said, following my eyes to the flower. There was a long silence in the room while he stared at the petals. I wondered if he was listening with his heart. Did he mean to tune in to God on a deeper level?

"When you listen with your heart, you put up sensors for God's words hidden around you and within you," he continued. "You listen for Him in the sights, sounds, thoughts, feelings and awarenesses that occupy your silence. What does God say through a crotchety old man who feeds a pigeon? Or a child who skips? What does He say to you through your reluctance to forgive, or your inclination to visit a friend?"

"What does He say through a yellow daffodil?" I offered, swept into his grand exuberance for God.

"Exactly!" he exploded, making me jump in my seat. "You and I will never know what God is saying until we listen deeply and creatively to Him."

As I was leaving, he added one last thing. "Above all, Sue, remember you have not listened with your heart until you have risked allowing your vision to be changed. Listening can be very dangerous business."

As we listen, putting up sensors for God's words hidden around us, sometimes we hear a quiet something within our experience and begin to understand that it is God waking us up, calling us to Himself. In the moment we allow ourselves to become quiet, open and vulnerable, the journey can begin.

Listen Like a Child

During the holiday preparations, Ann continued to sing her song "Who's that knocking at my door?" Watching her pop open doors in time with the music, greeting the invisible knocker, I began to wonder if perhaps there was someone there. Perhaps she was hearing a knock that was lost to my grown-up ears.

So often we fail to hear God tapping in our experiences because our ears are filled with a grown-up disbelief, closed off to the mystery of His Spirit moving across the surface of each day. We hear what we've grown accustomed to hearing. Nothing more. Maybe we're too self-conscious for anything else. But children are still open to mystery and wonder.

We need to become like little children, Jesus told us, if we are to see His kingdom. That is, we need to listen with wonder and a willingness to let go of our deafness to anything that is out of the ordinary. We need not be childish—we can listen with an intelligent and critical openness. But unless we become childlike, God's knock may escape our ears.

When I worked as a nurse in the pediatric ward, before I listened to the little ones' chests I would sometimes plug the stethoscope in their ears and let them listen to their own hearts. One day I tucked the stethoscope in little David's ears. "Can you hear that?" I asked. "What do you suppose that is?"

He frowned for a moment as if he were lost in the wonder of the strange tapping in his chest. Then he broke out in a grin and startled me by saying, "Is that Jesus knocking?"

It is mostly those of us who listen with the wonder of a David who will hear the faint and holy sound of God in the experiences of our lives. How wondrous and open-ended life becomes when we look at something as commonplace and familiar as the thump in our chest and hear God in it.

So I tried to listen less like an adult with a closed mind and more with the openness and wonder of a child. And indeed the awakening experience began to come to life again. *Maybe there is something to this after all,* I began to think. *Maybe.*

Listen with Expectancy

Christmas Day began in a frenzy, torn open like a present. The children ripped into their gifts an hour after dawn. By seven thirty the room was a wading pool of wrapping paper. I gazed around at all the toys. While Sandy blew up a big inflatable plastic clown, I tramped outside in my robe to watch Ann pump her new scooter along the driveway. Standing there in the cold air, I remembered for the first time what this day was all about—*God coming.* And I wondered if it was true not only in a historical sense—that two thousand years ago God came in a baby at Bethlehem—but true in the present. That now in this season of stress and tranquilizers God was coming in the events of my life.

For the longest time I had lost touch with the very heart of Christmas—that Jesus came not just to show us what to do and what to believe. He came as a revelation of God's love. He came so we could have the same kind of intimate relationship with the Father that He had. He showed us how to love and be loved.

Then in the last days of December another lesson came along that helped me to continue. One evening darkness began to gather across the lawn and Bob was not home. He had ridden off on his bicycle to a friend's house with a promise to be back at six. At five past, the driveway was still empty. I went on preparing dinner. At 6:07 I turned to Sandy and said, "Bob's home."

"How do you know?" he asked, for there was no sign of him.

"Because I heard his bike tire on the edge of the driveway," I answered.

Inside the house I heard the tire the instant it touched the driveway because every fiber of me was waiting for it, expecting his coming. And so I heard what I would never ordinarily hear. It is the same for parents with babies—we can wake up because we hear them turn in the night in their little cribs down the hall. But if it had been a stranger rolling over in the night we would have gone on sleeping.

The ability to hear sounds on doors when there seems to be no sound at all has a lot to do with expecting someone. I was expecting Bob. To hear God, we need to listen with expectation, our ears open for the least whisper of His coming.

We must respond to ordinary events and experiences like a little girl full of anticipation, who swings open doors with a breathless curiosity and belief that someone really will be there. We listen for Him the way a mother listens for her son when he is late. That is when we hear sounds hidden in sounds.

It is possible, even in a noisy world, to hear quiet sounds. In the roaring city, one can hear the cry of gulls overhead, or the chirp of sparrows, if our ears are turned to hear them. A friend recounted to me how one day a bird lover heard the soft whistle of a white-throated sparrow from an eighth-floor window in the center of industrial Philadelphia.

While at the seaside last summer, amid all that radio noise, I picked up a conch shell from the sand, and put it to my ear just as I'd done when I was a little girl and my mother told me the voice of the ocean could be heard inside it. As I tuned out the sounds around me—the radios blaring, the people yelling—and tuned in to the shell, I heard that faint and haunting echo of the surf. God's voice is like the still small sound buried inside a shell. Only when I become quiet, cupping my ear to His presence, can I hear His gentle whisper in my life.

God comes in the events of our lives seeking to awaken us to His love. That is what we live in expectation of. We can't pin it down much more than that. For try as we may, we cannot predict God. Thus a gentle reminder that in our expectation we must allow God to be God, free of human demand.

So I tried listening again with a measure of expectation. And the more I did, the more distinct the knock of God became.

———————

On December 31 I felt a particularly keen awareness of standing on the crossroads between old and new, sleeping and waking. We had planned a stay-at-home evening. Sandy insisted. He had been home for two weeks during the college holiday break, and had spent much of that time reminding me to slow down. I had tried. But my efforts were frequently tinged with restlessness and guilt about not doing everything I had planned or was expected to do. That evening, however, I felt more serene inside, focusing more than ever on the spiritual journey that seemed to stretch in front of me into the new year.

Sandy made a fire in the fireplace. Around ten o'clock I pulled a spiral notebook out of my desk, sat before the flames and began to doodle in the margins. I noticed that I was drawing doors. Doors! I began my journal, the first page of many that would seek to record the journey ahead. I wrote:

"December was a door through which I embarked upon something holy."

There were great searchings of heart.
JUDGES 5:16

3

Am I Lovable?

LATE ONE AFTERNOON I refilled my little bottle of tranquilizers at the drugstore, brought them home and banged them on the dresser.

"What's the matter?" asked Sandy.

"Everything," I muttered. I was in a dark mood. Despite the sense of awakening that stirred within me, I often gave in to frustration and anger. The pills represented the worst of the experience. "I hate having this happen to me. These pills . . . I mean, I thought stress was for anxious people who are always wringing their hands over a crisis. People who can't cope with anything."

"You're not like that," he said. "You know you're not."

"I know. But still . . . " I dropped on the bed, so frustrated I barely suppressed an urge to toss a pillow across the room. "Taking the tranquilizers is like an admission of weakness, to myself, to everyone. Even the pharmacist looked at me funny when I got them refilled."

"People understand," he said.

"Well, I don't!" I cried. I looked up at him, lowering my

voice. "It's just that I hate having to depend on these pills to keep my life on keel. But I'm afraid not to take them. I don't know what to do."

All of a sudden my eyes were burning with tears. I squeezed the pillow I'd resisted throwing. "They're not doing anything about the real problem," I continued. True. Taking them was like sticking my finger in a dike to keep back the flood. It didn't do anything about reducing the flood itself.

"Look, why don't you try to understand the underlying cause of all this?" Sandy said, suppressing his exasperation.

I leaned back on the bed, feeling like a stranger in my own body. It seemed impossible that I could know so little about myself and the way I responded to life.

"All I mean is that it might help to look honestly at what is causing this bout with stress," he said. "Get to the bottom of it."

Darkness was gathering at the windows, and the panes looked cold and shadowed. "I'm not sure I know how to do that."

"It's worth a try, isn't it?" he asked. "You could start with the library."

I only looked at him. What made people like me—ordinary busy Christians with the usual modicum of problems—have chest pains or migraines or stomach ulcers or whatever?

"I'll try," I said, half-convinced.

Asking the Right Questions

As he left the room, my eyes drifted to the dresser. Beside the pills stood an empty picture frame I'd received as a Christmas gift. I hadn't taken time to put a picture inside it yet. The thing could easily have been a piece of silent commentary on my life. Looking at the empty frame was almost like looking at a picture of myself.

It reminded me of a hospital patient I took care of once when

I was a nurse. She told me that the most painful dream she ever had was that of staring at a mirror and seeing nothing there. She beat frantically on the glass, crying, "Where are you?" The thought of that haunted me for days. Now in a crazy way, it was happening to me. I mean, how much did I really know about myself or where I was in my life?

Lying there on the bed, I was finally asking myself the right questions. *What is going on inside of me? What drives me from one task to another? Who am I beneath the mask I wear and why is there no one staring back from the mirror?*

I have since learned that when a baffling or painful experience comes, the crucial thing is not always to find the right answers, but to ask the right questions. Self-questioning is a far more essential ingredient in life than I ever supposed. It's the water that keeps the modeling clay of our life from hardening into something forever rigid and unchanging. To refuse to ask honest questions of ourselves ultimately means shutting ourselves off from revelation. Often it is simply the right question at the right time that propels us on into the journey of awakening.

It's amazing how out of touch with ourselves we can become during the busy course of our days . . . how faint the image of our real self grows. Many of us float on the surface of our lives for years, riding the little dips and crests and never peering into the depths beneath. I certainly had not looked below the surface. There had never been much incentive to do it. Certainly I had never wanted to confront what I might discover. But now . . . now was different.

The next day I went to the library and checked out books on stress. Poring through them, I came upon all kinds of things that seemed to have a connection to me. But one thing especially. "Stress begins with anxiety arising from some imbalance within us."[1]

An imbalance within. The phrase reminded me of the buzzer that goes off on my washing machine whenever the load becomes unbalanced. Maybe we all had built in buzzers, alarms that go off in our body when the load inside gets out of balance. How was I out of balance?

The next morning I woke with the idea that if I was ever to discover my real self and find the answer to that question, I would have to take time to think. I'd have to have silent moments of reflection. And not just moments, but periods of time for gazing at my life like a spectator in the stands at a ball game.

Reflection is in many ways a lost art. It is an eyepiece to a world hidden away, the world within ourselves which is alive with truths and beauties and darkness we have never glimpsed. It seems sad that we slice our time too thin for dreaming long dreams and thinking long thoughts. We've grown uncomfortable with that sort of thing. For a long time I had been uneasy left alone. I would snap on the television or grab a book or make brownies. Anything. I suppose we are restless all alone with ourselves and our thoughts because it's like being in the room with a stranger. What if we face ourselves and find we don't like the person we meet? I didn't even want to spend much time in prayer because God might confront me and I'd have to look at myself.

Have you ever perpetuated little myths in your prayers? You fail to mention those sides of yourself that make you uneasy? You pray comfortable, usually similar-sounding prayers that do not probe very deep? And soon the truth about who you are becomes so obscure it is difficult to retrieve. I think I'd grown rather artful at it. As long as I failed to look at myself or tell myself the truth, I continued to become a stranger not only to myself but a stranger before God.

I hadn't reflected since I was a little girl sitting in my "secret place" under the mimosa tree outside my bedroom window, breathing in the scent, catching the pink blossoms as they fell and dreaming long dreams. Maybe that's why now I chose the little maple tree in the backyard. On many days, probably to the bewilderment of any neighbors who happened to be watching, I sat against its cold tree trunk and reflected. Sometimes I sat there only a short while. Other days I sat there so long my toes felt numb and I would have to go inside and rub them by the heating vent.

Despite how foreign it was, and how fearful I was, reflecting beneath the tree became routine. At first I had wondered how I would fit time for it into my schedule. I usually worked at my desk, writing in the mornings, then after lunch, the children came home and there were housework and errands. But I squeezed time here and there. I did it because I told myself that it was a necessary adventure and the only hope I had.

But mostly I sat there out of sheer curiosity, and because God somehow drew me there. The first time I sat on the tree roots and heard the silence and looked at the patches of soft color spread across the grass, I felt a great rush of "homecoming." A coming home to myself. That's why I kept going out to the tree in spite of how foolish the whole thing might have looked to others. Sometimes I peeled away layer after layer of my life, each one evoking a response from me. At other times it was more like being inside a crystal deep within myself, looking from the inside out, seeing it from new sides and in new lights. And sometimes I would spread a drop of my life across my mind and ponder it like a child with a microscope.

Uncovering the Past

One day in my reverie, I was a young girl growing up in a small Georgia town in the fifties. Sylvester was a safe, sheltered place, full of trees and churches and a peanut parade every year when the crop came in. A place where everyone knew your daddy and you could charge a soft drink at any store in town.

Daddy owned an insurance business, but he had a love for farming, and on weekends and after work he could be found growing crops on Monk Farm. Mama was home raising my three younger brothers and myself, sewing most of my clothes and canning all Daddy's beans and tomatoes. Warm memories from my past stirred to life among the golden shadows of the tree. Yet along with the nostalgia came the awareness that even as a child I was driven to get involved in everything possible. Church activities, ballet, Girl Scouts, speech classes, cheerleading, school plays, choirs, swim teams, candy striper, and endless clubs and committees. Despite the slow, small-town pace, I was nearly always in a hurry.

I remembered applying to the Medical College of Georgia Nursing School and receiving a summons. "Sue, frankly we don't see how you've managed academically with all your extracurricular activities," the dean told me. "We want to be sure you understand how demanding your college work will be, and how important it is not to become overly involved in other things."

I was uncovering a pattern of living that had roots way back in my childhood. To alter it would take time and effort if I really wanted to deal with the stress and imbalance that had produced the chest pains. But I knew, too, that there was more to all this than cracking old patterns of rush and the tendency to overextend myself. I kept going to the bare maple.

Another day I saw myself as a nine-year-old, being baptized in the Baptist Church that stood one block from the courthouse where my granddaddy was the city judge. I remembered being plunged down under the water and coming up sputtering and wiping away the strands of hair wet on my face. Reliving that moment with fresh joy, I heard the preacher say something about rising to walk in newness of life. *Rising to walk.* I had made such a marvelous beginning. But what had taken place since I splashed out of the water? What about the "walk"? The thought swept me to other memories—a collage of them.

I saw myself marrying a young seminary student, moving to Texas and plunging immediately into teaching Sunday school, attending Bible studies, working on church committees, organizing religious programs, activities that grew, especially after the seminary years. Sandy became assistant minister at a large church in Georgia, then there was a year in Africa as missionaries. Now in South Carolina, I seemed busier than ever. It seemed I'd worked hard for God. So hard . . .

Suddenly beneath the tree I got very tired thinking about all my ceaseless activity for God. It wasn't just church that kept me busy. Life had grown more complicated every year since that simple day I had dripped baptismal water down the back corridor of the church to put on dry clothes. For the first time I recognized that my last few years had been swamped by days so hectic and crammed, it seemed the seams would split.

Then something popped into my memory. Such a small scene, but I could see it clearly. It was a day in a department store when I had balanced Ann on my hip and rushed about looking for Bob who, it turned out, had climbed beneath a dress rack. A friend of mine, having similar troubles, looked at me and said, "I don't know about you, but I live every day in quiet desperation." We laughed.

But afterward in the car driving home, hurrying to prepare dinner so I could attend a meeting, her words were so unexpectedly true of my life, I wanted to cry. I remembered feeling empty and off-key, as a terrible yearning welled up in me.

The memories of that event faded as a wind came and rattled the limbs of the tree, making me shiver back into the present. The gnawing was always there, I thought. Never far away. I had never really admitted that to myself before. Now it seemed clear to me that not only was there a muffled hunger in my life, but that I had always responded to it by doing even more, anything to smother the peculiar hunger away. I remembered after the department store episode I had had the restless feeling that I was not doing enough. Not for my family or myself or God. *I will do more,* I promised one Sunday morning in church. I did more. I volunteered to lead a youth Bible study. But now beneath the tree I knew the hunger had not gone away.

Even as I reflected on it, I felt it come and throb inside me. Swept clean, it ached almost like a wound. I was not able to name it, only recognize it. It was the hunger that had smoldered deep inside of me over the years as the waters of my baptism dried away.

So I came to the tree and looked deeper each day. Why was I hungry? What was I so hungry for? What did this have to do with the stress in my life?

The Algebra Pie

"Do you think I'm overloaded?" I asked Sandy one night as I mulled back over my appointment calendar. It looked like a dictionary.

"Hmmmm," he said, coming to peer over my shoulder. "Looks like all that congestion just might be dividing you up. Look," he continued. His finger ran down an assortment of notes on my calendar during the past months. My days—my whole life—were divided up in countless ways. Children, home, God, church, work, committees, hobbies, organizations and a myriad of other daily demands.

A light flashed in my head. I saw a woman whose life was split in a hundred different functions. I had been dashing about like a committee of persons, divided and scattered in different directions. Maybe the essence was not only the weight of all my tasks but the divisions I allowed them to create within me.

Once long ago in algebra class the teacher had drawn a pie on the blackboard and divided it into fractions. I closed my eyes. Somehow in my walk from the baptismal pool to the present, I had become divided up, and dished out in every direction. An algebra pie. Or a jigsaw puzzle spilled on the rug in a little mound of clutter and confusion. And beneath it all I now felt more strongly than ever the hunger which none of the activity could quite conceal.

I cannot tell you how torn and fractured I felt as I walked inside my own spirit. It was not only strange territory, but frighteningly barren beneath all the chaos and noise. In my rush to achieve, compete, serve, do, cope, keep up, and be fulfilled, I had lost touch with something vital. Far inside, on the deepest levels of my spirit, I was starving for the wholeness that could bind up the jigsaw of my life and bring focus and meaning to a life fractured by daily stresses.

An overwhelming sense of hopelessness swept over me. I saw the congestion in my life about to swallow me up, the jigsaw pieces too scattered ever to come together again, the algebra pie so divided it could never become one complete whole. Things seemed worse than when I started. I didn't want to think any more. I didn't want to see the emptiness and deception in my life—all the dark little places.

I ran into the kitchen where I got very busy scrubbing the bottoms of my pots and pans, an activity that was sure to carry me back to life as it was before. *No more wasting time reflecting,* I thought. *I will stop this nonsense . . . now!*

It's inevitable when we reflect seriously on our life, trying to penetrate our secrets with the cutting edge of honesty, that we will have distressing moments. We will be seeing ourselves as we really are, warts and all. The portrait of myself that was coming together wasn't a pleasant one. I was the "kingdom divided" that Jesus warned about. The kingdom is within, He said. And a divided kingdom will not stand (Luke 11:18; 17:21).

I had discovered the "imbalance within" that I had started out to find. Mine was a divided life without a nourishing whole. And the disharmony of all the competing pieces, the desires and conflicts that pulled in every direction within, led to inner tensions which had actually become so intense they had created physical changes in my body. Chest pains and a galloping pulse.

"Stress creeps up on you," the doctor had said. For the first time, I really saw how it had happened. Richard Foster in *The Freedom of Simplicity* talks about our many selves, "the business self, the parental self, the religious self, the literary self, the energetic self." All of them, he says, are "rugged individualists" trying to protect his or her interest. "No wonder we overcommit our schedules and live lives of frantic faithfulness," he wrote.[2]

But though I wanted to forget the reflecting and go on as before, chest pains and all, deep within I knew it was precisely this confrontation with the inadequacy of the real state of my life in relation to God that carried me to new possibilities. I could not evade the truths that could set me free. It was a painful necessity. Only as I entered the recreating silences within my spirit could I hope to nurture this new life waking within. And that was the knowledge that brought me back to my long thoughts under the maple, that, and some deep-drawing love that would not let me go.

Sometimes I stopped to wonder how all this searching of heart was affecting Bob and Ann. On a Saturday late in January they found me under the tree. "What are you doing, Mama?" Bob asked, nudging his kick ball through the grass.

"Just resting a minute and thinking about things," I said.

"What things?"

"Oh, about what's really important . . . like you and you," I said, touching each of their noses. I patted the ground. "Sit down with me."

So for a few moments they left their childlike business and crowded in on either side of me. Ann placed her cheek against my arm while Bob looked up through the branches. They seemed to fall into a kind of reflection themselves.

"I like it when you think about things," Bob said after a while.

It seemed to me that in some small way they sensed what was happening to me. I was saying "Hurry" less often. I was toning down the demands that pulled and scattered me about. Already I had resigned from a couple of committees, as well as the country club. Several times I'd taken a nap in the middle of the day! Yes, Mama was changing.

I knew that day that I was making some progress, but still I needed to find something that could nourish the deep and secret hunger I'd come upon. What could bring the wholeness I longed for?

God Is the "Whole Pie"!

One morning when the kids were in school I went outside

to empty the garbage. I leaned over the fence and dumped the trash into the can, watching the little pieces of debris spill down. I thought about all the "pieces" in my life. Then suddenly I was struck by something I had never honestly confronted before. *God was simply another slice of my life.* Another piece, disconnected from the rest. I had finally arrived at the cellar truth. It was God I hungered for. God.

If someone else had told me that, I wouldn't have believed it. But I had peeled away until there I was staring at my true face. It was undeniable. Despite all my activity on God's behalf, all my church attendance and all my commitment, I knew little about experiencing God as the heart of my existence. So much, so amazingly much of my life, was unopened to God's presence and didn't relate to Him in the least. He was like a moon orbiting the outer rims of my world. Or like a comet flashing through every seven days, with maybe another appearance once or twice during the week if I could manage five quiet minutes to read my Bible (which was more mental work than it was an experience of God) and to pray (which was more a list of needs than an encounter with Him).

I had little intimacy with God in the midst of my everyday life, and virtually no awareness of His presence in my daily routine. He was the familiar stranger in my life, far removed from the real essence of my days. And yet, I knew as most of us do, that God is omnipresent. He was there. But He wasn't. I "had" God in my life. Yet I missed Him. It was all a great paradox. There is a line in the prison prayer of German theologian Dietrich Bonhoeffer that captures the tender agony I felt. "God is the beyond in the midst of life."[3] God was out there somewhere, beyond me. Yet I knew in my head that He was living in me through His Holy Spirit. But where? How? I had no sense of Him at all.

I had spent the time since my conversion (at the age of nine), thinking I'd done more or less all I'd needed to do—I'd received the gift of salvation. Period. Now I had only to work for Him, obey the rules, attend church and hopefully I would

"grow" (I suppose by osmosis). Meanwhile I had never cultivated the inner spiritual disciplines which drew God from the
periphery to the center of my life and made him present and
real. I had never entered the depths of the spiritual life, the
inner realms of prayer. Oh, I knew a lot about God, but I did
not know Him in the kind of intimate, encompassing way that
transfigures life into an experience of His love and presence.

I came inside the house, lined the trash cans with plastic bags
and wondered if it was really conceivable that I had separated
God from much of my life, putting Him in a little box that I
could pull off the shelf at appropriate moments, just as I did
any other part of my life.

As I went about my tasks that day I was plagued by questions.
*Have I written about God more than I've prayed to Him? What
do I know about experiencing God as a way of life? How much of
my relationship with Him is based on someone else's experience of
Him, rather than my own? Do I really know for myself that God
loves me? When was the last time I encountered Him deep within?*

That last question set my mind combing back through the
shallow, on-again-off-again efforts of my praying, the rules I
kept and the good works I did. That pattern too went all the
way back, too far back, to the waters of my baptism.

That evening while Sandy was busy with a class lecture, I
put the children to bed and sat down with my journal. "I do
not know You so well, God," I wrote.

Then I read it back. The letters looked like little scars across
the paper. They were written with an awful sense of God's
absence. I felt naked in spirit, holding the truth in the palm of
my hand, wanting to get rid of it like a live coal. Yet wanting
to hold on to it, too. Mostly wanting to hold on.

How easy it is to miss the point of living, I thought. It is too
easy to become an algebra pie with only one slice for God.
God is the whole pie! Perhaps God's presence among us is
brighter and more extravagant than we have imagined. Perhaps
the very idea of life is to experience and discover God *in* it.
Maybe we are meant to journey not only *toward* God or even
for God, but *with* God. *With.*

It's hard to describe the impact that little preposition had upon me. It transformed life into a companion-journey, a sharing of God's presence. It threw the world into a new light and called on me to make God not just another reality—but *the* reality, the "whole" that shapes and colors and touches all I think and say and do. And all I am. The dimension of "with God" was one I had overlooked all my life.

We all have moments of illumination, transcendent moments, big and small, when something that was there all along grows clear, something we never quite knew before, at least on the level that counts. We may sense we have received a gift from God himself. And when that happens, even if the vision that breaks over us is humble, we want to pull off our shoes and declare the ground holy, or build a tabernacle as Peter did on Mt. Tabor. Or fall off a horse like Paul. That is how I felt.

The truths I had been discovering beneath the reflection tree over many weeks rose in me like a deep joy. Everywhere it seemed I could hear the soft words murmured over Jairus' daughter: "*Talitha cumi,* arise daughter, awake from sleep."

If . . . thine eye be single,
thy whole body shall be full of light.
MATTHEW 6:22

4

What's at the Center?

ONE NIGHT in February when the wind whistled around the
house, I walked into Ann's room and came upon her idly
pushing the inflated, plastic clown she'd received at Christmas.
It was one of those punching toys that always returns upright
to its rounded base, no matter how far over it is pushed. I
watched the clown flop back when Ann poked it, then roll up
on its base, which had remained stationary on the floor due to
some kind of grounded center.

A grounded center! That was what I needed. A center that
remained still when the rest of me shifted. That's what would
help me find wholeness, help me meet the demands of each
day, but also let me live intimately with God.

"Put God in the center of your life," was a phrase I'd often
heard from the pulpits of the churches I'd attended. We have
kicked that phrase around until we have nearly worn the
meaning from it. Do we have any idea what it really means to
"put God in the center"? Could it mean more than we have
realized? I never understood the phrase, just knew that it
sounded nice and spiritual. The words were seed that fell on

shallow soil, never going very deep. Now, through a clown, I understood what a center was. That was where I needed to begin.

"He who does not gather with me scatters," said Jesus (Matthew 12:30b RSV). I'd recorded that verse in my journal back in January. Now it seemed to say to me, "Gather your life together into Mine." I needed to experience God as the center of my life—where all my selves and all of life could be gathered, where every activity and moment could flow from the divine point of His presence.

It amuses me that God should show me something so important through a clown. (Who says God has no sense of humor?)

The Hollow Center

We all have this spiritual need for God at the center, a need that increases along with the inner and outer chaos spinning in our lives. Have you ever seen a centrifuge at work? The medical laboratory at the hospital where I used to work had one. Inside the drum of the machine a liquid is spun with such rapid force it impels everything away from the center out to the periphery, and separates the liquid into different substances and densities, breaking it down into serum, cells and other parts. The greater the centrifugal force or pull outward, the more hollow the center becomes and the greater the separation or divisions into different components. I saw the chaos in my life as a centrifugal force, pulling me from the center and dividing my life. The more it whirled, the sharper my need grew.

For most of my Christian life, I had been caught in a centrifugal pattern of working hard, spinning my wheels as fast as they would go in order to fill the deep hollowness within my spirit. I imagined the way to fill it was through an active, grasping approach and lots of strenuous effort: witness, church work, prayer, Bible study . . . the "total" commitment. All good things, but there was a drivenness to my religiosity and the rest of my life, too. Oddly, the more I had tried to do, the more chaotic and broken into pieces I'd felt within.

Every day it seems I discover more Christians like me who are searching for a response to the stress and intricacy of life. Christians do have stress. Lots of us struggle with lives that are fractured by everyday living. I'm relieved to know I was not the first nor the only one. I've met persons like myself, whose Christian life is active, even relentless, but by their own admission, hungry. Distances between themselves and God seep into their days just as they did into mine. And the presence of the God who is meant to be source and center slips to the outer rim, and He becomes another disjointed part of the chaos.

And then what? Maybe we sense we're disconnected from God somehow. He becomes superfluous to the business at hand. He lives on the periphery so long we begin to think that is where He belongs. Anything else seems unsophisticated or fanatical.

I must admit that while part of me was pure desire, part was utter rebellion. Did I really want to embark on anything so new and daring as this? I was afraid of where the adventure might lead. Frankly, the whole experience was making me feel different and even alone, as though I had stepped out of line and was marching to a rhythm no one could hear, much less understand. I sometimes longed for life to return to the way it was before, before the chest pains.

Yet I could not escape the mysterious, magnetic attraction that drew me, at times with strange intensity. I marveled constantly at the Godward tug I felt inside. Actually there were times when it seemed my desire for God would swallow me. Odd, but even now, I feel hesitant admitting the strength of my desire for Him. We Christians are schooled in moderation. But God's love has never been moderate. And to find yourself invaded by that love, incited by its fire, can be a consuming experience. In awakening to His love there is little that is moderate. Desire *or* rebellion.

One morning in a brave and probably brazen moment, I poured out the tranquilizers, sensing I no longer needed them. I was right. I never again had another chest pain. From then on the recurrent ache in my heart was something altogether different.

Remember David's psalm?

> As a hart longs for flowing streams,
>   so longs my soul for thee, O God.
> My soul thirsts for God,
>   for the living God.
>   —PSALM 42:1-2 RSV.

When I read those words that winter, I found in David a friend, someone to share my secret. David, too, had carried the intense longing inside him. *He sang those words for me,* I thought. *For the whole human family.*

The complexion of my journey was changing from those early December days. The chest pains had gone as mysteriously as they'd come, as if they'd served their purpose and moved on. Now at the end of February, my search was no longer for an escape hatch from a stressful world. It had become a quest for God. For intimacy with Him in the midst of the world. I turned attention to "gathering my life together in God."

A Shared Space

But reshaping a life so it is centered in God was an enigma to me—absolutely bewildering. I had a mountain of doubts to climb. Did such a place really exist, a place where life is gathered together in God? Was I making it up because I needed such a place to exist? How could I know? Is it really possible to live one's life with a growing, even habitual perception of God's presence? I wanted it to be so with all my heart, but I also wanted the truth. Life was too important to be shaped by an illusion. For a while I felt like Thomas who strolled into the Upper Room after the Resurrection, saying, "You'll have to show me." And that is exactly what God began to do.

One day at church a friend who taught a Sunday school class along with me handed me an old paperback. "I think you would like to read this," he said. I glanced at the title. *The Seven Storey Mountain* by Thomas Merton—a name I hardly knew. That evening I sat down to glance through the book. In the early hours of the morning I was still reading, turning the pages with that peculiar and rare wonder that only comes when you read a certain book at just the right moment in your life. It was the warm spiritual chronicle of a brilliant young man who, finding himself caught up in a life of growing restlessness and emptiness, encounters himself and his deep need for God, and finally enters a Trappist monastery, which he lovingly called "the four walls of my new freedom."[1] There he began to find wholeness by discovering God at the center.

Though much of Merton's story seemed alien to me, his extraordinary journey touched me deeply. The book led me to others—like *The Practice of the Presence of God* by Brother Lawrence,[2] the kitchen monk who transformed his whole life into a constant awareness of God's presence.

I found my way from one book to another, or sometimes they found me. I read with curiosity words I'd never encountered and ideas that seemed to touch the springs of my life. Phrases leaped out at me: "Center down," "Hold thou to the center."

Those were rich days of discovery, reading on the sofa till late in the night. Sometimes Sandy joined me, intrigued by the books as well, some of which he had read years before in seminary. Over and over I found described the very thing for which God had planted a desire in me—a centering in His presence, a focusing on Him.

Deep within us all there is an amazing inner sanctuary

of the soul, a holy place, a Divine Center . . . to which
we may continuously return. . . . It is a dynamic center,
a created Life that presses to birth within us. . . . It is a
seed stirring to life if we do not choke it. It is the . . .
Presence in the Midst.[3]

When I read these words of Thomas Kelly, I was so stirred
I could not go on reading but only sit in awe. I knew intuitively
those words were true, and that God was speaking to me. How
had it been that all my life I had possessed a center, a potential
for God's presence, and not known it until these days in which
I was awakened by God?

Yet what a center actually is was still rather vague to me. It
was a term, a concept in a book or in another person's experience. Then I remembered a vivid moment that had taken
place several years before. I had to wonder if maybe God
wasn't knocking then, too.

It was the first night of our family vacation on the Carolina
coast. I love the sea, especially the place where it meets the
land, and I have always thought God speaks most eloquently
there. So after unpacking I took a walk along the sandy corridor. The moon was round and white as a pearl. And in the
distance, pier lights shredded the darkness with yellow beams.
I had probably walked a mile when I sat down and gazed into
the magnitude of the night, at the stars and the encroaching
sea. And gradually I became aware of a great rhythm going on
about me, as though my fingers had inadvertently slipped upon
a pulse beating deep in the universe. The pattern of the stars
followed the rhythm. The moon and the tide also obeyed it.
Even the wind moved back and forth like a breath. Night, day,
wind, tide, stars and moon—it all seemed like a magnificent
dance done to silent music, orchestrated by God. It was a world
ebbing and flowing in harmony with His conductor's baton.

I had not thought about that experience since. Now I wondered if perhaps God designed the world within us like the
world around us . . . to be lived in a certain rhythm with Him,

to revolve around Him like a dance done to silent music. Maybe that *had* been my first stirrings for a center, or at least a clue to its meaning. And in some way it had prepared me for the discoveries I was making now. But I hadn't known enough then to recognize the moment or to follow the stirrings.

Perhaps a center is an inner space where your life and God touch. But like an experience of God, it is difficult, if not impossible, to define in an analytical way. Usually the best you can do is speak of it in pictures.

In the waiting room of a doctor's office one day I saw a copy of one tiny piece of Michelangelo's painting on the Sistine Chapel ceiling. It showed God's hand with one finger reaching out and Adam's hand with one finger extending back toward God's. Their fingers are almost touching, but not quite. The tiniest space is left between them. I remember staring at the picture while I waited for the doctor. For some reason my attention was drawn away from the fingers to the space between them. It brought to mind at the time the gulf of separation between human beings and God.

But maybe there is a different way to view that space. The mysterious inch on the fresco could as easily be where God and humans reach their fingers into a common space. It could speak to us of the place where our lives touch and mingle with God's. A shared space, a center.[4]

A center is not simply an inner place where you are in touch with God's presence. Most important, it is a space from which you can focus your entire life. Being centered is not so much a state of being as a point of beginning.

A brand new image was taking shape for me. Certainly not original, it is frequently used to describe a life centered in God's presence. Yet it entered my thoughts with such luminosity, I finally pulled out my journal and sketched it—a wagon wheel, with spokes around a hub, God. God, the axis of a spinning life . . . the still point, the grounded center.

While not as majestic as the image of a center in Michelangelo's *Creation of Adam,* a wagon wheel has something else—

spokes, an outward flow. Here the idea is more complete. The spokes moving out from the hub represent the multifaceted life, all our different selves, flowing from the center rather than scattered about without integration from within. The wagon wheel took on special meaning to me, becoming an image of what I needed—life with God, in God, through God, experiencing Him as the "whole" of life.

Yes, that's what we need. But I don't think for a minute that a centered life is the *solution* to all our problems. Rather it is a way to *respond* to our problems. We don't withdraw from the world to a center. We respond to the world from our center.

Instead of rushing about, accepting every job that comes, we get a sense of what's really important. Being centered allows us to bring that elusive quality of focus to our lives. It enables us to set priorities. From the center we can respond to the chaos by eliminating that which isn't meaningful and bringing order and calm to the rest. For in the center we are rooted in God's love. In such a place there is no need for striving and impatience and dashing about seeking approval.

We need not avoid our active lives, but simply bring to them a new vision and shift of gravity. We are called to live a life rich and full, but rooted firmly in the center where all is drawn together in God and then flows out of His presence. That is when life becomes the silent dance revolving around Him, alive with the music of His love.

Blessed Are the Pure in Heart

How do we shift our gravity to the center? How do we accomplish this matter of gathering life together in God? I imagine we are talking about a long time of growing into it. But we must begin primarily by refocusing our attention, keeping our minds and hearts directed toward God. The essence of the centered life is attention to God in all we think, say and do. It is the growing realization of His presence in our most down-to-earth living. It is *keeping* our finger in the space.

To be centered, quite plainly, is to be single-hearted. Jesus calls us to an inward re-formation. He advised us to seek first God's kingdom (Matthew 6:33). Obviously if we follow this advice, we will be more focused and unified.

"Blessed are the pure in heart," Jesus also said, "for they shall see God" (Matthew 5:8). Can we peel away the familiarity and discover those words anew? Pure in heart means to be single-hearted . . . to will one thing—God. From the center we see with a single vision everything in the light of God. This was certainly how Jesus lived His life. All His moments flowed from His single-heartedness, from His intimacy with God. That was His core.

Perhaps you wonder, as I did at first, if this is not a narrow way to approach life, aiming for it all to flow from a single divine point. Christianity is full of paradoxes and this is one of the strangest. When we are centered in God alone, we are able to relate to more of life and the world, and find more meaning in them. In some way a centered life becomes wider and fuller. To form one's life around this single perspective enables us to deal with more problems, not fewer, embrace more of life, not less of it. One reason is that we are not so divided, over-whelmed or bogged down by trivia and confusion.

These were the kinds of secret thoughts that filled my winter—discovering my need for a center, what it meant and how to shape my life in that direction. One day it was an affair of the head, as I read, sifted, pondered and questioned what it meant to center oneself in God. The next day it was all an affair of the heart as the longing for God and for wholeness in Him filled me up. And then there were the days I lived oblivious to everything, rejecting the entire notion, running wildly from it, absorbing myself in cooking and cleaning, committee meetings and running the children here and there.

Mostly I was not sure how far I could commit myself to all this. I did not know how much I could gather my life together in God. Even how much I wanted to. Paul asked in Corinthians, "Do I make my plans like a worldly man, ready to say Yes and

No at once?" (2 Corinthians 1:17b RSV). Jesus Christ is not Yes and No, he said, but all Yes. But I was full of conflict, wanting to walk two paths at once. I was Yes and No at the same time.

What if the things that mattered before no longer mattered to me, and the things that never mattered did? What if God asked too much? What if I became "different"—so different no one would recognize me? How would my life change? One thing about awakening, you open yourself to a newness you cannot always control.

One Saturday afternoon I helped Sandy prune the rose bushes climbing the back fence. I watched him clip until the poor bush was a stump of nubs and limbs. "Do you think you've overdone it?" I asked. It seemed impossible anything could bloom out of this. And I found myself staring at it with a sudden sense of kinship.

"Roses will be spilling all over the place in May," he said with confidence.

Could that possibly happen in my life? Could pruning and cutting away the old bring an unfurling of newness? I didn't know. I didn't even know if I wanted to grow back any differently after my upheaval with stress. My doubts and hesitations about going deeper into this journey seemed stronger than ever.

"Do you suppose that sort of thing happens to people?" I said, hardly aware I'd spoken the thought out loud.

Sandy lowered his clippers. "You're talking about yourself. About the past few months, aren't you?"

I nodded. "I suppose so."

"Well, why not?" he said. "Something completely new can come out of it . . . maybe it already has begun." He seemed to know I was moving through the passages of some sort of spiritual journey. But there was a question in his voice and he waited for me to answer.

We'd never really talked about the experience that had begun in me. Even now I felt myself slow to answer.

"Maybe you're right," I finally said, turning back to work, and the moment was over. But the unsettled feeling lingered. *Why am I so tentative with my answer?* I kept thinking.

But down deep I knew. I didn't want to be pushed into committing myself. It seemed frighteningly real to me that I was approaching a time when I must decide whether to commit myself to go on in this new direction. So far it had been a matter played out safely in my head, and perhaps even in my heart. But when God shows up on our doorstep, it is ultimately the direction our *feet* take that means the most.

What was I actually going to *do* about all of this?

By faith Abraham, when he was called
to go out to a place . . . obeyed; and he went out,
not knowing whither he went.

Hebrews 11:8

5

Deciding to Open the Door

All through March I had the sense of being pursued by the need to make a decision. I needed to step out, put my feet in this new path that my head had discovered and my heart was drawn to. But I kept resisting.

It had begun, I think, that day by the roses when Sandy turned his eyes on me and asked me quietly about the journey he had sensed taking place in me. And I could not speak of it. Somehow, to speak of it was the same as committing myself to it. And I could not do that—yet.

I returned to my journal frequently because it became a sanctuary where I could pour out in honesty my pain and joy. It recorded my footsteps and helped me understand where I was standing, where I had been, and even where God pointed. One morning in March I folded back a page and wrote:

Whatever am I resisting? Am I scared of a deeper experience with God? Am I lazy? Or just entrenched in my old familiar way of "doing" religion? I would like to enter into an ongoing, encompassing communion with

God in the midst of my life. I would like to gather my
life together in God and see and touch the world through
His eyes. But something tells me I cannot, I should not,
enter this lightly. I hang back. Oh God, I am weak and
I have no courage!

I was, in fact, scared of extremism. Scared of following after
God with such total abandon. The road of "God alone" struck
me with unsettling fear.

So I lingered in a kind of limbo. Unable to go back, unable
to go on. Uncertain. Tentative. The stream of resistance flowing beneath the ground of all my discoveries and good inten-
tions had caught my life in its current.

Something happened about this time that had a curious effect
on me, though it seems illogical that an episode so typical and
unassuming could affect me so strongly. I was having tea with
a group of young women whom I knew fairly well. We had
been involved in a number of community activities over the
years. The conversation, light and cheery, moved briskly about
our children, the books we'd read, our current fund-raising
activities, our future plans. There was nothing out of the
ordinary about the gathering and usually I joined in with
delight. But that day I fidgeted in my chair. My mind kept
drifting off and I had an ache in my throat, a longing for the
journey I'd glimpsed, but was somehow afraid of.

I managed to get through the tea, but the sense of no longer
belonging in situations where before I was comfortable stayed
with me for days. It was the distressing feeling of being
different, incongruent with my old friends and conversations.
What was happening to me?

I refused to go on like that. So I determined to put an end to
the spiritual upheaval in my soul, all the inner searching, and
return to the days when such things never happened. I would
take my hand off the plow and turn back. *But I couldn't!*

Though I wanted the safe, familiar world of before, I also
wanted to follow the challenge of dwelling deep in God . . . in

prayer . . . in His presence. I could not choose; I could only sit on the fence with a foot in each pasture.

How strange that we tend to stand ankle-deep in the spiritual life even though the grounding depth of intimacy with God is the most nourishing experience of our lives and affirms our very being!

I Will Choose

It was a simple line in a book that propelled me to face the dilemma.

> To live in the presence of God . . . is to live with purity
> of heart, with simple-mindedness . . . That, indeed,
> demands a choice, a decision and great courage.[1]

A choice, a decision and great courage. *Okay,* I told myself one blustery March morning—*choose!*

In awakening to God there is always a moment of choice, a time to say an absolute yes, to commit yourself as best you can to the life of God that is kindled inside you. The experience demands it. And there will likely be a need for a reaffirmation of that choice numerous times as we awaken to God. We are spasmodic, fickle creatures who must be brought back again and again to our journey.

At the window I watched the wind whip the clouds. I could hear the question asking itself in my mind: *Can you alter your life without surface games, opening yourself to a new and deeper level of experience with God, not knowing where it might lead?* The experiences of the past months were pressing upon me like the crest of a wave, wanting to take me somewhere. *I will go for a walk,* I thought abruptly. *And I will decide.*

I went to the back porch to put on some walking shoes and saw the boots that had belonged to Sandy's Gramp, who had died at the age of eighty-seven. He had been a little man, and he and I wore the same size shoe, almost. The boots were my only possession from this gentle man who was like my own grandfather. When I wore them on cold, nostalgic days, they recalled his presence to me. Now as I tugged them on, I thought, *When God comes knocking, it's the feet that give us away.* Feet are little appendages of our will. I would take a walk and decide about the direction I would follow. Enough is enough.

I had no idea what I might choose. Really. I think I was leaning toward calling some sort of halt to the whole thing. I felt my cowardice most keenly that day.

Outside, the sky was slung low, smeared with inky clouds by a wind swirling wildly out of the north. Sunlight gnawed feebly at one small corner of the sky. I shuffled along the street beside the silver mailboxes in our little neighborhood. Everywhere the trees pointed bony fingers at the sky as if trying to direct me. The boots clopped on the pavement. I sounded like a Clydesdale. Suddenly the light that was thick and dull around me grew bright for an instant as sunlight struggled through a break in the storm clouds. I felt kin to the sun as it tried to break into the grayness. Perhaps that was the fragile mystery going on inside me, too . . . breaking into a new way of experiencing God's presence, overcoming the darkness inside myself.

I stomped on in Gramp's boots, sensing I was moving along an inner path as well, traveling toward a decisive moment . . . a conversion.

The word leaped into my head. *Conversion?* How strange I would think of that. My interpretation of my own tradition (right or wrong) was that the grace of God came in one great dose as we accepted Christ into our lives and were born again. It was a one-time negotiation in which grace arrived in a lump sum. Conversion then was more or less over. There was nothing left to do except come to church, live for God and get other people to discover Him. But what if conversion, this turning of the heart to God, is a gradual, ongoing process that begins at that great outpouring of grace and then continues on? Is it possible that awakening to God is the continuation of conversion?

I Am Being Converted

This thought was so radical to me, I paused on the street to be sure I took it in. Of course grace comes initially as we respond to God's gift of salvation. Yet it is a good work *begun* in us that God brings to completion. The Apostle Paul had told us that (Philippians 1:6). We do not go to sleep one night and wake up completely new and whole in the morning. No, that is magic. And as far as I know God does not relate to us as a magician.

That means that conversion is a process of growth and change. It begins with God and goes on silently within us, flowering out at certain unique times as He calls us to decisive moments, rediscovery, awakening, just as that initial moment of conversion did. *I am* being *converted,* I thought. *I am being converted on the side of this road!* To embrace this new birth, I was discovering, would simply be a response to more of God's grace, allowing my conversion experience to continue.

I don't think *conversion* is too strong a way of putting it. Perhaps I am taking a risk using the word, but I doubt there is a more apt description for what was happening to me. For conversion is a way of living out the entire spiritual life. It is a birthing *process.* A sifting of life's deepest mysteries, coming to see things in new lights and responding in fundamentally new ways. John Claypool once commented that the Great Commission in which Jesus commands us to go into all the world, teaching the gospel and making disciples, applies to our inner world as well.[2] We should go into all parts of ourselves, into the dark, yet unconverted places inside. It seemed those were the inner places I was walking that morning.

Yes, *conversion* was a good word for the journey.

Since then I have recognized that God's way of working in

the world is primarily the way of process and passages. Our physical life on earth is the inevitable movement through certain passages—from the womb to birth, from infancy to childhood, from puberty to young adulthood, through middle adulthood, senior adulthood, to death. We move from one stage to another, and often the passage is painful, like squeezing through the narrow part of an hourglass. God has designed creation to move inch by inch, stage by stage, from incompleteness to completion. This is something we should always keep in mind as we relate to God. For it says a great deal about the way He works in the spiritual life also.

I had been moving slowly, and at times imperceptibly, through the passages of an awakening experience, though I did not know, really, where one stage ended and another began, just as I was not sharply aware when I left childhood and entered adulthood. Now, with the advantage of hindsight, I have come to name these passages in my spiritual journey.

First I had moved through the precipitating (or knocking) event, followed by the passage of self-discovery, then on into the discovery of God as the central whole of life. Now I was entering another passage, about to squeeze through perhaps the most painful of those hourglass experiences, into the dimension of decision and commitment. Would I, could I, do it?

The basic dynamics of conversion are summed up for me in the words *leave-arrive, end-begin, shed-emerge*. These are the tensions of conversion and spiritual awakening. They are the permanent poles we travel between. In conversion we are called upon to leave, end, shed in order to arrive, begin, emerge. That is the meaning of conversion.

Not long ago my daughter received a butterfly garden, a large box with big windows for viewing. Along with it came a package of tiny caterpillar larvae in a jar. We placed them prominently in the kitchen and watched with wonder as these larvae grew into fuzzy worms. After a few days we found them attached upside-down to the lid of the jar like little question marks. An incredible mystery was going on every day as the creatures seemed to migrate according to some sacred clock buried inside them. They formed the hard chrysalis around themselves, entering the dark silence of a cocoon, *leaving, ending* their old way of life.

Then one day we found one of the creatures emerging from its cocoon. A brilliant monarch butterfly wriggled out, unfurling its body and squeezing the extra orange color from its wings onto the bottom of the box. Ann and I watched, mesmerized by the process, captivated by the empty shell of the cocoon left behind.

This is the miracle of conversion that we experience. Life is one grand metamorphosis. We are creatures stretching into new selves, new levels of being, deeper ways of relating to God. And we leave our chrysalis behind . . . the husk of another time and place and being.

The Abraham Journey

These were the truths that grew inside me as I walked. The road curved. My coat whipped against my legs as the wind howled around the turn. I walked in the old man's shoes, suddenly thinking of another old man I liked very much, one who left his chrysalis behind—Abraham. I'd had a special feeling for Abraham ever since I learned the bold and scary thing he had done. "Go," said God, "from your country and your kindred and your father's house to the land that I will show you" (Genesis 12:1 RSV). At seventy-five, Abraham felt the vibrations in his life prodding him to a new beginning. It was time to leave and let go. And he did.

When the time comes, when God strums the chords, we too will feel the vibrations, if we are not too busy or distracted. We may sense Him calling us to set off in quest of a new interior land . . . to unearth new and deeper dimensions of ourselves, to leave behind old places and ways of relating to find fulfillment in new ways. Perhaps even to change our lifestyle, move physically. It is not easy to say yes as Abraham did.

As I walked along I decided I would name the inner movement I'd begun to sense deep in my soul in honor of Abraham. Why not, since I have an incurable urge to name everything? (As a child I once named my toothbrush.) It would hereafter be known as the Abraham-journey. I think we could say that conversion is a lifetime of Abraham-journeys in relation to God and life.

My boots clicked on the gravel. Gramp again. A man with the heart of Abraham. I recalled how he had been baptized at the age of sixty-five, wandering after a God he'd heard beckoning him to brave new lands.

Once I saw a poster on a wall in Atlanta that reminded me of Abraham, and I suppose Gramp, too. Attributed to Charles DuBois, it said: "The important thing is this: to be willing at any moment to sacrifice what we are for what we can become." Always in an Abraham-journey you and I are brought to the brink of deciding whether to remain where we are or move into the new and risky world of becoming fully born spiritually.

Anxiety at the thought of risking change rose in me and I was aware of the wind beating in my face. I looked up and saw a bare oak tree. It had shed, too, emptied itself, let go old leaves so new life could come. Everywhere I looked, every thought that filled my head, reminded me of it . . . this shedding of the old way in order to allow something new to grow in me. I crossed the brown field at the end of the looping road. Once more sunlight hit the lot and receded, leaving me stalking through the dead grass with my own fluctuations.

I went back and forth, my reluctance popping out from nowhere like my shadow leaping at me on the pavement. John of the Cross observed once that God has more difficulty in converting one soul than He did in creating the whole universe, because with the universe He met no resistance![3]

Had the fullness of time come for me, as it had for Abraham when he left for a new land? By far the more delicate part of any conversion is to be able to grasp the fullness of what is finished, to recognize the endings that can become beginnings. It came down to a question—was the ground where I planted my spiritual life worn out? I strolled on. Yes, of course it was.

When I was small, I was aware how my daddy changed the crops on Monk Farm from one field to another. I remember bumping along in the front of the old black pickup at planting time, wondering where the cotton and peanuts would show up. A farmer knows when the field has exhausted its nutrients and potential and it's time to move the crop on. A spiritual pilgrim needs to discern when his or her life is stunted in an old field and find the courage and determination to go to a "new land" that the Lord will show. Surely this is one of our greatest challenges and capacities—to understand and reorient our lives, aligning ourselves with the God-given rhythms of growth and awakening that vibrate within.

At the end of the road I turned around and looked back at the bare oak swaying in the wind, a winter tree that spoke eloquently of the promise of conversion. It waited for the new life of spring, just as the butterfly waited in the cocoon for a new beginning, just as Abraham waited for his arrival in the Promised Land. *Leave, end, shed,* the tree said, *so you can find the wholeness you seek.*

Somehow in that moment all the events and emotions since December converged. Chest pains, reflection tree, punching clown, wagon wheel—all of it flowed together. The awakening passed from simple recognition of my need for God at the center of my life, to a depth where the will is stirred. And that is a deeper place by far. That is the place of response, of unifying one's heart, mind, soul and feet around a decision.

Yes, I thought. *Yes! I must leave this old way of living out my life and somehow set my feet for the grounding center which can bring the wholeness and presence I need. I must do it even if it means a re-formation of my life. I must.*

So, by the grace of God and nothing else, I set my feet for a new interior land while Gramp's boots shuffled me home.

Later I was surprised to learn that a bare tree was instrumental in the conversion of Brother Lawrence, the French monk I had read about during the winter.[4] A bare tree in winter. What is it about that, or about anything, which can speak a sentence from God and prod us to change our lives? Only in the mystery of God, I suppose, do such things happen.

I had chosen. It was nearly like turning loose a trapeze and pivoting in the air . . . hoping God would swing another trapeze to me. When I came inside after my long walk in the cold air, I could not stop shaking.

My decision tossed in me for days. About a week later, as Sandy and I watched an old movie on television, I couldn't carry it alone any more. I began to tell him about my experience, my decision that I wanted God as the whole of my life, to experience His presence in my everyday life. There was a certain tentativeness to my voice as I spoke, and many of the questions and doubts I'd struggled with came pouring out.

Sandy looked at me. I thought I saw a flicker of recognition cross his face, a look that suggested he knew exactly what I meant. And I saw a quiet strength in him. This gentle, solid man. I knew that I needed him very much.

"What is happening to you is very important," he said. "Hold onto it."

I reached over for his hand. I would not have to make this journey alone.

The Gleam of the Pearl

In the days ahead I felt new, tugged by love for God welling up in me. Yes, there was pain that came with it—fears of the new and nostalgia for the old "easy" days lingered like old ghosts. But the joy and challenge, the voice of God in the distance, Sandy and the children's warm support, and some inner propulsion I couldn't even explain saw me through all that.

I think if we hear, really hear in the depths of our hearts, God knocking, and wake to the adventure of experiencing the world in His presence, we will not turn back. Sandy was right. We should hold onto it, for embarking into a conscious awareness of and intimacy with God is the great treasure of life. It is like Jesus' story about the pearl of great price (Matthew 13:45). You remember that the merchant who found it sold all that he had to buy the pearl. Perhaps Jesus was referring to those priceless moments when we discover the voice of God calling out to us, summoning us to a new creative experience with Him. He tells us bluntly that if we buy the pearl, it will cost us everything. But—the pearl is worth it. The merchant didn't think twice about his decision.

It is the gleam of the pearl, the lure of the Spirit, that sees you through everything else, everything that pulls you back and makes you doubt your decision and wonder what you're doing this for. I had caught the tiniest spark of it, the desire to be united with God's presence in the midst of my moments. Only that. I was a million miles from achieving it, but still I had the audacious hope burning within. I knew it was probably the finest flame God had ever ignited in me, and that God would not let it be extinguished. I felt His hand cupped around it with great tenderness.

They that wait upon the Lord shall renew their strength;
they shall mount up with wings as eagles.

ISAIAH 40:31

6

"I Will Speak Tenderly to Her"

SOMETIMES IT SEEMS God is doing nothing at all. Nothing happens. The psalmist says, "God hides his face" (Psalm 13:1). That verse always reminds me of the time I saw two old gentlemen in overalls sitting on soda crates at a filling station in North Carolina.

"Times are bad," one said as I passed by.

The other cast a look at the sky. "Looks to me like God hung a gone-fishing sign on the pearly gate." He chuckled, but it did not hide the pain in his little joke. Beneath his mountain humor I think I understood what he meant. Like the psalmist he was expressing the human anguish we all feel when God can't be perceived in our affairs. And this was the darkness I had come upon.

I'd gone for a walk in March. I'd made a commitment, or at least I'd determined a new course—to enter into a deeper walk in the presence of God. Okay, I was ready. Now I combed the skyline for a ray of guidance, a place to begin, some small light. Anything at all. But there was nothing. God had hung His sign and left. March wore on. April arrived. I grew impatient. At times I felt almost foolish for getting myself into this. After everything that had happened, I even thought of walking away from the whole experience. One "pearl" flung over the fence. For the experience that had been unraveling since last December seemed to grind to a halt. Now, only silence. And aloneness. That I couldn't bear.

It often happens this way. We are awakened to our true self, to the need for God at the center, even to a moment when the will is stirred and yields. But what of that delicate time that follows? The experience of awakening can become so fragile and crystal thin at this point, we are likely to look right through it and see nothing.

Outwardly I went about my life as usual, but inwardly I fretted about centering my life. I thought of my sketch of the wagon wheel and was frustrated because nothing changed. But then, I'm prone to impatience. I am a child of instant oatmeal and Polaroid pictures that develop before my eyes. And really I had no idea how one went about the spiritual life.

Early one morning I sat at my desk before waking the rest of the family. Desire for God beat inside me and at the same time confusion washed over me. "What do I do now, Lord?" I prayed. "I need insight."

I must do something, I told myself. *I have to make some attempt to break through and grow.* My history was to grab any ball tossed to me and run deliberately with it. I was very much action oriented. That was the one thing plain to me. This time I wanted to be sure it was God who was doing the leading. There at my desk I decided. I would return here every morning, earlier even than this, and pray. Not the traditional way I'd always prayed, which was mostly asking. But something different. I had no idea what.

So each morning for the next few weeks I crept out of bed at the worst possible hour and sat at my desk in the den with the aim of praying for about twenty minutes. I decided to "meditate" upon a piece of Scripture. I had little idea what I was doing. My mind was either hopelessly distracted or lying down between two thoughts going to sleep. Mostly it was torture. It seemed nothing was happening. I suppose I clung to it for no reason other than the memory of bare trees and the hope hidden in them.

One morning on my way to one of those prayer times, I stopped to make a pot of coffee and flipped on the fluorescent light in the kitchen. The bulb didn't respond as usual and I stood in the dark kitchen thinking the fuse was out. But just as I reached to turn the switch off, the bulb flickered and the room leaped into light.

Days later, as I sat in the pre-dawn stillness trying to pray, that insignificant episode returned to me. It seemed a crazy thought, but I began to imagine how God's coming could be like the fluorescent lights in our houses. Sometimes we flip on the switch, opening ourselves to Him, and there is nothing but darkness. If we are impatient, we might flip the switch off and decide the fuse is out and the system isn't working. But if we wait just a bit longer than usual, the light blinks on. *God will come,* I thought. *He always comes—in His own time. The important thing is not to get lost in the delays.* That bit of insight kept me going. *O God, how subtle You are!*

I quit the doubting and fretting. For the first time I realized the need to wait. Wait, pray, be patient. "I am still at work," God seemed to be saying to me. I reflected on the implausible idea that waiting actually had a role to play in all this. Was there a time in the process of awakening to God that called for waiting? Could it be another "passage" in the journey? Could something crucial be happening during those silent days when it seemed God had vanished?

The Work of Waiting

One Saturday morning at seven I woke to find my son standing by my bed fully dressed in his Little League baseball uniform, cap, batting glove and all. "Mama," he was whispering into my half-conscious ear. "Is it time?"

I knew what he meant. Is it time for the game? Today he would play his first baseball game ever. It was no small thing. He had been excited (and nervous) about it all week. "I know I'm going to strike out," he had said at least a dozen times.

"No, son, you have six more hours," I told him with a yawn.

"Oh." He shuffled from the room. I drifted back to sleep.

Soon it came again—the eager little voice reaching into my dreams. "What about now? How much time now?"

"You're going to have to wait," I said. He looked at me with real anguish. "But I just can't wait any more."

"All right," I muttered, dragging myself out of bed. "I'll wait with you."

We passed the time pitching, catching and batting. Bob thought it was a useless waste of time. But without knowing it, he grew far more confident about his abilities during those hours. He sharpened his swing, smoothed out his throw and loosened his arm.

When it was finally time for the game, his team won 6-2. Bob's first time at bat he hit the ball, surprising himself so much he momentarily forgot to run to first base! It hadn't been easy waiting, but the time we shared, the work going on, was important.

This little episode was another turning point. I began to understand that in my own way I'd been doing much the same thing—poking God in the side and asking "Isn't it time? Nothing's happening." But even the distracted time spent praying, those dry moments spent groping around for Him, every little turning of our desire toward Him tills the ground of our spirits. Waiting is important work. It is a space of time that is needed. We can't fathom what God is doing. Nothing, it seems.

But we can often look back, can't we, and see that something was indeed happening, when at the time it didn't seem so. So much of God's work goes on in the deep places within us, on a secret level too deep to recognize. And this quiet creative action, this ground work in which He prepares the soil for growth, takes time. "A lot of the road to heaven has to be taken at thirty miles an hour," wrote Evelyn Underhill.[1]

During the dry waits we learn a kind of naked trust. We learn to grow still and listen. We learn to hope. Waiting time allows the loving call of God to sink into our marrow and become one with us. Any time we move into something new, we need time to process the changes. Changing too rapidly can mean inviting a journey that will not last. God knows that well.

So now I began to question each fragment of my experience, the awarenesses that had entered my life. I tried to understand their authenticity and to relate them to the goals of loving God and loving others.

Jesus gave us two commandments. Love God with all your heart, mind and soul, and love your neighbor as yourself (Matthew 22:36-40 and Luke 10:25-27). These two goals are the center of our faith, and everything we do, especially when we are breaking new ground in our spiritual walk, needs to be tested against them. Does what is happening to me make me more loving within and without? Is what I am doing enhancing my love for God, for other people? Such questions keep us safely grounded.

As the days of spring peeled away, I eventually came to recognize that God had not hidden His face at all. I could almost hear Him saying, "Sometimes you have to wait. But come along, I'll wait with you."

I had wanted to come immediately into a new sense of inner calm, a new closeness with God, a discovery of His intimacy and nearness. Now, even though it seemed things were not progressing and I was going nowhere at all, I began to yield to a gentle waiting. I adopted Isaiah's words, "I will wait for the Lord . . . and I will hope in him" (Isaiah 8:17 RSV), and wrote them across a journal page. I whispered them at odd, unlikely times during the day. They seemed to rejuvenate a spirit of anticipation, listening and stillness in me. And I began to feel terribly silly that I had anguished over my spiritual life. We are much better off when we relax with patience knowing that in all that happens the Eternal is there with us, drawing us steadily, almost naturally, forward.

Lured by the Spirit

As the weeks went by I kept at the meditative prayer, though my efforts struck me as futile much of the time. I would focus on a Gospel scene, especially some event in the life of Christ, in order to chase away the distractions that swooped upon me.

One morning I reflected on the events surrounding Jesus' baptism, and in particular the scene where the Spirit of God descended on Him like a dove. In my mind's eye I pictured Jesus striding out of the Jordan River into the wilderness, led by the Spirit. I envisioned the dove flying over His head, riding the desert wind, leading Him away into solitude. And for some reason I saw myself trailing after them, too far behind to be noticed. That was all. I admit I forgot it right away.

In May an extravagant leafing was going on outside. All the green bumps on the branches of my reflection tree had sprouted and were unwrinkling into green umbrellas. Spring had reached its peak and the world looked newly scrubbed, ripe as a piece of fruit. I felt the vibrations of it inside me, as if time was being ripened too.

Early one morning before sunrise, I went out to get the paper. The air was quiet, and a band of pink light ran around the sky just above the horizon like a ribbon. As I walked along the driveway, a bird flew up off the grass right in front of me, soaring up into the pink sky. For a few moments I stood transfixed, watching it disappear over the glazed rooftops.

The solitary bird rising high and alone kindled a strange impulse in me—a hunger to taste solitude myself, to climb heights and find myself alone with God, to follow the little bird. Then I remembered my meditation on Jesus' baptism. He had encountered a dove and had gone out into the wilderness.

I was still at the edge of the driveway, my slippers growing damp in the dew. This was the moment I'd been waiting for, I knew. Of course, it was only a bird rising up from the earth. But because I needed it to be more than that, it was. From then on I had a new recognition, a sharp, emphatic, deep-drawing pull. God was inviting me to a time of solitude. The need to go away, to follow the "dove" into the wilderness, had broken out in me like a little geyser of flame.

I looked back and saw clearly how the prayer and waiting had been breaking up the old ground beneath my feet. Strange, isn't it, how God's touch is often so light and so deep, we do not know He has been there at all . . . until later.

The light was spreading. The bird had vanished over the glare. I carried the newspaper into the house, and went to thumb through a Bible concordance for the word *wilderness*. I came upon these words that touched me to the core. "I will allure her, and bring her into the wilderness, and speak tenderly to her" (Hosea 2:14 RSV).

For the first time in many long weeks, I sensed God's guidance again. This is all we can do, I suppose. Just wait and pray, and when the guiding ray flashes, we catch it with our hearts and play the hunch. When we wait on God there is hardly anything more crucial than openness. We set our feet on a new course. We wait. Sometimes in the dark. We even pray in the dark and wonder why we are doing it. But if we manage to wait and pray with even a little openness, listening to the inner prompting and to the world around us—even to a bird winging toward the sky—then all will not be lost.

God was calling me aside.

I had never considered that centering in God was linked to anything like solitude. Richard Foster puts it clearly: "Don't you long for something more? Doesn't every breath crave a deeper, fuller exposure to His Presence? It is the discipline of solitude that will open the door."[2]

In the Gospels I discovered the value that Jesus placed on solitude. I hadn't noticed it before. He would climb some hill or trek out into the wilderness or search out some place around the Sea of Galilee in order to be alone with His Father.

Not long ago I came across the story of Carlo Corretto, a contemporary writer who led an active Christian life in Europe. He appeared to be one who was always doing for God. At the age of forty-four he heard an inner voice speaking to him. In his diary he described it as the most serious call of his life. "Leave everything and come with me into the desert. It is not your acts and deeds I want; I want your prayer, your love."[3] Like Christ Carlo went straightway into the desert . . . literally.

He went to the Sahara and learned the secret of being with God. At Tamanrasset, he lived and prayed under the fierce white sun. He made sandals for a living and became a friend to the children and cripples around his shop. His experience reminded me of the furnace in Babylon where those three young men, Shadrach, Meshach and Abednego, encountered God moving in the flames. Solitude is a furnace of encounter with God and through it we can offer him our "acts and deeds" and find them burning with new fervor and meaning.

Carlo found a real desert. But I think God calls most of us to a "desert-experience" . . . to a desert that is hollowed out of our day-to-day lives. That is what I sensed God beckoning me to. A few days out of my routine . . . simply a time and place to seek Him and Him alone.

Running from Solitude

The pull refused to slacken as the days went by, no matter how much I discouraged it. And I certainly discouraged it. I know it makes no sense. I was so eager for God's guidance, so ready, I thought, to move on to new and deeper spiritual paths. But the moment God opened a way, I rebelled. Solitude was not what I had in mind. That was something I'd been conditioned to avoid, not seek out. Even though my need and desire were there, another part of me did not like the idea of aloneness.

Jesus' words tolled at me like a bell, "Come away by yourselves to a lonely place, and rest a while" (Mark 6:31 RSV). But solitude and lonely places were so foreign to me, I didn't know where to begin or even if anyone could understand if I explained my need. I had never done this sort of thing—go off to be with God and God alone. The dominant spirituality of my tradition was full of the American work ethic—plunging into the world with active involvement and dousing activity with prayer, rather like shaking salt on the main dish. I met God in my Sunday school class, in church through hymns and sermon. At least I thought about Him there. A withdrawal for quiet attentiveness to God without structure or program was, well . . . unusual. I pondered whether anyone would condone anything so solitary and "inward" as this. It had always seemed safer and more acceptable to get to work in the "field of the Lord."

Anne Morrow Lindbergh may have a clue as to why so many of us respond negatively to the idea of solitude. "When the noise stops there is no inner music to take its place," she wrote.[4] Most of us spend our lives running from the moment when the noise stops and we are alone in the silence. For there we come to the end of ourselves and arrive at the truth that reaches to the underside of our soul—that we are all, ultimately, alone. We are born alone, die alone and decide alone. And in the end we must find the music of God alone, within ourselves.

As the tug to solitude pursued me, I tried to talk myself out of it and talk God out of it, too. I understood in a small way how Francis Thompson felt when he wrote in *The Hound of Heaven* of fleeing God "down the nights and down the days." That was my initial reaction. Run. Escape the distasteful and extreme and figure out another way. "I don't really need to go away and seek God in solitude," I wrote in my journal one evening just before I fell asleep. "I can work all this out right here among friends, family and church." That sounded very correct to me.

"Come away to a lonely place." I heard the words all night weaving in and out of my troubled sleep. When I woke up I knew I could not avoid it any longer.

Something inside me gave way. "God, I'm willing to go to some lonely place, if that's what You want," I prayed even before getting out of bed. "Only please guide me. I don't have the slightest idea how to go about this."

And there I was waiting again.

Where Is My Lonely Place?

A few days later I attended a writer's group. I hadn't wanted to go, but I went anyway, propelled by the thought that a good member ought to go. After it was over, I found myself standing beside, of all people, a nun, who was visiting that day. Her eyes smiled my way, full of a soft, disarming peace.

It must have been her eyes. For though I had never actually met a nun before, I astonished myself by telling her the prompting I felt to withdraw for a time of solitude.

"Sister Colette, I have no idea where to go or how to begin," I concluded.

She smiled at me, her eyes flooded with joy. "If God is calling, I'm sure you will find your solitude," she said simply. I halfway expected advice, maybe a suggestion. But that was all she said. As I drove home I thought of the sister's confident words. I almost wished she was wrong.

During the summer a letter turned up in the mailbox from Sister Colette. I pulled it out with the inscrutable feeling that opening it would be like opening a door.

"I am sending the names of a few places where you can go for your solitude. God bless you," she wrote.

My eyes scanned the brief list, pausing at a place called the Oratory of St. Philip Neri, a community of the Oratorian Fathers and Brothers. It was a place of prayer, but also a place where the little community ventured out to confront the needs of the world. And those in the world could go there for a time to receive renewal.

Maybe it was the wonder I'd experienced as I read about Thomas Merton's monastery, because it didn't seem all that strange to go to a place so far flung from the roots of my little church back in Georgia. Despite how "unconventional" it seemed and how scary the thought of real solitude, my attraction for the Oratory was immediate. Even from between the lines of the letter, God whispered at my spirit. "Deep calleth unto deep" the Psalmist wrote (Psalm 42:7).

Emerging out of the buffer zone of waiting, where our spiritual decisions are carved deeper and refined, God's guidance does eventually come, especially if we open our hearts for it. And hope. But His message may make us bristle in surprise. Never in all my strict Baptist years would I have guessed that God would lead me to an Oratory. Such wonders!

On a pleasant Sunday afternoon I held the letter in my hand and sat beside Sandy while he read the paper.

"I've been thinking—just a little—about going off for a few days on a retreat," I said. "Some time alone might be good for me."

He lowered the paper. "I imagine it would. Where are you thinking of going?"

"Oh, I'm not sure. Maybe the Oratory. It's a Catholic community of priests and lay brothers and it's not that far away," I said.

And for the first time, I had succeeded in making my husband, the Baptist minister, speechless.

He could only look at me. "A community of priests and lay brothers," he finally said, as if he were trying to be sure he'd heard right.

I showed him the letter. "Maybe it's a ludicrous idea," I said.

But Sandy looked beyond how strange it all seemed and simply said, "God's ways aren't our ways, are they? Why don't you go?"

His wonderful openness unlocked something in me. I was going to think about it. Really think about it.

The summer burned away and I never wrote the Oratory as I intended. My procrastination had no limit. I'd pulled out stationery more than once, but always put it off for another day. Was it fear? How could I be so decided on one level and resist so slyly on another? Whatever it was, I kept the sister's letter tucked in my desk, part of me wanting to return to the old safe places in my life. See what a difficult case I can be? I absolutely exasperated myself.

I discovered within the peculiar urge known well to the band of Israelites, who decided halfway to the Promised Land they wanted to go back. Bondage and Egypt weren't so bad after all. (Some things never change!)

The urge to go back is normal. But most of us, if we have caught the flash of the pearl even momentarily, will inch ahead sooner or later. In my case, later.

Oddly it was my birthday that nudged me on. That morning when I crept out of bed to pray, I paused at the living room window. I could see the sun sitting on the horizon like a nest high in a tree. Another year. It had been one of inner movement, awakening, discoveries. So much, yet . . . I turned away unsettled.

Propped on the kitchen table was a birthday card. I opened it. "May this day bring new beginnings. Love, Sandy."

I turned it over in my hands. With time moving past me like the silence in the house, I heard God's voice calling to me from the card. "What are you waiting for?"

To grow older physically and not spiritually suddenly seemed a ridiculous waste. It is our friend, Brother Lawrence, who tells us, "Time presses, there is no room for delay. . . . Not to advance in the spiritual life is to go back."[5] Back to Egypt.

I pulled the letter from my desk. There is a season to wait and a season to press ahead. I had come upon the time to move and forge on. What was I waiting for? The question put such determination in me that day, I finally wrote the letter to the Oratory, asking to come. In the end you swallow hard and take the risk.

The reply was prompt. "Come in October."

In thy presence is fullness of joy.
PSALM 16:11

7

Love Songs from God

THE SUN WAS fading as I drove north, climbing into a golden late afternoon light. The country rolled by . . . wheat-brown, sloping silence, hay stacks, old barns. So much simplicity. I found myself letting go a bit. October had arrived. I was headed for the Oratory.

The past weeks had been ones of waiting. There were days when my thoughts seemed marked with a quiet stirring of love and desire for God. And then days when I was so immersed in everyday concerns and pettiness of all sorts that I did not give God a second thought. Or even a first. I might even have forgotten the thread of awakening that had run through my life, except for this date penciled on my calendar. I had looked forward to it with a mixture of anticipation and reluctance, sensing it was something I must do to continue moving toward wholeness, but scared of entering so much newness. I was worried about what friends would think, of being alone with myself, of how I would be received at a place I knew nothing about. But intimacy with God does not develop without sacrifice. Mostly it is our reluctance we sacrifice.

Temperatures dropped as I drove. A light mist started and finally turned to rain.

Things will be fine at home, I told myself for the tenth time. I'd stocked up on the children's favorite snacks, frozen a couple of casseroles. Sandy was going to pick the children up from school and get them to all their activities.

As I'd left, they all stood in the driveway, waving goodbye, Sandy holding a list of menus and the children's schedule. "I'm going to draw a picture for you while you're gone," Ann called as I drove away. I was relieved there had been no forlorn looks when I left. Thank you, Sandy.

I arrived at the Oratory gate precisely at dusk, that brief window between day and night that has always been such an engaging time to me. As I turned in the drive, I had the sensation of slipping through the window into a time and place of mystery, depth and beginning. "In solitude we meet God," wrote Henri Nouwen.[1] It sounded awesome to me.

The rain had stopped, leaving the air misty and cool in the half-light. I parked the car and walked toward the dormitory beneath dripping trees. All around me buildings sat darkly on the grass, quiet as midnight. Behind a curtain of tall shrubs the roof of the church arched up, raising an eyebrow at me. I spotted a little bird perched on the side of a bird bath across the yard. I wondered with a smile if that could be my "dove."

I rang the bell. A gray-haired man with a tan face peered at me through the doorway. "I'm Brother Eugene," he said warmly, lifting my bag. I followed him into the hall.

"It's lovely here," I mumbled, feeling incredibly awkward.

"Oh, you should come again in spring," he said, then added, "I'm the gardener here."

I suddenly relaxed and liked him even more.

He led me into a small room where a pot of swedish ivy grew long and gangly at the window. He rearranged the vines as he gave me instructions about meals, mentioning that they were a bit short on kitchen help and evening meals were "do-it-yourself." Then he was gone.

Shouldn't I Be Doing Something?

I listened to his footsteps trailing off into the evening. The effect of that moment was unforgettable. Quietness . . . an almost bottomless quietness . . . surrounded me. I thought, *What on earth am I doing here?*

I fidgeted with my suitcase, hanging up the clothes that would see me through the next few days. I hadn't brought much. A change of clothes, a Bible, my journal . . . that was all. I sat down on the bed. Now what? I jumped up and wandered around the room, full of a sudden compulsion to do something. Already I wanted to return to the world of "relevance."

I thought of a sign I'd read on a bulletin board. "Don't just do something. Stand there." But simply being *with* God, open and alive to His presence, was proving far more difficult than the active counterpart of doing *for* God. The aim is an ongoing awareness of God . . . opening ourselves to His loving presence. But when you are all alone in the middle of a strange place, face to face with the prospect, you decide it sounds a lot easier than it actually is.

My discomfort was so strong, I opened my notebook and actually made a list of things to do while I was there: "Read a chapter of the Bible morning and evening, take a walk, chart goals for the future, jot down article ideas, visit the library for books to read, ask if I can help in the kitchen."

When I read back what I'd written, it dawned on me what I was doing. I'd come here to be with God, to listen to Him and experience His presence. But already I was making lists of activities to keep me busy. I was like Martha in the Bible who worked in the kitchen for Jesus while her sister Mary sat at His feet. I was back to the old struggle between inward movement and outward movement, between being and doing, between prayer and involvement. I had been a Martha all my life, with all my activities for God. Was there a Mary inside me? This old Mary/Martha conflict can be a divisive one for Christians. I don't think I'd ever felt it so acutely as I did then.

I've learned since that it is really wrong to separate the inner movement toward God in prayer from the outward movement toward God in ministry. They are meant to be intertwined and balanced in a way that makes them inseparable. We are called to be both Mary and Martha together. One without the other is to miss the point. But I am convinced that our "Martha-hood," our involvement with a needy world, must flow like a by-product from our contemplation at the feet of Jesus. It is the Mary in us that must form the core of all we do. "The more we receive in silent prayer," said Mother Teresa, "the more we can give in our active life."[2] In fact, when we are immersed in God's presence, our active involvement itself becomes a prayer.

Not long ago, a friend of mine who is heavily involved in the social imperatives of the gospel suggested I concentrate more on awakening to the suffering in the world rather than awakening to God's presence. My response was that in the end they are one and the same. Intimate communion with God brings the suffering world sharply into focus, and breeds authentic and compassionate ministry. Once awakened in the depths of our souls to the presence of God as a way of life, we will also hear a voice that whispers, and sometimes shouts, "This is My world. Touch its wounds. Heal its injustice. Love it for Me." Inward movement ultimately becomes outward movement, borne on a wave of God's presence.

There in the little room with my silly list, it was clear I'd spent most of my life on the road leading out with nothing inward to nourish it. *Okay*, I thought to myself. *I will find the Mary in me. Somehow.*

I struggled almost desperately the first two days. I wandered in and out of the church and walked the grounds, usually ending up on a bench beside the bird bath, restless and search-ing. My mind was choked with thoughts, words, needs and plans. Even my attempts at prayer were strained. "Are You sure this is what You had in mind, Lord?" I asked, as I watched my second sunset casting shadows across the lawn.

Alone, with everything stripped away, my inner chaos seemed

to rise to the surface. But that is not always so bad. Perhaps it is necessary in the beginning. As Friedrich Nietzsche wrote: "One must . . . have chaos in oneself in order to give birth to a dancing star."[3] Nietzsche, who was an atheist, would probably object to my interpretation, that if we are willing to wade through our chaos in search of the door where God knocks, we will sooner or later give birth to an encounter with Him. And perhaps it will help us move again to the harmonious dance of God.

Surprised by Love

On Saturday evening a pale stream of moonlight fell across the wooded hill behind the window of my room. I watched, feeling out of sync with such peacefulness, but not nearly so distracted as in the days before. Finally I poked my head into the deserted hall. More silence.

I ambled along not really knowing where I was going. Remembering the mention of a chapel somewhere on the second floor, I climbed some stairs, following the enormous silence up the stairwell.

The second floor stretched along like a dark tunnel. A few feet away I noticed a door. Hesitating a moment, I pushed it open and stepped into the darkness of a tiny chapel lit by a single candle. The flame flickered in a red glass, moving shadows around the room in rich, wavy lines. The reverent spell of the room pulled me toward the altar. At the front of the chapel I sat down on a bench.

"Better is a handful of quietness than two hands full of toil" wrote the author of Ecclesiastes (4:6 RSV). I thought of my old pattern of religious striving, of that image of myself crawling on my knees, scraping papier-mâché off the church floor just so God would love me. I felt exhausted by all the years of trying to gain his love.

In the dimness I opened my hands and let everything go.

"God," I said out loud, "I'm not going to talk to You any

more just now. I'm tired. I'm simply going to sit here and be with You. I turn loose everything else. I want only You."

The words of my prayer ran around the chairs of the empty chapel like echoes. The longing and love I felt for God, which I hardly knew was there most of the time, swept through me with unaccustomed intensity. I closed my eyes, growing still, really still for the first time since I'd been here. The tensions began to melt away.

The wick on the candle burned lower. I lost concern for time. Something was happening to me. The stillness, the silence, the dark holiness were drawing me into a new level of awareness, clearing a space inside me . . . a visiting place for God. After a time it seemed there was only Christ in the little chapel. Just Him and me and a powerful reality of His nearness. It came stealing over the room, welling up from hidden places within me and spilling out of the moments around me. That in itself was memorable enough to last a lifetime.

But as I knelt beneath His gaze, awakening to this mystery, a beautifully delicate moment took place. A moment of grace. There rose up within me a profound sense of being loved. I felt "gathered together" and encircled by a Presence completely loving, as if I were enveloped by the music of a love song created just for me. It was not overwhelming or even emotional. Just a warm knowing that I was in God's loving embrace . . . centered and unified there.

"Lord . . . " I whispered.

"I love you, My child," He said in a still small voice inside of me.

The truth reached me like a finger of light that touches the deepest place there is within. It was God's joyful surprise. There in the little chapel I found myself loved.

Of course encounters like these are almost impossible to put into words. Surely they cannot be analyzed, only shared. If you take a butterfly, Robert Frost said, and pin it down into a box, you no longer have a butterfly.[4] This is true of our meetings with God. We should live our mysteries, without trying to dissect them. So I will not try to explain it except to say that the impression that struck me later was that some inner window had been momentarily polished, permitting God's loving presence to break through. It was the same presence that was always present, but rarely experienced because of all the busyness and trivia in my life. It had been a moment of spiritual clarity breaking into my darkness. I had entered into the miracle of Emmanuel, God-with-us.

But on my knees in the candlelight, I did not try to put words to any of the music I experienced inside. I simply felt caught and held in the midst of it. *God loved me!* He loved me for who I was, not what I did. He didn't wait until I became perfect. He loved me now, through and through, forever and ever.

As I left the chapel that night, I felt reoriented to everything around me, as if withdrawing from the world had helped me discover it anew. I noticed small things with a new delight. The plant in the stairwell, a simple row of books in the lobby. God was shining in them all.

Alone in my room, everything seemed joyfully alive to me. I sat long by the window where the moon reflected on the hill with the same warmth as the chapel candle.

The Marks of Love

I do not want to overdo my experience. It was after all, only a step. Dag Hammarskjold wrote, "Never measure the height of a mountain until you have reached the top. Then you will see how low it was."[5] Our experiences with God are "low mountains" nestled against taller unseen ones. They are steps on a continuing journey, never ends within themselves.

But I do not want to wave away my experience either. It happened. And it brought about a curious regrouping of my spirit. I don't understand exactly how God forges a new sense of wholeness and meaning in us. But I do know that drawing near God's love, one is sure to change, just as drawing near a fire one is sure to get singed. "God is a consuming fire," the

Bible says (Hebrews 12:29). To come near Him is to find His marks left in our lives. Invisible marks of love.

One of these markings is the remarkable process of bonding that goes on inside us whenever we experience God's presence. Bonding is the unseen, silent thing that passes between two souls and meshes them together. During those moments in the chapel God was bonding me to Him in a way I could scarcely perceive.

The night my first child was born, the nurse tapped on my door at 4:00 A.M. and woke me for his first feeding. After she disappeared into the darkness of the hospital, I gathered him close to my breast. It was our first meeting alone. I looked into his face, and in the silence, with his little chest pressed against mine, I suddenly felt his heart beating on my skin. It was one of the most vivid moments of my life. It seemed his heart entered mine and beat inside it. And we were so close that for one instant I could not tell where he ended and I began. We were woven into one. Bonded. I don't doubt for a minute that because of the marks left inside me from that experience I was somehow a better mother, closer to him than I would have been otherwise.

In the mystery of bonding our souls are knitted to God. You may experience Him in overwhelming holiness or simply catch His presence beating in the small moment. In a stranger's eyes. In a violet sky. And if you open yourself to God in that moment, His presence enters your heart and beats inside it. You and He are one. The hidden knotting of your life with His is strengthened. Because of the markings left in your life from that experience, you will be closer to Him. And You will be tugged to seek Him again. And again.

Bonding burns a craving inside for God that is not easily extinguished. Even a small taste of His intimacy leaves us hungry to form a continuing intimacy with Him in the midst of a busy world. It fills us with hope for a life in God's presence, peeling away all that fills the spaces between ourselves and Him. These things were a deeper hope than I had ever known. And I was afraid I would never be the same. But more afraid I would.

The next day I put my suitcase in the car and took one more walk around the grounds. The bird bath was empty and Brother Eugene's brown garden was full of last summer's seed waiting in the earth. I bent down and ran my hand into the soil. I thought back to the December day when I had the EKG. It had been a journey full of seeds. One blooming, leaving another behind, then another. Awakening blooms slowly, I thought, beautifully . . . like a garden. I felt sure there were still seeds waiting in the soil, so much to discover and experience in the days ahead. The spiritual journey is a thrilling adventure, a coming alive! And I did feel so incredibly alive and at peace crouched beside the garden.

All of a sudden I began to laugh. Laugh right out loud. A young man approaching on the sidewalk glanced over and smiled at me, then continued on his way. I covered my mouth with my hand, wondering what had gotten into me. Later I would read the words of Samuel Shoemaker "The surest mark of a Christian is not faith, or even love, but joy."[6]

I drove through the gate out into the countryside. It was all autumn haze and plowed furrows. Clouds. Sun. Peace. My heart was dancing. The deep-rooted sense of being centered in God's love and aware of His presence had not passed. Not yet. But I was trying not to be naïve. I knew about mountaintops and valleys. Somehow I expected the radiancy of these events to dim as the natural course of things, even though this retreat would always be an important event in the course of my life.

As the miles took me further away from the Oratory, something in me felt sad about leaving. I missed my husband and children and was anxious to see them, yet it was as though I had encountered God at the Oratory and was driving away. Would God be back home, too?

Sandy met me at the door with such relief, I felt a little like the cavalry. "I have a new appreciation for motherhood," was all he said. Ann rushed up behind him with the picture she had promised when I left.

She had drawn a stick figure walking on a road that wound through a lot of flowers and buildings with crosses on top of them. Her conception of where I had been, I supposed. There were other figures in the scene, too, all of them with yellow haloes around their heads. "Guess which one is you?" Ann said.

I pointed to the first figure on the road. "Right!" she squealed.

It was easy. The first figure on the road was the only one without a halo!

In quietness and confidence shall be your strength.
ISAIAH 30:15

8

I Am a Word of Love from God

HAD I GONE to the Oratory to find a halo? Perhaps I did hope that some of the holiness I felt there would rub off on me. But realistically I knew that was unlikely. I had wanted a breather from my hectic life. But that was not my main reason for going "into the wilderness." I had gone to find *solitude.*

The best definition of solitude I have found comes from Jesus Himself: "When thou prayest, enter into thy closet, and . . . shut thy door" (Matthew 6:6). Anyone can retire into a quiet place, wrote Evelyn Underhill, but it's the shutting of the door that makes the difference.[1] Solitude is a time for stripping away everything in order to focus on God. In other words, we don't go into our solitary closet carrying along the newspaper, engagement book, correspondence and all the fuss and demands of our life.

It's easy to think of solitude as just a breather from the fuss and breakneck speed of life. When life becomes a spinning whirlwind of activity—like being in one of those revolving doors in hotel lobbies—we are apt to think longingly, *If only I could slip away for a while, have some space all to myself, and get my bearings.*

When Bob and Ann were both pre-schoolers, I often had that longing to get away. They were the kind of precious toddlers who wrapped their arms around my legs and clung there half the day. I sometimes cooked and straightened house while dragging them about latched to my leg. (I remember vividly the time I tried on shoes in a store and noticed that I had peanut butter fingerprints on the knees of my slacks!) I often longed so for a place to sneak away and have my own leg back, without the demands or busyness of children, that I would sit in the car in the driveway where they could not find me. But that was not solitude. That was only a breather, a bit of privacy. It was slipping out of the revolving door for a bit, but I still had my world and my cares with me.

Solitude is a time for "God and God alone." In solitude we leave our cares outside the time and place set apart, in order to enter the silence of our hearts and immerse ourselves in God's presence. Who knows what can happen when we focus only on God.

But we don't stay in solitude. To be human is to live both in community and solitude, and to let them nourish one another. I don't think we should put more emphasis on one than the other. Though Jesus spent much time alone, He also returned to the crowds that followed Him, renewed in His power to heal, forgive, feed the multitudes and teach His followers. Paul, who spent three years alone in Arabia, afterward traveled up and down the Roman world, preaching in large, crowded cities, making many close friends. (We read their names in his letters.)

Another misconception we have is that loneliness and solitude are somehow the same. I once heard an interesting comment made by a widower: "Since my wife died I live with solitude as my companion. I feel alone and I despise it." I can understand that. He was suffering from a cruel loneliness that haunts millions of persons in our society. Loneliness is the agonizing sense of being isolated in the world, without friends, completely alone. In solitude, however, we sense our deep oneness with God and keep company with Him. Solitude, says Sean Caufield,

> is not a time to sit staring at the four walls, to give way to an early senility or boredom. It is a call to contemplative prayer, if for no other reason than to discover that being alone is not the whole of one's reality.[2]

While there may be some loneliness in every experience of solitude, we should not confuse the two. Solitude is breaking through my isolation into sharing, and being in touch with my Creator. In fact, we can begin to heal our loneliness by transforming it into solitude.

Confronting My Real Self

Times alone have helped me in many ways. In solitude I am able to cut through all the layers I've built up in my busy schedule, layers that keep me from hearing God, from being centered in Him, and from knowing who I am. Solitude helps me realize that, yes, I do not yet have a halo! Because, first of all, spending time alone means that we spend time *with ourselves.*

Who are you . . . really? Who am I? Are we summed up by the labels and categories assigned to us, such as age, sex, marital status, race, weight, economic attainment, occupation, professional and personal success level, nationality, social standing, family tree? Our true identity goes beyond these things. If I took all the above items that belonged to me and changed them around, I still would not change what is the very heart of me, that which is "purely and truly my 'I'."[3] Our real selfhood or deepest being does not depend on what the census takers or society say. Our true identity flows from our "center." Therefore we are living the fullness of who we truly are when we are living out of our center.

But often we get confused. We tend to believe that our identity lies essentially in these outward things. So we work hard to build an identity based on society's values. Unfortunately, we build an illusion.

Part of the purpose of solitude is to collapse this private illusion about our identity and help us come home again to who we really are—beings who, apart from God, are nothing.

About a year after my first experience of "going into the wilderness" with God, I spent a weekend at a retreat center in Indiana, across the river from where Sandy and some students were attending a missions conference. The first evening I was restless, unable to stay in my room. I wandered outside under an icy moon, and followed the sound of organ music to the side door of the church. Inside, the only light was a tiny lamp burning beside the young man bent over the keyboard. He didn't seem to notice me as I sat down on some side steps to listen to this private concert. The music swirled up into the arches and seemed to stay there, rolling over and over on top of itself, surrounding me with echoes.

I began to feel a part of the music, like an echo from God that had spilled into the world. What was it Thomas Merton had said? "God utters me like a word containing a partial thought of himself."[4]

What a gripping image! Each life a living word, spoken by God, and like no other word ever spoken! God shapes each one with tenderness and love to be unique. Each one is meant to resonate throughout the world, echoing the Speaker, because a word cannot really separate itself from the speaker or the speaker's thought without losing its true meaning.

My life, I realized, would always be garbled and unclear unless I remained true to the thought of the One who spoke me. Otherwise I would be a false word. So who I truly am and am meant to be is found only in my rootedness in God.

The music continued to echo around me while I asked myself, *Am I acting like who I really am?* Back at home it seemed I spent a lot of time struggling to be someone other than my true self. Did I have an external, everyday self that was mostly a fabrication? To what extent was I a "false" word?

I began to think of times I'd tried to fashion my own identity, an outer identity, that would coincide with what people thought of as success. I saw myself competing with others, trying to achieve little glories here and there in an effort to enhance my identity. Why did I rush after status and recognition like they were badges of identity? That was not the real me. No wonder my life left me so hollow and ill at ease.

I acknowledged, too, my desire to have and possess, as if what I had said something about who I was. It had been so important to me to acquire the little collection of ivory and all that antique brass. Why? Did I think my identity flowed from what I owned?

The thoughts were disturbing, but they would not stop coming. I recalled how I tried miserably to say and do the pleasing thing, sometimes at great cost, just to nurture a certain image of myself, how often I looked to others for a sense of worth about who I was. My heart sank. Alone in the church it struck me clearly. All of that was a false self.

I had been in the church a long while. The music had stopped and the organist had slipped away. Now, trying to turn loose of that outer shell—my false identity—was the thing that glued me to the steps. I wondered if I could turn to God as the source of my identity and let that say it all. Could I turn loose the compulsions for greed, achieving, competing, self-serving success and all the rest? For quite a while I wrestled with those questions.

Above me a dark rose window caught little glimmers of reflected light from somewhere outside. As I stared at it, it spoke to me of just how empty and hopeless an identity apart from God is, as futile as a dark rose window trying to give light by itself.

It was distressing to confront pieces of my false self. But it was important. In the solitude of "God-Alone" I began to know once again who I was and where I belonged. "I want to be the true me, the real me, the one that exists only in You!" I prayed.

During those moments it seemed the true part of me was being affirmed. I knew without any doubt that the more we are rooted in God, the closer we come to being ourselves, with more potential and creativity than at any other time.

Confronting our false selves can be a dark and painful process, but it is crucial. And it is an important and even blessed function of solitude to give us the time and the space to clarify our vision, so that we can struggle against all that makes up our false self and return to our true selves—to God who speaks His word in and through us.

Face to Face with God

Solitude also allows us to confront God, to come face to face with Him in a deep, free and re-creating way. Solitude ushers us into the freedom of listening. It is not all struggle and heaviness. Perhaps we picture it as Jacob wrestling with an angel, struggling and then limping away with a hip out of joint. But solitude is also being light and happy like a child in a field of flowers.

> Solitude is like a tea ceremony, the celebration of life in all its homely movements taken out of time. The wonder of the commonplace; the mystery of ordinary life . . . listening to God's secrets and jokes, a sense of delight, of dance, of coming to fruition, learning that solitude is not something we need to scramble to fill up, but that it is full and overflowing.[5]

The first morning in Indiana I woke to a great clattering of bells. After breakfast I bundled up and struck out along the road with no idea where I was going. I passed the church I had been in the night before—an imposing structure with sunlight glinting off its jutting stones. I curved around the hill, feeling light and free, trying to let thoughts of myself go. *Today there will be only God! Today I will listen, just walk and listen,* I thought.

Was that also why I was here? To walk in a great and happy freedom of listening? To hear God whispering? To be re-created in the sounds I was able to hear in this place? The questions filled me with hope. Perhaps I could spend the day confronting God in a free and concentrated way that was lost to me at home.

I strolled off the road, down the steel gray hill toward the woods and came upon a pond that gleamed like a big silver tray, with a bench beside it. There I watched the pond for at least an hour. I'd never done anything so impractical—or so wonderful—in my life. The hillside was so deep and full of God's presence it seemed to be singing. "You are singing love songs to me everywhere," I thought in a burst of joy.

Love songs!

In the silence it was easy to hear the wind singing over the water and through the trees. Unseen, but heard. Like God's Spirit. The Hebrews were right when they used the same word for moving wind and for God's Spirit—*ruach.* I heard squirrels pattering overhead in the tree branches. A clock chiming far up the hill. Leaves rustling. My heart beating. Love songs. I wanted to gather up the sounds and hold them inside me.

My Bible was in my coat pocket and I dug it out, deciding to open it at random and read, though it had always struck me as rather silly to let the Bible flop open and take the first thing you saw as your word for that moment. But at that moment I didn't care if it was silly. I opened it down the center and let my eyes fall on the page. Isaiah 5:1: "Let me sing for my beloved a love song," is what I read!

It was as if God had audibly confirmed to me His presence on the hillside, His voice in my soul, His love . . . immense, vulnerable, heart-stopping! *O God, is there anything more healing than hearing the love songs You sing?*

All the rest of the morning I walked. And listened. The hours became one seamless garment of love. The deeper I walked into aloneness, the fuller my aloneness became. I felt very close to the joyous "now," as if time were cracking open and I was dwelling in the immediacy of it all with an overflowing new awareness of God. There were moments I wanted to prance and run.

At the summit of a hill I paused and looked back at the rooftops sparkling in the sun. *This is the essence of life,* I understood suddenly. To dwell fully in the moment I am in, listening to incarnation in the midst of ordinary time.

In solitude we are "not called on to do anything in order to communicate with [God]. He does his being in our being, thinks himself through to us through the medium of our loving thought."[6] In times like these God knits us together in secret. He whispers words into us that we may not hear for a long time afterward.

The sounds we do hear in our solitude help us become born anew. Moments alone with God, untethered by time, noise and inner compulsions, nourish the places where our spiritual energy is depleted and regrounds us in His love. We taste again the fullness of living and praying on the edge of the present moment. Solitude allows us to listen with delight and celebration to God. We are renewed by the unfettered simplicity.

Responding in Love for Others

Solitude has a third role to play, one that surprised me in the beginning. For the last thing I expected was that in solitude we not only confront ourselves and the voice of God, but we confront *people*. Not in a physical sense, of course, but in our hearts.

What often grows out of our aloneness in solitude is a sense of our connectedness to other people. We are drawn not away from people but closer to them. I believe it was Albert

Schweitzer who said we should never consider any person a stranger. The more we enter solitude the more difficult it becomes to think of others as strangers.

On the second morning in Indiana, I awoke feeling unusually happy. I had experienced such an intensity of God's love in such a short time, it was hard to keep a straight face. I walked outside thinking, "Thank You, thank You, thank You. What am I going to do with all this?"

Gradually a new and puzzling sense of love for every person I saw or even thought of began to rise in me. Two men in overalls were walking toward me along the road, and I felt a great surge of compassion for them rise in me. Faces floated into my mind: people back home, my family, others. I began to think of ways I could touch them with the compassion welling up in me. What could I do and say and be to make them happier? How could I respond to them in ways that would bring us closer together in love?

In the past I was more inclined to think of what *they* could do to bring us closer. But now in my solitude everything had shifted. It had stirred up a love that wanted to pour itself out.

Then the faces of people whom I generally avoided because we were on opposite side of an issue joined the others in my thoughts. Usually I was caustic and disapproving where they were concerned. Now I was feeling my oneness with them, with everyone. I didn't want to be alienated from them any longer. *How can I reconcile myself to them in love? How can I accept them?*

My thoughts soared out all over the world to where people were separated, suffering. People I didn't know, but whose faces I had seen on the six o'clock news. Hungry children, refugees, warring tribes. Somehow they were there inside me, too.

I have learned since that weekend that true solitude in God's presence always leads us to discover others. Love and community are born in our times alone with God. Thomas Merton wrote that on a trip to town from his monastery, as he came to the corner of Fourth and Walnut he saw the people bustling back and forth. "I was suddenly overwhelmed with the realization that I loved all those people, that they were mine and I theirs."[7] In that moment he understood what solitude had done to him. It had given him his brothers.

It will do the same for us. We cannot enter solitude, this great "God-Alone-ness," and hold the world at arm's length. In solitude we are awakened more fully to people. The joke is on us.

Solitude opens our hearts to love in new and deeper ways. Back from my solitude I began thinking about a person whose face had come to me while I was away, someone who viewed things completely opposite from me. I could hardly stand to be in the same room with her for more than five minutes. But I called and invited her to lunch. All through lunch I looked at her, thinking to myself, "You are more important than what separates us." And it was true. By some miracle that had happened in my heart, she was.

Since then I have tried to make two solitary retreats a year. One result has been a burning concern for the hungry and homeless, two groups that had always raised my sympathy. But now I cared more intensely than I'd imagined I could. I began raising money to buy seeds for an African village and volunteered in a homeless shelter in Atlanta, cooking and befriending the residents. Now I could do it without the drivenness and need for approval I'd had before. I could do it purely for love.

How to Make the Most of Times Alone

Are there some specific things we can do to make our times alone meaningful, not just lonely times?

I think, first, we do need to get right away from our familiar surroundings, particularly in the beginning. At home, it is too easy to think of all the things waiting for us to accomplish downstairs or outside our "closet" door. But it is not essential that we leave home. Place is not as important as who you meet there.

Second, we should not try to program our time too much, but let it unfold. If we set up schedules and a list of things to do, we are usually only running from the moment when we are alone with ourselves and God. I have attended religious conferences at a large retreat center in the mountains. Those times were enriching, but they were not solitude, not when my time was programmed with seminars and services from morning to night. I believe we need an agenda-less approach to solitude. Then we can listen to the little impulse voices inside us. If we are impelled to walk across the hills, we can. If we are nudged to read the Bible, we can. We simply allow things to happen. We allow God to happen to us as He will.

Third, we should not come to solitude with a lot of stringent expectations. When we expect God to act, speak, come only as we envision, we are liable to miss Him. Some time ago I traveled to a nearby city to speak at a luncheon, and walked around the dining room for some time looking for someone in charge. One woman smiled at me and walked on by as if she were looking for someone. *Could it be me?* I wondered. So I caught up with her and introduced myself. She blushed. "Oh, I knew you were a visitor here, but I didn't expect our speaker to look like you." I have no idea what she expected. I was afraid to ask! Because her expectations were so specifically defined, she walked right by me.

That is the kind of thing we sometimes do in our times alone. We are looking for God to meet us in a certain way, at a certain time. Perhaps we imagine what the encounter will be like. We narrow the focus of our expectations so tightly that if God comes outside them, we do not notice. "Again and again he comes and the revelation is not a bit what we expect," wrote Evelyn Underhill.[8]

Yet we don't want to enter solitude without *any* expectations. We expect God. We set our hearts on Him. But we leave the rest to Him. If He comes to us through an organ playing in an empty church, fine. If He speaks through the wind on a winter pond, or faces that invade our thoughts, or a verse from the Bible, that is fine too.

Fourth, we need to simplify. Solitude is basically an emptying of ourselves, a stripping away. We try to do that not only within but without. When we become simple outwardly it is easier to be simple within.

I begin with material things. I have found it best to carry as little into solitude as possible. One or two changes of clothes, one pair of shoes, a Bible, one small notebook. That's all. I try to leave behind the extras. No radio, jewelry, magazines, makeup or stacks of books. The idea is to clear things away and stand before God free and unencumbered.

It is important to simplify not only the outer baggage, but also our daily practices, particularly those which have to do with our bodies. A strong connection exists between body and spirit, an interflow. We have tended to separate them, but the biblical tradition is that body and spirit are one integrated whole. What we do with our bodies affects our spirits.

Eating simply while I am being solitary draws me toward an inner simplicity. In solitude I try to forego caffeine and sugar-drenched, fatty foods and eat instead fruit, raw vegetables, bread and cheese.

I also try not to use the time to oversleep or nap all day. It is a strong temptation to overindulge myself with too much sleep, especially when the din of normal activities suddenly ceases. The challenge is to find rhythms of rest that are balanced, wholesome and simple. I usually wake very early, take a brief nap after lunch, and retire early. We need rhythms of exercise or movement that are equally simple and balanced. We don't need to carry along fancy exercise equipment, tennis rackets or golf clubs. I find that simple walking, the most basic exercise of all, puts me in touch with God and enlivens my spiritual life.

These are some of the things I have learned about solitude in the last few years. But immediately after that first retreat, I was still trying to make sense of the experience. And I was still asking the same question I'd asked when I'd left the Oratory: Would I find God at home?

Whither shall I go from thy spirit?
or whither shall I flee from thy presence?
PSALM 139:7

9

God Lives on Oak Street

IT WAS NOVEMBER. Leaves covered the lawns and sidewalks, the wind whistled through bare branches, and a deadly routine had swallowed up any sense of God's nearness: groceries, bills, phones, laundry, schedules, work. Plain old life. I felt homesick for God as I had experienced Him while I was away, for the embrace of His love across my life. What I felt was a sharp sesnse of His absence. As it closed in, I grew restless, wondering where or how I could find Him again. I knew God met me in solitude. He was there in the Oratory chapel, in all that holiness where so many prayers were said you could almost feel them against your skin, as later I was to feel Him on a retreat hillside. But now . . .

Even the new sense of love for my family which I'd brought back with me grew thin at times. If Sandy lingered too long at work so that we missed going out to dinner as planned, I grew unforgiving, and fell into my old pattern of holding a grudge. My temper grew short with the children. Ann was right. I had no halo. No sense of God's nearness in the nitty-gritty of routine and relationships.

"How was your trip?" Sandy had asked when I came back from the Oratory. I was bouyant with the experience and tried to tell him, even the parts that had no words—the moments on the bench beside the bird bath, the chapel . . .

"God's presence was so vivid . . . so real. But—"

"But what?"

"But I'm afraid of it dimming." Even as I spoke the ripples of God's absence had begun to move through me. "Maybe if I stopped in church occasionally during the week for some solitary, quiet moments, some silence . . ." My mind was racing ahead. "Is our church sanctuary locked during the day?"

"I imagine it is, but do you think that's necessary? God is not partial to stained glass," he had said, grinning at me.

What on earth did he mean by that? I was not impressed with his comment.

Where Is God?

I really did want to continue to awaken to God, but it wasn't until three or four weeks later that I drove downtown to my church one Monday morning while the children were in school. The sanctuary was locked, but I finally located a housekeeper with a key. She couldn't understand what I wanted to do there on Monday. "Church was yesterday," she told me apologetically.

"I know. I just want to sit inside a while."

She looked at me oddly and nodded. *Why did I feel so foolish?*

I eased into a pew and tried to collect myself. My mind felt impervious, like a piece of stone. I fidgeted with the hymn book. The housekeeper's vacuum cleaner whined loudly in the corridor off the sanctuary. The stained glass beamed down on me. Maybe it was the vacuum cleaner, maybe it was me, but even the window didn't look particularly holy at this point. When I tried to pray, the words came out like little cardboard cutouts. I began to feel confused. Where was God? He was supposed to be here!

Longing rose inside me. A terrible ache. I'd reached the exasperating point in hide and seek when you say, "Okay, I give up, where *are* you?"

"Oh, please God," I breathed. "Where are You?"

I knew I would have to scratch beneath easy, pat answers and search my heart and soul to get the answer.

The psalmist had this problem, trying to live between two worlds. He was forever standing in the pit of God's absence and the next minute being pulled up by some inexplicable rope of God's presence.

Listen to him. "O God . . . I seek thee: my soul thirsteth for thee, my flesh longeth for thee in a dry and thirsty land, where no water is" (Psalm 63:1). In these words I hear the same question I asked in the emptiness of the church: "Where are You, God?" The psalmist seeks after God even at the black bottom of the well. Then, on the heels of the question comes this intimate awareness: "In the shadow of thy wings will I rejoice" (v. 7). When he acknowledged God's absence, when he asked the question of God's whereabouts, then he began to make his way toward God's presence.

Perhaps this is the most shattering truth of all. God is present even in His absence. It sounds contradictory. But still I believe it. For when God is scarcely perceived, when longing squeezes your heart, He is near. The sense of God's absence and the sense of His presence are two circles that overlap. When God seems absent, ask the question, probe the boundaries, seek, knock. You will eventually end up in the other sphere. You will find Him. "Ask, and it will be given you; seek, and you will find; knock, and it will be opened to you" (Matthew 7:7 RSV).

But at the time I was not so sure. As I sat in the stillness of the church and listened to the moan of the vacuum cleaner, I wasn't sure I'd ever know His presence again. I did not know that presence often grows out of the very sense of absence that causes so much pain. The point is, you don't search for what you don't miss. If I don't miss God, if I don't burn inside with need for Him, I will probably not seek Him. It is just as Jeremiah wrote: "You will seek me and find me; when you seek me with all your heart I will be found by you, says the Lord" (Jeremiah 29:13–14 RSV).

Just where is God, this One I had known as the "beyond in my midst"? Where could His presence be found? Where did He show His face? There on the pew, I found myself face to face with the questions. I felt them so strongly I even wrote them down on the back of an old church program I found. And frankly, it's impossible to set out on a journey toward deeper intimacy with God without confronting them sooner or later. Perhaps it is another passage of awakening.

That Monday I knew I would have to settle one thing. If I am intent on centering my life in the presence of God, then what do I believe about where this presence can be found? Do I imagine Him as far off, elusive, here and gone? Do I think of Him present only in certain times and places? More here than there? Of course, I knew what I was programmed to say: "God is everywhere."

But what did I really believe? The way I lived my life and prayed my prayers would tell me the answer. Had I unknowingly limited God's presence to what I perceived as sacred—to holy places and church-sponsored moments? Had I restricted my companionship with God by assuming that the material world was more or less empty of Him? Was there somewhere in the back of my mind the notion that I was either doing what was "religious" and spiritual, giving time to God, *or* I was doing what was secular and worldly, giving time to everyday life? Had I separated common things from spiritual things? And routine moments from holy moments?

My thoughts were spilling over one another like waves. I shifted in the pew as the whining in the corridor ceased. *What does running a vacuum cleaner have to do with God?* The question seemed important. Crucially important. *Do I live in two different worlds,* I wondered, *one marked "God" and the other "vacuum cleaners"?*

Perhaps this was why I'd experienced such an acute sense of God's absence since returning from the Oratory. Because I hadn't really expected Him in the common events of daily life. Had separating and compartmentalizing everyday experiences from experiences of faith blocked my experience of Him? It did seem that He had tapped my shoulder there, and when I turned around—He was gone.

It reminded me in a way of the childhood trick I used to play on my neighbor's front porch. Ring the door bell, dash for the bushes and watch poor Mrs. Graham poke out her head and look up and down Oak Street. Oak Street, where I grew up, was as ordinary a street as ever was. Oak Street was the kind of place you never expected God to turn up.

Mrs. Graham would always sigh and disappear back inside. One day, however, she came off the porch and scoured the bushes and found me! I got quite a tongue-lashing that day.

But God does not play tricks. He does not ring bells and then disappear. But perhaps He does beckon us gently out the door with an encounter that rings like a bell in the depths of us, and then He waits and watches for us to discover Him out among the common bushes and along the plain ordinary streets where we live our lives. Wasn't it a common bush that burned with God's presence for Moses?

Sitting in the church, I wondered if God wasn't telling me to go scour some common bushes for Him. "Go discover Me in plain ordinary life, on the street where you live." "God is not partial to stained glass," Sandy had said.

I looked again at the window, then slipped out of the church and went home.

Two Benches, Two Worlds?

Late that same afternoon I drove Bob to the downtown square across from the courthouse to visit a historical monument. It was part of the requirements for a Cub Scout badge. Bob scampered off to view the Civil War statue and old cannon, while I waited for him on a city bench, surrounded by city buses and crowded streets.

The sun was sinking in a great smear of red. I gazed at the courthouse roof, at the bank on the corner, the bus stop and the people lined up. Especially at one old woman who, for reasons known only to her, had a blue sweater on her head buttoned under her chin like a scarf. Two blocks away was the church where I'd sat during the morning, expecting God.

The well of absence I'd met there resonated inside me. Suddenly there came a powerful sense of *déjà vu*. I felt as though I'd been here on this bench before, doing the same thing, thinking the same thought. And in a way I had. Not this particular bench, but the other one. The one on the Oratory lawn beside the bird bath. The one I'd sat on while the sky turned red just like now. But though there was the same rush of feeling, the two benches seemed a galaxy apart.

One had been tucked in a quiet sacred place, where crosses flamed and holiness is a silent thing. This one sat beside a red light, enveloped by exhaust fumes, with cars and buses rumbling back and forth. This seat looked out on a slice of life at its most ordinary and mundane.

Two benches. Two worlds. One sacred. One secular. One had seemed ripe with God's presence. The other inhabited by His absence.

"Why do you limit where I can come to you?" a voice seemed to whisper in my thoughts. It was the same message I had been getting in the church. "Find Me in the ordinary and mundane. Look for Me *here*."

Yes, solitude, being with God alone at the Oratory, had been a necessary thing in opening me to God's presence. But now I must extend the experience to the "whole" of my life. As soon as we discover God at the heart of our existence, we will want to discover Him in all the rest of it too. Withdrawal to be with God is only valid if it leads us to transform all the rest of life into a prayer.

I must find God where I am, I thought.

I slid up so I perched on the edge of the bench. And when I looked around, it seemed as though a veil slipped off all the pedestrian sights and sounds around me. "God is here," I whispered. The thought of it, clean and full inside me, nearly knocked me breathless. It swept me up like a feather. I was blown high and free, liberated from something I hadn't even known imprisoned me.

A wind rose on the grass, twirling the leaves beneath the bench and turning them end over end along the gutter. God's presence was in the wind, in the leaves. I could sense it slanting off the courthouse roof, in the fume-laden air, in the rhythms of life moving on the gray street. And most especially in the woman with the sweater on her head.

I found God in those moments. I found Him on Oak Street. And I did not have to track Him down with feverish activity and struggle. I only had to be aware of Him everywhere. It was the improbable mixture of absence and seeking, openness and grace melting into a common moment.

The path of God leads through the very middle of my most daily routine. It does not bypass Oak Streets. In fact, these noisy, busy, boring places are not in the way of God's presence but the way *to* it. The content of prayer is life itself.

"Hey, Mama, I got all the history from around here," Bob was saying to me. So we left. Bob with his history and me with a new realization. Life doesn't stop for the holy to happen. Holiness occurs in the course of life—or never. You simply open to God here and now. In other words, you don't view life from two different benches, separating life into where God is and where He is not. There is only one bench, one view. All is holy. Every breathtaking moment. As Madeleine L'Engle puts it, "There is nothing so secular that it cannot be sacred."[1]

The Swiss physician and spiritual writer Paul Tournier looked at a few biblical texts that have been used to support this split between "heaven" and "earth" and noted that we have misunderstood them when we suppose they are telling us to deny the world or declare parts of it void of God's presence.

"The message of the Bible as a whole is the very opposite of a contrast between heaven and earth. It is their unity. In the biblical perspective there are not two distinct worlds, the profane and sacred. Everything is sacred."[2]

Our time on earth should not be spent trying to transcend "worldly" things or the material world, but finding God in the midst of them. Jesus never denied the world. He went about instead discovering His Father everywhere in it. He saw spiritual significance in common things and actions: a lily, a grain of wheat, a mustard seed, bread, wine, water, doors, mending, sweeping, sewing. For Him, all was prayer and presence.

The bottom line is that since God created the world, lives in the world and works in and through the world, we find Him here with our feet on the ground, living and interacting with the world in the presence of God. Of course I don't mean that we should adopt all the world's values. Rather, we are to view the world and all creation as the realm of God's presence. We are not to count the work of a missionary any more holy than the work of someone who sweeps a street. What I am talking about is a way of seeing all of life as incarnation, seeing God in it. And even beyond that, to an Emmanuel-way of approaching all of life—being with God in it.

Pearls on a String

During the days after my experience on the city bench, I found my whole consciousness about God's whereabouts and availability to me being transformed. It was as though I was being opened to a much bigger, more freeing vision of God and the potential of encountering Him. God was not "up" and me "down." He was horizontal, under, above, in and through. His presence was not restricted to certain times or places or actions. It was all-embracing.

I remembered the time in my childhood when conflict between the two worlds perhaps first appeared. One Sunday my parents took my brothers and me to the farm for a picnic.

You would have to visit Monk Farm to understand the special way it talks to you about God. It is five hundred acres of Georgia woodland, ponds, red soil and pine trees that brush against the sky. There was a rusty fence we climbed to pick berries and cows we chased and an old green boat that floated us, it seemed, on the face of life itself. I loved those times. The problem arose when it became evident we would not make it back to church for the evening service, which we never missed. I mean, never. I remember the rush of guilt I felt when Daddy looked at his watch and said, "The time sure got away from us." Miss church for a picnic? How unspiritual! How secular! And I wouldn't make my eight points!

For the rest of that afternoon I didn't have much fun at all. A tug of war was going on inside me. Part of me seemed to say that God is here in Monk Farm, just as much here as in the Baptist Church. And part of me said, no, you cannot experience God here, only in the proper religious setting. The split that began then was only now beginning to be mended.

I wondered whether I was bringing up my children to celebrate God's presence everywhere. "Where do you think God is?" I asked them at the dinner table one evening.

"Up in heaven," said Ann.

"Yes, but church is God's house. That's where He lives," Bob added.

"How about right here in the kitchen?" I asked them. They looked at me oddly. I had work to do with them.

As for myself, I saw plainly how I had saved God for worship services, religious acts, Bible readings and church work. I had to admit to myself that I had believed God preferred stained glass. But if we are sensitive, we can just as truly discover Him in the rust on a fence or a fallen leaf. His presence touches all points of creation, making the depth of His availability staggering.

Did that mean God had been there while I cooked out of the same pots on the same stove night after night? Did it mean He had inhabited that filthy-looking, graffiti-scarred subway train I rode once in a big city? Yes, it meant that.

I had been picking and choosing when and where I could meet God and experience His love. I had thought . . . *I can find God alone on a retreat; I cannot find Him running a carpool. He can speak to me from the Bible; He can't speak to me from a museum painting.* But when I arbitrarily decide where God can be found and where He can't, I have sharply curtailed His avenues of coming to me. It's about as silly as not opening a gift because we weren't planning on its coming wrapped that way. Each moment of our day holds the possibility of encountering God's love. I have tried to think of these moments as pearls strung on one holy string of God's presence. To tear the string and divide the pearls up into two piles is like casting them before swine.

"Take off your shoes," God told Moses. "You are standing on holy ground" (Exodus 3:5 TLB). I think that's what God said to me that November while I sat on the city bench. He's probably saying it to all of us all the time, if we would only hear Him. For every ground, even the ground of common experiences, is holy. I think if we ever grasped that fact, we would go barefooted all the time.

Through my turning point on the city bench, God was moving me to stretch and broaden my concept of His whereabouts. It begins with seeking and asking. We follow the pain of God's absence like breadcrumbs through the forest, until we find Him present more than we first expected. And then we discover what has been the single most important awareness of my life—that God is intimately present with us, everywhere, all the time. He seeks us every place, in the exalted and the humble. Imagine! There is no place, no moment, no event, no person, where we cannot find Him.

Every day the nearness of God collected in me like rain water. I sensed Him coming and coming and coming . . . in a sound, a smell, a touch, a movement, in common things that shaped my day. Those late fall days were some of the most joyful days of my life. I would stare at the most mundane things and be aware of His love. A pitcher of milk in the refrigerator, an old sweater, the steam rising off my soup, a quiet sky, an uprooted tree . . . all were gifts of love.

"Enjoy. Drink Me in," He seemed to say. "Find My love everywhere."

In every common moment God is cherishing us, pouring His love upon us. That thought would seize me unexpectedly like a shout of surprise, like trumpets going off in the night. And I was the city of Jericho, my walls falling down, walls that had kept God out.

One warm November afternoon a hot air balloon sailed right over our house. The children rushed inside to tell me. We stood under the sky and watched, mesmerized by its silent, floating beauty, the fullness that held it aloft. It made you think of mother Earth floating along, trailing her round black shadow across time.

I was deeply touched by the presence of God and His love in that moment. When I said as much to the children, Ann looked at me and exclaimed, "Me, too!" Bob, more reserved, only smiled.

I came inside and scrawled in my journal, "God, if I could only wake up and pay attention to things as they really are, I would see that Your presence fills this world like a hot air balloon. I would see it is Your very presence that holds the molecules of the universe together and keeps it all afloat. I think if You left us for one second, the world would deflate into a scrap in the universe."

Those were the kind of days they were . . . days of waking up to where God is. Nicholas of Cusa, the fifteenth-century bishop, is attributed with the saying, "God is he whose center is everywhere and circumference is nowhere."[3] If you think about that for very long, it will fill you with awe. There is the same feeling surrounding Paul's claim, "From him and through him and to him are all things" (Romans 11:36 rsv).

Back to the Bible

I was just beginning to come to grips with these ideas when I shared them one day with a group I belonged to at church. One woman spoke up: "That sounds pantheistic."

I think I stammered trying to answer her. What I wished I'd said, but never got out, was that it is vastly different to say God *is* all things, as a pantheist does, than to say God is *in* all things, as St. Paul did (Colossians 1:16-17).[4] But I'm grateful to her. For her comment made me study the Bible to get the biblical perspective about God's presence among humankind.

In Genesis I discovered that God's original intention seemed to have been an intimate and perpetual communion with us. God walked about in the Garden of Eden with the first man and woman. But after the Fall, human beings began to lose touch with the sense of God's presence everywhere, all the time.

In Exodus I saw the Israelites beginning to think of God's presence localized within the Ark of the Covenant. As Old Testament history progressed, His presence was considered to be enthroned in the temple in Jerusalem. The splitting of secular and sacred had begun. To some God seemed limited to the space behind some curtains in the Holy of Holies.

Then with the coming of Jesus, the Incarnation, there came also a dazzling expansion of the perception of God in the world. God was now present with us in human form. He walked the "garden" of earth again. It was Jesus who reestablished the fullness of intimate communion with the Father, pointing us back to God's original intention of encompassing intimacy. At His death the curtain in the temple was torn in two. God was no longer hidden behind a curtain.

Jesus told His disciples, "I will ask the Father, and he will give you another Counselor to be with you forever—the Spirit of Truth. . . . You know him, for he lives with you and will be in you. I will not leave you as orphans; I will come to you" (John 14:16-18 NIV). As he was ascending, He also said, "Lo, I am with you always" (Matthew 28:20 RSV). Jesus promises

His continuing presence in us through the Holy Spirit—intimate, immediate, always, and in all places.

In the Epistles, I found Paul at the Areopagus in Athens proclaiming that God is not far from each one of us. "In him we live and move and have our being" (Acts 17:27-28 RSV). In the Scripture I saw history become incarnational. People in the Bible woke up to God's whereabouts. God dwells *within me* and everywhere *around* me. The world is a cup running over with God's presence. And we can have the same intimate communion and awareness of God's presence that Jesus did.

But, we rarely do.

Why is that?

God in My Own Backyard

We are surrounded on all sides by God, Evelyn Underhill observed. But often we are no more conscious of Him than we are of air pressing against us.[5] We don't turn our attention to Him.

In my little hometown of Sylvester, Georgia, there used to be a drugstore called Mullis Drugs. One afternoon when I was small, my mother carried my younger brother and me in for a soda. Wade was the sort who galloped through store aisles, drank shampoo and knocked over mannequins in display windows. (Today he is a sedate attorney!)

As I sat on the big swivel stool at the fountain, Mother tried to cope with Wade, alternately chasing him and picking him up, then letting his writhing little body go. At one point Mother, who was usually quite sane, rushed by me crying, "Where is Wade?"

I giggled and Mr. Mullis, who was drying a glass behind the counter, stared at her with a sympathetic smile. "Why Leah," he said, "he's in your arms!"

We laugh about it to this day. Mother carrying Wade around, crying, "Where's Wade?" It's the sort of nonsensical thing we do with the presence of God. He is already in our midst, under our noses and in our arms. Just now, right here, God's heart can be found brimming over with love for us, while we cry, "Where is God?" Isn't this how it always turns out? The treasure we seek is inevitably in our backyard. Sometimes just figuring this out is the beginning of a new life.

I was beginning to figure it out. One rainy day in December, the children played hide and seek in the house. It reminded me for some reason of the little games of hide and seek we play with God. I reached for my Bible and began to read the story of the first game recorded, picturing it in my mind.

Adam and Eve were tiptoeing in the world's first garden. They heard the sound of God moving in the cool of the day. They decided to hide from God's presence among the trees of the garden because they were ashamed of disobeying Him. So they shut themselves off, closing their eyes and ears to God's presence that resounded everywhere through the world.

I lowered the Bible, closed my eyes and listened to the rain. Suddenly I was Eve, squatting behind a tree, hiding in my own insensitivity and guilt, while the footfalls of God fell all around me.

Breaking into my fantasy, my daughter's muffled voice came from the linen closet. "Re-e-e-ady." Then came Bob's sock feet moving through the house after her. She'd given herself away.

I picked up the Bible and read on. The Lord called to them, "Where are you?"

When I read that question I could scarcely believe it. It was the same question I'd been asking Him: "Where are You?" We ask it of God and He answers, "I'm here. Where are *you?*"

I had the odd feeling that at that very moment God was looking at me as Mr. Mullis had looked at my mother in the drugstore. "I'm present, Sue. It's you who are not always present to Me."

What a crazy turn of events! We seek, only to find we are sought. We ask, "Where are You?" only to have the same question thrown back at us. God's question in Eden showed me who is really hiding and who is really seeking in this mystery.

It is God who loved us first. His unceasing love sends Him after us. He is the seeking Lover, the one who has made us for Himself. From the very beginning we were created to be found and loved by Him. He has woven this secret into the very fibers of our soul and when we seek Him with all the longing He has planted in our hearts, in the end, we simply discover Him seeking us, loving us—in all times and all places.

I sat there with the rain sloshing across the windows and my children hiding and seeking through the house. Ann's voice from the linen closet grew in me. "Ready," she had said to the one padding silently after her. That was the key word, the one Eve failed to say when she hid in the trees.

"Ready," I whispered as I sat on the sofa. "I am ready to be found by You everywhere."

The Lord is with you, while you are with him.
2 CHRONICLES 15:2 RSV

10

Putting Out the Welcome Mat

THE DAYS GREW cold and shiny. Christmas was once again in full swing. Once again I climbed the ladder to hang cedar over the mantle. This time the whole family was there. Ann handed me the train of greenery while Bob and Sandy poured popcorn into the popper.

On the rungs, I paused a moment, remembering the year before: the pain on the ladder, the panicked trip to the doctor, the hospital, tranquilizers, stress. And then, somehow in the mystery and grace of God . . . the quiet sense that in all of it God was calling out to me, beckoning me to wholeness through His love. I was just beginning to discover the grand sweep of God's presence across my existence, the voice of His love whispering in my life. A whole year had passed, but only a blink in the process of becoming.

Yet much had changed in that year. My perfectionist approach to life was slowly dissolving. Because I was finding myself loved as I was, the need to do and achieve in order to prove my worth and excellence—the compulsion to be supermom, superwife, super-career-woman and super-Christian all at

126

once—was slowly losing its hold. I was becoming more patient and kind with myself. For the first time, I was allowing myself to be human. There were days I didn't make the beds. Days I gave myself permission to play instead of work. Even times I missed a church meeting to be home with my family without wallowing under a blanket of guilt.

"There are two things to remember in avoiding stress," I heard a physician say on an early morning talk show. "First, don't sweat the small stuff. Second, it's *all* small stuff!" I was peeling away the "oughts" and the "small stuff," finding my way to the real center.

I thought back to the day I'd stood in front of the mirror and watched myself form the word "no," saying it over and over, building my courage for the moment I would need to say it to someone else. I called it "the creative no." That meant saying no so I could say yes to something more meaningful. Yes to time with my family, time with myself, time with life, time with God. But when I actually had to tell someone no, the word was like a brick in my throat. It took all my strength to pry it out. The next time was easier. And one day I said no to another activity with little explanation and no apology. What a milestone!

Slowly through the past year God had nudged my spirit toward the horizon of a new life, one in which I was clear about what was most important in my life and lived by those priorities.

Being Present

As I tacked up the cedar, enjoying the crisp, green smell of it, I thought about the question that continued to rise in me with that quiet kind of insistence I have learned not to ignore. If God is forever and always present to me, why am I not present to Him? To be honest I had always half thought, if I thought of it at all, that when distance crept in between me and God, or when I could not perceive His presence, it was God who was not around. He was the missing party, not I.

But that idea had been exploded. Now, reflecting on my past I saw that it was I who was missing. Even during the past year, with its joyous flashes of awareness and moments of knowing His love, I knew I had mostly been absent to God. The words of William of Thierry capture perfectly the puzzlement I felt:

> This much at least I know and that most certainly, that you in whom we move and have our being, are in a manner present here with me. . . . But if you are with me, why am I not with you?[1]

A gust of frigid wind barreled down the chimney, blasting into the room. I had left open the glass screen in front of the fireplace. As I climbed down to close it, the awareness of my condition moved through me like the wind. "God, I know that You are here even now with Your love," I prayed silently. "I have been absent, unaware, sleepwalking through Your glorious presence. Please, God, help me learn to be present to You. Teach me, Lord."

It is a fearful awareness that you and I are responsible for the extent we will be present to God. We choose. God has made it that way. His presence is magnanimous, yet He leaves it to us to notice Him or not, to enter His presence and commune with Him on whatever level of intimacy we choose. His desire for communion with human creatures is surpassed only by the enormous freedom He gives us to enter this intimacy with Him.

Once in high school, when my homeroom teacher called my name, I didn't hear her since I was staring out the window, wrapped in my thoughts. After my name was called three times, my friend Cynthia elbowed me. "Present," I said while the class snickered. And of course I was. I occupied a space, filled a desk. I was even located in close proximity to the teacher. That was spatial presence. I was present, but in a deeper, richer way I wasn't present at all.

Not long ago I sat in the waiting room of a dentist's office together with another woman. We sat without a word, thought or the simplest awareness passing between us. We were present beside each other, but we could have been two logs sitting side by side in a wood pile. We were not present to each other.

Just so, being present to God is far more than locality. Knowing God is everywhere and realizing you're located near Him in time and space is only a beginning. There is a deeper mystery still. We must move beyond the idea of spatial presence and tap into the essence of what creates real presence, or what I call "relational" presence.

The Apron Lady

An experience I had while I was a public health nurse describes for me what this kind of presence is, though it is only now, many years after the event, that I have come to understand what happened that hot summer day.

I hadn't embraced my job wholeheartedly as I should have, and as I stomped up some flimsy steps to a wooden boarding house under the smokestack of a nearby factory, I expected this visit to be like the others—awkward, dreary, boring. I would fill out the report on the old man who'd had tuberculosis, be sure he was taking his medicine and slip away as quickly as possible. A stout woman opened the door at my rap. She was wearing a white organdy apron that draped over her like a curtain with big ruffles trailing over her shoulders. I could hardly introduce myself for staring at that apron. The apartment was as tidy and grand as she was. She had spread round little crocheted doilies on everything. I could see a box of yarn beside a faded chair with another doily in the making, though for the life of me I couldn't figure where she would put it.

No, her husband wasn't there, she said. Then she looked at me and said, "Would you like some lemonade, dear?"

I tried to think of some excuse. I didn't want to sit down with a stranger and make polite small talk. My eyes roamed the room as I groped for something to say. I saw she had an open Bible displayed on the mantle. It sat on a doily, naturally. I smiled at it and something thawed in me. "Sure, why not?" I answered, surprising myself.

We sipped lemonade facing each other in chairs drawn close together in front of a rotating fan that blew hot Georgia air in spurts and made the ruffles on her shoulders flap. I forgot my report and the distractions that had followed me all week. I forgot the way I'd expected to be. I even forgot time itself. Instead I sat back, let go and concentrated on the unique person in front of me.

I listened—really listened—as she spoke about her husband, the way he coughed through the nights so the bed springs squeaked, and how she sat in her chair and crocheted while the sound raked her with fear. I found myself telling her about my work and the helplessness I sometimes felt when I knocked on doors where there was nothing but suffering. That was something I hadn't even known myself until I told her.

Time deepened. I saw her and heard her words as if I had just been born. She talked about when her last sister died and a few tears trickled across her wide face. Amazingly, tears welled up in my eyes . . . because she loved her sister . . . because she seemed to miss her so. And when she saw my tears, she reached over and held my hand. I don't know how long we sat there, just holding hands, looking at one another, mystified by the intimacy we were sharing. But I remember being penetrated with her presence. It filled the moment.

Before long she broke the silence and refilled my glass. I finished the lemonade and left. She stood on the porch and waved till I was gone from view. I can see her still, framed in my rearview mirror, wearing her apron.

I did not know it until I sketched that encounter in my journal years later, but she had been with me ever since. I even got the peculiar feeling that she had come into my life for the very purpose of teaching me what it means to be present to someone. Now it was the fullness of time, and God seemed to say to me in that silent voice of His: "Search the experience. Search for the threads which wove the delicate sense of presence into it. Then you will begin to understand about being present to Me."

It seemed an odd way to approach something so lofty as being present to God, sorting through an experience with an old lady in a boarding house, but I entered into it nevertheless.

When I was younger I read the poetry of William Blake and didn't have the slightest idea what he was talking about. I still read him, with a little more luck than before. I persist because now and then I catch a shaft of truth that is unforgettable, like these lines I happened to read that December.

> I give you the end of a golden string,
> Only wind it into a ball,
> It will lead you in at Heaven's gate.[2]

Blake started me mulling over my experience with the apron lady, trying to find the end of the golden string I knew was there. As I began to wind it into a ball, I found that it contained three strands.

Being Open

First of all there is *openness*. Being truly present to another requires that we open ourselves to them as I had opened to the apron lady. I hadn't wanted to sit down and spend time with her, but when I did I opened a way to be present to her. I forgot the report I came to fill out, all my inhibitions, even time. I let everything go and relaxed before her, becoming emptied and willing to let in the unique person before me.

So with God we must be willing to pause, to clear away the distractions, the inhibitions and whatever else fills our minds, and stand unoccupied, vacant and free before Him, desiring to let Him in.

A group of scholars came to see a religious teacher. The

teacher surprised them by asking what seemed obvious. "Where is the dwelling place of God?" They laughed among themselves and replied, "What a thing to ask! Is not the whole world full of his glory?" But the teacher smiled and said, "God dwells wherever man lets him in."[3]

Until I open myself to God He is not present to me, just as the woman wasn't really there at all until I opened to her, until I made time and inner space to be with her.

One evening not long after Christmas, I was driving home from church thinking of the apron lady and about how I had opened up and let her into my life. Suddenly I made a decision that here and now I would open myself to God. I would put aside the thoughts and preoccupations that kept me from being present in these moments with Him. I would simply make myself available.

Mentally I cleared away the worries and details pressing on my mind, saying them out loud and imagining them blowing out the car window onto the cold black currents of air. I was driving by a yard where a giant evergreen strung with tiny white Christmas lights blazed like flames and cinders in the darkness. On an impulse I parked the car on the side of the road and watched the tree for a while until it began to look for all the world like a burning bush. "Come, Lord Jesus," I prayed. "I open myself to You. Maranatha." Then I cranked the car and drove home, with the warmth of God deep in my bones. I *knew* that God was wherever I opened myself to Him, in church or beside an evergreen. Being open to Him was pausing and inviting Him in. It was going about with "Maranatha" ("Come, Lord") on the tip of your tongue.[4]

When I was first married we lived in an apartment complex where a thin Irish setter went about pulling sheets off the clothes lines. His favorite thing, however, was to pick up my neighbor's welcome mat and carry it around in his mouth. You would come across it practically everywhere—the laundry room, the parking lot, the sidewalk—wherever he had dropped it last. One evening I found the little brown mat out beside the trash cans. "Welcome," it said!

In a way, to be open to God is to carry around a welcome mat. In the Middle East Muslims carry around prayer mats, which they unroll to kneel on at certain times of the day. They've got the right idea. We need that kind of willingness, an inward prayer mat we can drop any time, any place. A maranatha-mat which says "Welcome" to God.

Another way to say it is that being open to God is to carry around an inner solitude in which we can meet with Him. Going away, finding exterior solitude, is beneficial mostly because it helps us create this inner solitude. It is possible to live peacefully in God's presence, even in the midst of a confusing and crowded world, because we carry with us a chamber of inward calm.

We all have more times that we are aware of when we are momentarily alone. The weekend our mate goes on a business trip, or visits parents. The nights the children stay with a friend. The hours we lie awake. Even riding a commuter train when we do not have to give our attention to anything outside us. We can use these times to focus on God, rather than on our aloneness, and allow them to nourish and maintain our inner solitude.

My driving time has become my time for solitude, when I consciously put out the welcome mat for God. I spend parts of every day alone in my car driving to pick up the children from an assortment of activities. I have learned to cut off the radio and enter into the solitude of the car. God and I can be alone there.

We can create special places where we are solitary for a while. A seat in the garden, a special chair in the den, a window seat. There we can peel away everything but God alone, even if it is only for three or four minutes. Or we can use the office desk at noon, when everyone else has gone to lunch, or early in the morning before others get there.

Sometimes I manage a solitary space in my children's

treehouse at night. That is just about the best solitude of all. Up in the dark branches of an oak tree flat on your back looking at the night, being alone with God.

God's presence is out back where trash cans sit in the twilight. In parking lots, beneath clothes lines, on busy streets, by kitchen stoves. But the truth is you and I will never be present to Him there or anywhere else until we find a kind of welcoming openness becoming part of our response to life. A willingness to pause and make ourselves available to Him.

God dwells where we let Him in. But we must make an opening. How beautifully simple!

Being "All There"

As I reflected on the encounter with the apron lady, I kept remembering how keenly aware I'd been of her while we sipped lemonade in front of the fan. But it was difficult to label what it was that had made her so vivid.

One evening after Sandy had had a little father-son talk with Bob about clobbering his sister with the pods off the magnolia tree, he plopped in his chair with an exasperated shake of the head. "What's the matter?" I asked. "Didn't your talk go well?"

"He kept bouncing a ball while I talked, like he was a million miles away," Sandy muttered. "He just wasn't all there."

All there. That was the phrase I was looking for. Back on that summer day, I was engaged by the presence of the woman beside me. She filled the moment I lived in. To be all there is to gather the energy and awareness of your mind and heart and focus them like a floodlight toward a given person. It is to enter the moment at hand and take the person to heart.

To be present with God is, in a way, to be all there with Him. Relating in this way is not so rare and impossible as it may sound. This is the way Jesus undertook life. In His encounters with people and with God, we see Him focusing on them with total awareness, dwelling on one person at a time.

He gave Himself over to them at that moment. And there was a compelling, nourishing, even exciting edge to His encounters. In "all-thereness" we cultivate self-forgetfulness. We allow the one before us to become "all," losing thought and awareness of ourself. This is a power we develop and expand, for it is essentially the power to tune in to another with love and listening and awareness, while becoming less conscious of self.

I talked with people all the time, even my family, without seeing and hearing them. When Ann and I stopped at an ice cream parlor for a cone one day, she started one of those long stories children sometimes tell in which they repeat every sentence twice. It buzzed around my ears like a fly. Something about her friend Jodie's puppy. My mind roamed. I looked around the shop, everywhere but at Ann, until my gaze came to rest upon a mother and her little boy seated at another booth. He was talking away with his strawberry ice cream cone dripping down his hand. But amazingly, his mother didn't seem to notice. She didn't even interrupt him to wipe the ice cream off. She simply looked at him and listened as if that voice, that face, that moment were the most important in all the world.

I knew that we had come into that store just so I could see the ice cream wind down the boy's hand and the way his mother was all there for him. I turned then to focus on Ann, almost as though I were seeing her for the first time all day. I discovered she had been telling me that her friend's puppy had been killed by a car. "Jodie cried," she told me with concern in her eyes.

"Jodie cried because when you lose someone, it hurts," I explained, knowing I had almost missed a significant moment with my child.

But I was even less "there" for God. Even in church my mind drifted far from Him. When praying, part of me was steeped in self-consciousness. I would catch myself thinking all kinds of self-indulgent thoughts. What am I getting out of this experience? What am I going to have for dinner? How can I use this experience later in my work?

One morning a verse in James leaped off the page as I read, "Draw near to God and he will draw near to you" (James 4:8 RSV). Be present to God and He will be present to you. In being all there before God, we are to draw close and take Him to heart at any given moment, and better yet, at *every* given moment. We draw the focus of our minds and hearts upon Him and find His presence magnified in that moment, just as the apron lady's was for me. God fills the moment.

When Bob was around four, I saw him one day stop still and draw so close to the patio doors that his nose flattened out against the glass. He seemed to pour his whole little being into something on the other side of the door, watching with complete absorption. You could almost see a circle of fascination fall around him like a lasso and hold him to the door.

Finally out of curiosity I wandered over the glass. He was engaged by a tiny yellow butterfly that had lit on a chair just on the other side of the glass.

Maybe that is the best way to describe what it means to be all there with God. It is to draw near Him like a child before a butterfly . . . to flatten our noses against the moment, not shutting out the world, but being engaged by God in the midst of the world.

I began to turn my attention, whenever I thought of it, to being all there before God, especially in the early morning prayer time. But I also became more conscious of paying attention when I was cooking or shopping or tucking my children in bed. To do so was not all sweetness and ease. Sometimes trying to tap into the deeper levels of my awareness, to concentrate, to open myself to the presence of God was pure aridity. While God is constantly and abundantly available, it is plain silly to think we will always "fly to God with great facility," as Thomas Merton once pointed out.[5] We must remember how blind we are, how attached to other things.

One day, pushing a grocery cart through a store aisle, I tuned into a loving awareness of God as I shopped. Bob and Ann walked along beside me asking for every box of cereal on the shelf. But still I seemed to step outside myself and concentrate in a gentle, unfretting kind of way on God, something like Bob and his butterfly. Oddly, I didn't want to possess God or "feel" Him or even get anything from Him. I only wanted to be there, close, alive in that moment and aware of Him. A closeness deeper than words spread over me, the overwhelming sense of being so cared for that every hair on my head was known and numbered. At the same time, I saw everything around me with unexpected love. For those few unlikely moments I believe I may have been "all there" with Him.

Being Vulnerable

In January a thin layer of ice covered the ground, white and crinkled like tissue paper. I stepped into the backyard one afternoon, making black tracks across the ground. Invigorated by the iciness of the air and a sudden spirit of playfulness, I made a figure eight. The children, barely visible beneath hats, scarves and gloves, took my lead and began creating grand black and white pictures with their feet, using the whole backyard as their canvas. I watched them for a while, then wandered to the back fence.

There I discovered tiny tubes of ice encasing the wire of the fence like a suit of armor. I thumped it with my glove and the ice fell away like eggshells. There was the old wire fence, clean and naked in front of me. The sight brought to mind something I hadn't thought of before in this mystery of being present. It also involves *vulnerability*.

The day I visited the apron lady, I told her about the helplessness and frustrations of my work, exposing to her the weakness in my life, until I felt clean and naked. For that space of time I shed the cold, pretending part of me, which was the face I usually wore, and revealed something of my real self to her. And I found her doing the same thing. We had become vulnerable before one another. No suit of armor, no masks, just the two of us—exposed. I had sat in her living room and cried tears! How often did that happen? Suddenly it seemed very amazing that I could have let down my guard and allowed anyone, much less a stranger, see such a vulnerable side of me.

Could it be that self-revelation and vulnerability breed intimacy and the sense of real presence between us as much as anything? Perhaps we need the ice thumped off of us. Madeleine L'Engle wrote once that she thought it was impossible to be Christian while refusing to be vulnerable.[6]

Back inside the house I got out my journal. As I wrote down my thoughts about vulnerability, I began to see how frozen and layered I was inside. How I held myself in, before others, before my family, even before God, afraid or unwilling to reveal the hurts and weaknesses. Afraid to cry—because that sort of thing made me powerless and defenseless. I had decided early on in life that I had an image to keep up, the happy Christian who coped with everything, perfect minister's wife, supermom . . . pretend. Pretend.

If I wear a little mask before God and never let my guard down, if I keep on one of those ridiculous grins that we Christians seem to wear much of the time—which suggests that "nothing ever gets me down 'cause I'm a Christian," then I would probably never be present with God on a very deep level. To be vulnerable before God is to be honest before Him. It is turning loose our rigid self-control for a moment and revealing ourselves. We simply let go and trust Him enough to be who we really are. It often happens that we are best able to be present when we have been reduced to a sense of our own weakness and helplessness. I hadn't allowed that to happen much at all since last winter beneath the reflection tree. Now I felt God prodding me. "Do not be afraid to turn loose before Me and reveal your real self. No pretense. No false images. No holding back. Remember, I love you as you are."

That moment was like a small dam bursting inside me. I could be vulnerable with God, knowing He would not condemn me or pull away from me because of my repeated failures, my stupid ideas, my anger, hatred or fear. Covering them up and wearing a silly grin only stood in the way of my presence to Him.

Growing toward Openness

I had been winding my string into a golden ball, and with all these strands God was showing me how to be present to Him: (1) trying to walk through my days with more openness to Him, seizing new opportunities to welcome Him into my life; (2) discovering how to focus on Him with more loving attentiveness and being all there to Him; (3) learning to respond to Him with honesty and vulnerability.

But none of this happens overnight. We must learn new behavior like a child. We must be told over and over. But that's okay. And the more we incorporate what we learn into our way of relating with God the more we are enabled to do the same with others. Being present to God inevitably makes us more present to those around us.

I began opening myself up to Sandy and the children, becoming more available, laying down the welcome mat for them more than ever by gazing deeply into their eyes when we talked, entering more fully into my moments with them. Instead of reserving all my free time for my work, now I would spend evenings with the family, singing songs, telling stories, forgetting myself and the things I had to do, and focusing on them with a new awareness.

Probably most unusual were the moments of vulnerability I shared with the children. It started one day when I overreacted to something small and annoying Bob had done. Exploding, I banished him to his room for the evening. Later, though, I went to him and admitted I was wrong. "Mothers make mistakes, too," I said. My honesty drove him right into my arms. "I know," he said. "But I didn't know *you* knew."

Even more uncharacteristic, on the day I learned my grandmother had died, I broke down and cried in front of Ann. I wondered how she would respond to seeing her invincible Mommy dissolved in tears. She put her hands on either side of my face, kissed my nose and told me, "When you lose someone it hurts." In that moment it seemed we had never been closer or more present to one another.

When we are present to God, when we are "all there" in His loving presence, He fills us with the knowledge that we are utterly treasured and held dear. Such moments set us free to love ourselves and love others.

Can we be present to Him all the time, every moment? Because I am a hopeless idealist, I believe the potential is there. I read Brother Lawrence and believe it. I read Frank Laubach and believe it. There are too many saints who have made their lives into an encompassing and ongoing awareness of God's presence and who tell us unashamedly that every moment may be open to God. I am not much of a saint. I am not present to Him all the time. Yet I do know in those moments when I am that the possibility is there for all of us. We can grow toward it. But we must want it very badly. We must want it with love in our hearts and a lump in our throats, with dance in our feet and steel in our wills.

Lift up your eyes round about, and see.
ISAIAH 60:4 RSV

11

Surprised by God Everywhere

AT THE END of January I was waiting in the car to pick up Ann from her ballet class. Gray clouds scudded across the sky and the spire of a church protruded into the bitter cold air. I was filled with desire for my experience of God's love to continue. "Don't let it grow cold," I prayed. I was afraid I would find myself stuck on a plateau. That seemed the worst fate of all.

For a moment there was only my desire and the warmth of my words fogging the window of the car. Then out of nowhere I was remembering a piece of Scripture from John. "He that loveth me shall be loved of my father, and I will love him, and will manifest myself to him" (John 14:21). The promise vibrated inside the car.

Ann came running out of the dance studio without her coat, clad only in a pale blue leotard and bare feet, though it was thirty degrees outside. She had been sniffling the past few days and I'd debated over letting her come to ballet. "Ann, where's your coat?" I demanded.

"I'm hot," she told me. Indeed her face was red from twirling on the floor inside.

The next day her temperature was 102. Being a former nurse I couldn't resist looking down her throat with a flashlight. It was red as an apple peel. I bundled her up and headed for the doctor.

Outside the sky was fat like a feather quilt, full of bulges and creases. You had the feeling at any moment the whole thing would tear and there would be feathers everywhere. But only a slight chance of snow was predicted. Ann whined pitifully as I nosed the car through a fine fog that washed the color out of the world. The minute we crossed the threshold of the office, however, she wriggled out of my arms and bounded to the playroom looking embarrassingly healthy. Moments later she held a children's magazine. "Let's read," she said.

More Than Meets the Eye

I flipped through it for something quick and easy and came upon one of those hidden-object puzzles. Spread across the page was a familiar scene from the woods with eight hidden objects drawn into it. "What do you see in the picture?" I asked.

"A hammer," she cried quickly. It was grafted into the trunk of a tree. Her eyes scanned the scene. "A snake." It was curled into a cloud. "A shoe."

A shoe? It took me a while but I saw it disguised in a pile of rocks. We finally discovered four more things. A rabbit in the leaves, a frying pan in a stream, a walking cane in the tree roots and a key in the limbs. That was seven. Where was the eighth? We couldn't find it.

Ann tired of the scrutiny and wandered back to the playroom. I went on with the game because I had an aversion to being beaten by a game designed for a six-year-old, and because I was enjoying it. I had to find the last item. I knew I was looking right at it, but I couldn't see it. I tried going over the scene in sections. Nothing.

Finally I tossed the maddening thing on the table where the

page landed upside down. And there it was! A light bulb designed in the big round hill in the background. It was huge and transparent. I was speechless. Now that was all I could see! It looked like a million-watt bulb burning on the page.

What kind of vision looks at something and doesn't see it? *There is more here than meets the eye,* I said to myself.

Sometimes a thought strikes you with such velocity you figure it can't be your own but must come from God himself. I was about as sure of it as I could be. God had manifested Himself to me just as the verse in John promised. He had given me a message: To continue to awaken to the fullness of God's love, you must begin to envision daily reality in a new way. You have to learn to "see" God in it. For there is more here than meets the eye. The world is a hidden object puzzle. It is mystery upon invisible mystery and infinite layers of holiness. It is God's presence hidden among the leaves.

Vision is an important and holy art of the Christian. We "can and must always re-learn how to see," wrote Karl Rahner.[1] Our most sublime effort is to seek the vision of God around us. This is nothing less than prayer. It was wonderful to think I could pray with my eyes.

As we left the pediatrician's office (yes, she had a mild virus) a flurry of snowflakes was falling. I told Ann it looked like a pillow fight outside. Snow feathers. She was glued to the car window. A snow in South Carolina is quite an event. But before we reached home she had fallen asleep against the door. I carried her inside to bed.

What Do You See?

I could not get the hidden object puzzle out of my mind. I constructed a blazing fire in the fireplace and sat on the carpet leafing through the Gospels, looking for accounts about Jesus and blind people. In a way I felt blind. I wanted to "see."

In Mark 8 I came upon the story of the blind man, but it was the incident immediately preceding that which grabbed my attention. Jesus was out on the Sea of Galilee with His disciples. He had just performed a miracle of feeding over four thousand people with seven loaves of bread and some fish. There were baskets of bread left over, yet somehow the disciples managed to get in the boat without enough bread for the trip. They had only one loaf between them. So when Jesus mentioned "the leaven of the Pharisees," they thought He was being literal. They looked at Jesus and murmured, "We have no bread."

It doesn't say so, but Jesus must have sighed at this point. When He had fed the five thousand, He'd said to them, "I am the bread of life" (John 6:35). But already they had forgotten. They were a group of spiritually blind men seeing things in an ordinary, superficial way—the way most of us go around seeing all the time. They saw the one loaf, heard the word "leaven" and thought of hunger. That's all.

The fire in my living room was now centuries away. I was on that boat with the disciples. I could see their faces and smell the fish in their nets. Strangely, Jesus responded to their murmuring by saying, "Having eyes do you not see? . . . And do you not remember?" (Mark 8:18 RSV). It seemed to me Jesus wanted the disciples to look at that loaf and see through it to the center of things. He wanted them to glimpse the spiritual essence of the moment, the presence of God in their midst that could nourish all their hungers. He wanted them to look at bread and see more than bread.

A minister friend of mine once told me that if God came to you with a message, He usually confirmed it shortly thereafter. I didn't put much stock in his comment at the time, but from now on I will listen better to him. It did seem that God was underlining the message I'd heard in the doctor's waiting room. *You have eyes but do not see.*

I read on. The boat landed and right away some people showed up with a blind man for Jesus to touch. It couldn't have happened at a more opportune time. I could almost see Him look around at His disciples and raise His eyebrows just enough to stir the question in them again: *Having eyes, do you not see?*

Drawing the blind man aside, He spat on his eyes and touched them. "Do you see anything?" he asked. The blind man looked up and said, "I see men; but they look like trees walking."

I am that man, I thought. *I look, seeing trees instead of men, emptiness instead of presence.*

But Jesus did not give up on the man. That alone gave me much comfort. He touched him again. This time, Mark says, the man "looked *intently* . . . and saw everything clearly" (Mark 8:25 RSV, italics mine).

Is there more here than a man recovering physical sight? Is there a parallel to the recovery of spiritual sight? I closed my Bible and heard Jesus say to me, "Do you see anything?"

Even when Bob arrived home from school, the question echoed inside me. Finally, late in the afternoon as Bob stomped outside in the little patches of snow, I decided to answer the question. I curled up on the carpet again with my journal. The curtains were wide open on the double glass doors. The snowflakes had stopped. And in the sinking sunlight, the snow on the ground was pink as flamingo feathers.

"Touch my eyes," I prayed.

"There, now do you see anything?" I imagined Him saying back to me just as He said to the man in the story.

A sense of wonder and reverence poured over me. I gazed through the doors and the world looked like trees walking, and then, surprise, I saw it clearly! The presence of Christ.

"You are here," I wrote. "I see You in the pink shadows on the snow, in the way my son tosses flakes in the air. I see You in the wind and the stillness, in the bony dead limbs and the round evergreens. If I had better eyes I would see that I am standing on a hill that is really a light bulb. In a world that is really an epiphany."

These moments of seeing imparted to me such sudden

nearness to God that to this day, if I see pink sunlight on the snow, my eyes fill almost instantly with tears.

Emilie Griffin writes:

> Each one of us must make the discovery on her or his own . . . that God invented the universe to delight us. That his love is so much for each one alone that it seems as if the moon and stars had been made for our nursery windows and no other creature had occupied God's mind since time.[2]

Learning to see, really to see God in our world returns to us this special childlike sense of being cherished and loved.

Look with Wonder

We can begin to see the world around with new eyes by practicing looking at everything with a sense of wonder.

Tilden Edwards has listed five "responses on seeing a flower":

"Ah!

Oh, beautiful—I want it, but I will let it be!

Oh, beautiful—I want it, I will take it!

Oh, beautiful—I can sell it!

So?"[3]

The response that opens us to see God in the world is the first one, the "Ah" response. The other responses make us increasingly impervious to God's presence in His creation, blind to His wonders, deaf to His voice.

Dr. Ernest Campbell once told his congregation at Riverside Church in New York, "Our television sets have progressed from black and white to color, but our daily lives have regressed from color to black and white!"[4] He went on to suggest that we are so mesmerized by technology, so wrapped up in our drive to produce and our need to succeed, make, acquire, amass, display, that our faculty for awe has been anesthetized. We no longer notice how the pavement of our streets glistens after a rain.

We no longer view the world as full of mystery, because we think we can explain it all. "We post-industrial adults have become so programmed to solving problems," said French philosopher Gabriel Marcel, "that we lose our capacity to wonder and be . . . ecstatic at mysteries."[5] Instead of being caught up by the mysterious, we approach it as something that bars our way, a problem to be solved.

There's an old story I heard about the farmer and the child who were standing at the edge of the Grand Canyon for the first time. Dancing with wonder, the child threw out his arms and cried, "Look! Oh, look!"

"Yep," muttered the farmer, scratching his beard. "That's a heck of a place to lose a cow!"

Whether it is a seed pod or a canyon wall, falling snow or a drop of water, the voice that spoke it into being still resounds inside it. If you listen lovingly enough, stand before it in awe, you may hear it. The moment of "Ah!" will come.

But it takes time and inclination to stop and look at God's world with wonder and awe, just as it takes time to be in God's presence with prayer. I've found that people of prayer seem most attune to "Ah" moments. I was visiting a friend in Winston-Salem who has woven her life into a fabric of prayer. As we were leaving to keep a lunch appointment for which we were already late, she spotted a minuscule violet still blooming in her November garden. While I drummed my fingers on the car's dashboard, she stooped over the violet.

"Why, look at you!" she said as if she were speaking to a child in a lavender bonnet. "You are glorious today. Magnificent . . . " Her voice trailed off into her own silent reverie, her moment of "Ah!" I on the other hand was feeling nothing much for the violet but a great deal of impatience for me.

When we are willing to stop and look, to step out of the

busy "relevant" activities of our day to see what is around us, we will be surprised.

One summer while I was a college student I served as a counselor for a church camp. Each evening I taught a Bible study to the children in a stuffy little room. We were on a verse in Jeremiah one evening when a firefly flew through the doorway and began to dip and soar over the children's heads, flickering its tiny incandescent mystery of a light at them. Smothered giggles and squeaks of delight broke out. I could feel the Bible study dissolving away as Jeremiah was forgotten.

I was on the verge of shooing the disrupting bug out of *my* classroom to regain control, when I caught sight of one little boy's face. His mouth hung open in a circle and his eyes glittered with joy as he stared in awe at what was happening. His wonder gave birth to my own. With a flash of inspiration I reached over and flipped off the light. A hush fell over the room as we watched the creature fly about the darkness, meteorlike, trailing his light behind him.

Many years later one of those children, now grown up, told me that event was the one thing she could vividly remember about being at camp that year. "It was the best worship service we had," she said.

Look with Vision

Our senses are vastly unaware of most of the reality around us. Just because I don't see or process something with my five senses may have little to do with whether it's there or not. I don't see radar waves or hear the sounds that make our spaniel Captain howl into the wind. But they are real.

If I dip a ladle into the pond on Monk Farm and peer at the contents, I see only a few ounces of murky water. But that's only a superficial perception. There is more there than meets the eye. Deep in the water percolates a tiny universe: swimming amoebae and diatoms, minuscule eggs, algae pulsating with chloroplasts. Hidden objects, all of them, but there for me to discover and see if I will. The pond is a puzzle of invisibles like the rest of life. To really see is to look beyond the murky surface of people, things and events to the inner reality, to the life and presence churning deep inside. It is not to look *at,* but *through.* It is to look with vision, insight, sensitivity.

Once we admit to ourselves that there is more here than meets the eye, more love, more wonder, more presence of the living God, then we begin to see it. "The great mystery of Christianity is not exactly the appearance, but the transparence of God in the universe."[6] It is only a matter of learning to look profoundly into everything.

Thomas Merton described the spiritual life as the movement from "opaqueness to transparency."[7] I like that description. It seems to capture the symbolism of the verses in Mark—the blind man begins in darkness, seeing not at all; gradually he sees men that look like trees walking, or with opaque vision; finally he comes to see clearly. The spiritual walk is a journey from perceiving God dimly or not at all to seeing His love shining in everything, making Him the whole of your life.

Once when I was in New York on business, I attended a Broadway play. Because I was late I rushed into the theater from the glare in the lobby and froze in the aisle, absolutely blind. I felt as though I'd run into a train tunnel. I couldn't see the usher who moved in front of me, couldn't make out a row or a chair or even my own hand. I had to take baby steps. Gradually shapes emerged in the darkness, shadows lightened. Finally I saw the usher far down in front.

The spiritual life is like walking down a theater aisle while your eyes adjust to the darkness. Our ability to see gradually increases as we learn the art of seeing in the dark, seeing spiritual reality in a material world. We grope our way through the darkness of preoccupation, inattentiveness, surface reality, all the things that cloud our vision, until we can open ourselves to the presence that is already there. If we will only keep moving down the aisle, things will eventually grow three shades lighter. And then—watch out for the hill with a light bulb!

"What are you writing?" Sandy asked me one day when he found me scribbling into my journal.

"I was thinking how fundamental seeing is to the spiritual journey," I said. "Our vision, the way we see, transforms our lives and keeps the experience of God alive in us."

"That reminds me of something Simone Weil once wrote," Sandy responded. "She said that real spiritual awakening was something like this: 'You go down a road at dusk. You see a stooping man through the mist. But as you draw near you begin to discern that it is not a stooping man at all, but a tree.'[8] I think she meant that when you discover the reality of God's presence, you do not see things in the same way."

And, I thought, *the hill is not a hill, but a light bulb. And the world is not darkness but glittering presence.* It sounded like the verse in Mark all over again.

The next day Sandy brought home some books on the writings of the Hasidim, a Jewish sect that began in the eighteenth century in Europe. Their writings did wonders for my concept of vision. They say that at creation God scattered His splendor throughout the world in the form of divine sparks that are hidden everywhere. Therefore, everything, every person, every moment, is to be approached with an effort toward seeing and hallowing the hidden sparks. What a magnificent way to approach the world! *See* and *hallow.*

The Hasidim gave me the impression that the world was like a fishbowl of pure glass that we have blackened with layers of blindness. If we ever scrubbed it clean with prayer and vision and wonder, we would find ourselves staring right into the eye of God. His love would be nearer, more vibrant. I underlined 1 Corinthians 13:12 in my Bible, "Now we see through a glass, darkly; but then face to face."

Look with Faith

Could I believe this and embrace it? It is so easy to lose the ability to see, the sense of wonder, when everything around you is the same old stuff. Teilhard de Chardin said we must *believe* that everything is charged with the possibility of God's presence. We must have faith. Then everything begins to take shape around us. Then even "suffering becomes a visit and caress of God."[9]

Bob was playing basketball on the church team that winter and was having trouble getting the ball through the hoop. Sandy was forever telling him that he could do it if he practiced. One day I asked Bob if he believed his team would win their next game. "No, but I'll practice believing until I do," he told me!

Practice believing. That was not a bad idea, I decided. I started going around the house, the yard, the store, wherever I happened to be, looking at people and things and saying, "I believe it's possible to see God through this task, that salesperson, this book, that sunset." Maybe it was foolish, but I practiced believing. We can get so mired down in our usual way of perceiving. I tried to look at things more closely, realizing the nearness of God in them. I was doing conditioning exercises for faith and vision.

It would be wrong, though, to become compulsive about such exercises. Learning to see is a gentle, natural process, a gift we receive as well as an art we learn. A bit of practice doesn't hurt, if we keep it in perspective. Practice doesn't make perfect as much as it makes permanence. It may help us wear a little groove in our thoughts so that this way of looking at life becomes a basic orientation.

The important thing to remember is that we can learn. We can change. We can reform our perceptions so that we come to view things through the eyes of prayer and wonder.

Have you ever taken an ink blot test? For a year I taught in a college of nursing. One day, for fun, a professor of psychiatric nursing flashed a handful at me. "Say the first thing you see," she told me.

I looked at them and blurted out things like spilled oatmeal (I taught pediatrics, often feeding babies in demonstration sessions), two crabs back to back (we had recently been to the beach), a shirt on the clothes line (my dryer had just broken down).

My colleague pointed out to me that the images I saw in the blots were based on my experience. I hadn't consciously planned to answer with those images, and hadn't realized that that is how everyone reacts to ink blots.

When I looked at a tennis ball, the nursing professor went on to say, I did not really see a tennis ball. I saw a round sphere that would fit in my palm. If you showed the ball to a person who had never heard of tennis, that's all she would see. But because of our experience and the way we have learned to interpret life, you and I translate that sphere into "tennis ball."

In other words, vision is far more than an impulse hitting millions of rods and cones on the retina. Vision is also influenced by our experience, our faith, our way of thinking and interpreting the world. We ourselves determine how we will tabulate what flashes across our brain and along our optic nerve. That means that we can learn to look at something and see more than an ordinary object. With the eyes of faith we can begin now to discover the holiness, the sign, hidden in each common thing, the reality and love of God all around us, by deciding to look for it. Because it is possible to look at the same object, the same surroundings, and see only what makes us bitter and angry. When I was growing up my father would quote that old verse to me whenever I started complaining:

> Two men looked out from prison bars.
> One saw mud, the other saw stars.[10]

We learn to see the stars with our inner eye, our spiritual sense. That is what the Apostle Paul called "the eyes of your heart" (Ephesians 1:18, NIV). When we are centered in God, we view things from that center. We see all things in the light of God.

Sensing Our Unity with Creation

When our eyes have been opened and we are practicing seeing God and His love in the world around us, we will begin to have a completely different relationship with the natural creation. For one thing, we will recognize in a far deeper way that our "pulse beats with nature," as Thoreau put it.[11] Perhaps this is why Francis of Assisi referred to Brother fire, Sister water, Brother sun and Sister moon in his "Canticle of the Creatures." Because Leonardo da Vinci was sensitive to the underlying harmony that flows through the universe, he perceived the connection between sap moving through the veins of a leaf and blood flowing in the arteries of his human hand. He was willing to be taught.

Now that I was weeding out the excessive busyness from my life, I had more time for Sandy, time in God's healing creation. On a warm Saturday that winter, Sandy and I went backpacking in the Mt. Pisgah national forest. Late in the afternoon we sat down in a thick glade of trees and brush. Eventually we quit talking and grew perfectly still. After a while a bird flew down beside us and perched on a branch so close I could have stroked his feathers. For a moment I thought he was going to land on my arm. The bird didn't even notice us. We were part of the woods.

Later, Sandy and I talked of how much a part of the woods we felt when the bird joined us. We both sensed a oneness with creation, and with the Creator.

I will never forget when Bob was studying plants in school. He burst in the door one afternoon to exclaim dramatically, "Did you know that we can't live without plants? We'd be dead without them."

It was the first time he'd been aware of the great interdependence between himself and creation. Plants give off oxygen, which we breathe in, and we breathe out carbon dioxide, which plants take in. He was very impressed by such unity, and his new awareness affected me as well. For a while I looked at every green plant I passed thinking what harmony we shared, how much we needed one another. I felt the nearness of the Harmony-Maker.

When we gain such awareness, we will treasure every part of God's creation, careful how we hew, cut, maul, kill. We will live in love with our neighbor earth.

Seeing Creation as Gift

As our vision of God grows, we will also learn to open our hands and receive His creation as a gift. Because God created the natural world, I will treasure it. I will encounter it without the need to manipulate, acquire or use it. I will marvel that it simply *is*. It's easy, as Tilden Edwards reminded us, to want to *use* what is around us for ourselves, to exploit it, to see nothing as beautiful or worthwhile unless it benefits us in some material way. But God speaks His love for us in nature when we are willing to let go and let it be.

A few years ago I visited a ninety-year-old man in Albany, Georgia. He grows the most beautiful roses I've seen, and much of his joy comes from giving them away. As I walked among the rows of glowing velvet-petaled blooms, he told me about the time someone offered to buy some roses from him.

"Sell a rose?" Mr. Carter exclaimed. "Can you imagine! A rose belongs to everyone!"

For him, creation was a gift.

With open hands is the best way to walk with God through this world. When we go about thinking that we must "have" in order to be happy, we will live in constant grasping and fear that what we have will be taken away. Stuffed hands can't receive very well. They are full already.

At Garden City Beach, South Carolina, the shoreline is sometimes sprinkled with small prehistoric shark's teeth, which beachcombers delight in finding. The teeth are treasures that whisper of another time—eons of creation, the primordial deep and the Bible's promise that even there one may descend and find God. And of course they touch us with the mystery and sometimes terrible beauty of God's underwater creatures. If we relate to it properly, even a shark's tooth can lift us into God's presence.

One afternoon as the tide was slipping out, Bob and I wandered along searching for teeth. After an hour he spotted one lying on the sand. His exuberance was evident by the way he picked it up and exclaimed over its ebony color, the curve of its body, its sharp point. Having it made him happy. So having more of them would make him even happier, he decided.

The next two days he endured a small obsession with finding shark's teeth. He quit swimming, designing sand castles and daydreaming at the water's edge to spend every possible moment hunting for teeth. I noticed he was not particularly thrilled any more when he did find one, only anxious to see how many more he could acquire. He found over twenty—his hands were stuffed with them. But the joy was gone from it. There was no awe, no presence, no prayerful wonder. They only returned when he stopped hunting for gain and began to receive his finds as gifts.

Willing to Be Surprised

During the frigid evenings of that winter, I had been reading *Alice in Wonderland* to the children, not with the compulsive need to be Supermom I'd had when I'd read the Narnia Chronicles, but with a new and unpressured sense of delight in my children. As I read, I kept thinking about Alice plunging down the rabbit hole into the strange risky world of Gryphons, Cheshire cats and soldiers that looked like playing cards. Alice left the safe, familiar bank where she tweedled away time making daisy chains, and made a daring leap. She went down, down, down . . .

It seemed to me that was the key to unlocking our tightly reined control and coming to see with the inner eye. We need to turn loose and plunge down the rabbit hole into a fresh way of seeing. Then we will find a world rinsed with holiness where even common things are crucibles of God's love and presence. To do that takes a certain amount of imaginative courage, peeling away "the veil of familiarity from things."[12] Children are especially good at this. On a clear afternoon in February, Ann called me outside from my desk and all my "important" work to "see something."

"See what?" I asked, reluctant to be interrupted.

"Come and I'll show you."

A year or so before I might well have refused such an "unproductive" breather from work, but today I followed her to the backyard where she pointed to a strangely shaped cloud. Her eyes were dancing with discovery. "It's a unicorn!" she announced as if she had sculpted it herself.

I gazed at it, trying to peel the veil away, turning loose the idea that this was simply a shapeless mass of condensed moisture in the sky. And when I did, I saw it perfectly: the four legs, the graceful neck, the head with its long single horn.

"Why, it *is* a unicorn," I cried. Ann and I sat on the cold ground, shivering against each other, and watched him. As the wind blew the clouds along the sky he appeared to be walking on air.

"Did you know that long ago the unicorn used to be a symbol for Christ?" I asked her.

"My teacher read a story about a unicorn who died so all the other animals could live," she said.

We sat and thought of Christ, seeing Him in the shape of a cloud, feeling the beauty of His love. What joy! And certainly far more important work than the papers on my desk.

As February turned into March, I began to understand that I

was far more tight-fisted with my vision than I realized. I was often like Alice on the bank. "Lord," I wrote in my journal, "give me the courage to risk seeing the world in new and holy ways. Help me to plunge down, down, down . . . ."

Not long after that God taught me another important lesson through my children. It was a rainy Saturday morning and the children were reading inside. Bob, a reader of Charlie Brown and old Archie comics, sauntered up and handed me a comic book. "Read this, Mama," he said, pointing to a sign at the top of the page.

"Paris in the spring," I read.

He grinned. "Read it again."

I looked at the words. "Paris in the spring!"

His smile grew. He looked like a cat with feathers on his face. "Look close and you'll be surprised."

I'd been had. I knew it, but I wasn't sure how. But when I opened myself to the possibility of surprise, I saw something else in the sign. What it really said was "Paris in the the spring"! An extra "the" had been slipped into the sentence, so that the first line ended with *the* and the second line began with *the*. I was positively amazed. It took me three tries to see what was there. Why? Because I saw only what I expected to see.

We do the same thing with God. We see Him in precisely the same old ways we've always seen Him. We see what we've come to expect. Nothing more. We are so selective. We shut out what we don't choose to see. We aren't willing to be surprised.

And so we won't be—unless perhaps God knocks hard on our door! The vision of the inner eye requires that we pay attention to the unexpected because if we don't expect to see God, the chances are we won't.

A friend who had been used to a formal, structured worship experience recently married someone in a very informal church. After visiting his church, she told me that God simply was not present for her in such a loose and casual service. I realize that there are different ways of worship that appeal to our different personalities. But to fail to expect God no matter where we are is like wearing blinders. This young woman was not willing to be surprised, and of course she was not.

It happens the other way round too. The first time I spoke at an Episcopal church, I did so just before the communion service. I knew that the Episcopalian way of serving communion was different from the way I had taken it all my life, and my first reaction was not to partake. God would not be in this for me. I did not expect Him.

But as I looked at the altar, at the minister holding the elements of the Lord's table in the air, it became such a moment of suspended beauty that instantly I gave in and became willing to be surprised. With wobbly legs I went and knelt at the altar rail with the others—and sensed the invisible Christ all around.

Can we live our lives willing to be surprised, thinking that God is going to turn up any minute, any place, any way? If we will, that is when we begin to see what is really there.

As the Father has loved me,
so have I loved you;
abide in my love.
JOHN 15:9 RSV

12

Making a Home for God

IN APRIL, afternoon light filtered through unfurling new leaves on the reflection tree, filling me with nostalgia. It had been over a year since I'd sat here. Though so much had changed, I still needed to reflect now and then on my life. So I spent a little while sitting underneath it again.

Before I could settle into my thoughts, Ann wandered up and nestled beside me. "Make up a story," she said.

This was a little game we played, making up stories never before heard. My father had made up stories for me, creating such notables as the mule who went through the cafeteria line, and a not too bright boy named Chewing Gum Bum. Now I kept the legacy alive.

"Once upon a time, there lived a damsel all alone in a castle, which was surrounded by a moat. One day in her tower she heard the royal trumpet blow outside, announcing the coming of the king. She was excited that His Majesty had come to her own humble castle."

Ann gazed at me expectantly.

"She hurried down to greet the king who had arrived at the

gate. But she discovered that a great pile of rocks had collected against the drawbridge and she could not lower it. While she wanted to entertain the king in her castle, she hated much more the task of clearing away those rocks. So she left them there and waved to him from afar."

Make Space for God

Ann bounced off to play and I leaned back against the tree. It was obvious I was talking about myself. And God. Our imaginations often unfold truths to us in hidden ways. I had just been reading a book by Teresa of Avila in which she compared the soul to an interior castle.[1]

I knew the castle in the story was my own inner life, the "kingdom within." The story was a gentle warning that I still had work to do. I had to remove the rocks blocking my life in order to create space for God to enter and take up residence. That meant effort and discipline. And I spent very little time practicing any spiritual disciplines, except for the half hour each morning I used to pray, read some Scripture, write in my journal or just sit and think. (And yes, sometimes daydream, doodle on the margins of scratch paper and once in a while fall asleep.) My approach was haphazard, on-again, off-again. In an odd way the early morning discipline was undisciplined. I never really knew what I'd be doing.

I could feel questions rise in me as I sat under the tree. What was I doing to nurture God's love in my life? Did I think more about the spiritual life than I lived it? How could I weave a disciplined approach to God into my life without becoming rigid, legalistic, pious and "overboard"?

Now it is time to find the disciplines to live this new life consistently, a voice inside me seemed to say.

There is a time in our awakening to God, a crucial juncture, when we shift from saying "the kingdom of God is at hand," and begin to take some concrete, consistent steps to usher it in. If we are serious about the spiritual journey, we must eventually seek out the disciplines necessary to keep our lives open to Him. We must be willing to clear a space for Him, and find a discipline that carries us beyond an initial burst of spiritual enthusiasm or a kind of dabbling in the spiritual life whenever the mood overtakes us.

But at the thought of discipline, I rebelled. *Keep things the way they are,* I told myself. Wasn't I learning? Wasn't I growing? Why mess things up now?

Abruptly I decided to plunge into spring cleaning, mostly closets. When I begin cleaning out closets, everyone in the family stands back. It is usually a frenzied occasion. The closet in the hall was so stuffed, every time you opened it, the ironing board fell out on the floor. I went at the cleaning with unusual determination, dumping incredible piles of debris on the floor, making the closet as empty as I could.

Yet all the time my thoughts kept going back to the rocks against the castle door. I had to wonder if I was trying to make up for not clearing away the rocks in my soul—the things that piled up to keep me from making a home for God. Busyness, blindness, laziness, uncertainty, selfishness, sin. *Make space. Create discipline. Get rid of the debris.* That was the message of the story I'd told Ann. Now it was the message of the closet.

Consider how carefully God has designed space into the world. It's the spaces that shape and define creation. Walk through a forest. Instead of the trees, look at the spaces between them and you'll know where the peace of the woods comes from. Think of the spaces between the notes of a concerto or symphony. Without them there would be no music. It's the spaces in this book that make it readable. And it's the spaces we make in our life for God's love that bring us peace and make sense of everything else.

Once Ann insisted on "typing" a letter to her grandma. She climbed up to my typewriter and pecked out a sentence one key at a time, very proud of herself. But unfortunately, you couldn't read a word of it. She never hit the space bar. The words were all run together in one long meaningless jumble. If we looked at a sentence like that, we might see our lives. Throughout many of my days I never hit the space bar.

Yes, I needed to make space. But I didn't want to go back to living by a pious little check list. That would only be a substitute for the eight-point system I revolved around before, when I had turned my faith into a list of "oughts."

Go Where Love Is

I have found the answer to that problem in a remark made by Henri Nouwen in an interview. Christians "must go where love is."[2] That's the best definition I know for a spiritual discipline.

Brother Lawrence wrote that in order to practice God's presence, "the heart must be empty of all other things because God will possess the heart alone."[3] Making space for God in our lives means entering special places that put us in touch with God's love. It is deliberately returning to the center, that inner sanctuary where our life and God's touch. Discipline, then, is in reality a turning to love.

Recently I acquired a potted plant and placed it in a window where it would get the morning sun. Weeks later I took a good look at it and discovered that the back side of the plant had become brown and sickly while the side facing the window was flourishing. The sun had been shining through the window, but catching the light was a matter of turning the pot.

Like the sun in the window, God's love shines—continually available, close, abundant. It is grace. Pure grace. But entering into God's love, finding the healing and wholeness we need, is a matter of "turning the pot"—turning our lives to receive His loving presence. "I cannot cause light," wrote Annie Dillard. "The most I can do is try and put myself in the path of its beam."[4]

There is nothing we can do to earn God's love or make it

shine any more or less in our lives. But there *are* attitudes and responses that make us more available to receive it. We need to learn some gentle and loving ways to put ourselves in the path of His light and love during the routine of our days. When we do that, we will be practicing spiritual disciplines.

Making a Covenant

I fell into bed that evening after cleaning the closet, but sleep would not come. I felt scrambled, full of chaos. Finally I slipped quietly out of bed and walked barefooted down the hall, out the front door and sat down on the porch steps. I'd never done that before at two in the morning.

Beneath the black dome of space, I stared unfocused at a thin crescent moon, then at the tiny blue flicker in the gas lantern across the yard. I was at the point of decision again. *How important is this journey to me? Am I willing to discipline myself in order to create space for God? Am I willing to lug rocks from the castle door?*

The questions made me nervous. I picked up two little rocks from the ground and shook them in my hands as I used to do when I was a child and someone asked me a question I couldn't answer.

Listening to the plaintive hum of the insects and the rocks rattling in my hand, I finally gave in to the utter quietness of the night and the spell of the darkness. As I grew still, it was as if God had joined me on the steps.

Why am I reluctant to find disciplines to undergird this journey? Don't I need a concrete discipline to keep my awakening to God alive? Am I afraid I will fail?

I thought back over my history. I would decide to read the Bible and have a prayer time. After a few enthusiastic days my efforts usually dwindled into sporadic attempts that had little to do with the rest of my life and were soon forgotten. Somehow I couldn't bear that kind of thing happening again.

Everything in the night seemed to be telling me to create

space. The air that rippled over me, the sliver of moon, the small voice inside. Suddenly I felt a great surge of desire for God inside me, so intense it burned away whatever reluctance remained. Nothing could be as important as making space for God. Nothing. It was worth the effort. Besides, there would be no "success" or "failure"—only the deep joy and wholeness of life *with* God.

"Lord, I am willing to create discipline in my life," I said out loud, startled to hear my voice break the stillness. "I am willing. But I am not sure about being able."

"I will be your strength," God seemed to say in my thoughts. "I will make a covenant with you."

Now a covenant is not a bargain. It is a promise that goes very deep. It is not like making a New Year's resolution. It is entering with your whole life into a trust. I believe there are moments when we should make our own private covenants with God and He with us.

God and I made a covenant. It is still hard for me to put it in words. But it seemed that God was saying, "We are in this together. You create space for Me, making Me the center of your life. I will never forsake you. I will be your strength and guide. We will journey together."

The darkness was soft all around me. My eyes blurred with tears and the flame in the lantern smeared in the black night. *O God. Light of light. True God of true God.* Tears splashed on my bare feet.

I took the two little rocks from my hand and set them on the steps to mark the covenant. The two of us . . .

After that I expected to feel tied down. Instead I felt incredibly free, as though I had unshackled myself from selfishness, shallowness and a vague, unfocused approach to the spiritual life. Yet as the days went on, I began to feel stymied, not knowing exactly what to do or where to begin in the matter of creating my own disciplines. Finally I prayed one morning, "Lord, I feel so inadequate. Please guide me into a spiritual discipline."

Seeking a Sign

On a bright afternoon a few days later, I took the children to Cater's Pond not far from the house. I gave each one of them a tall paper cup of torn bread to feed the ducks while I sat on the grass and watched the ripples move over the pond like muscles on an old face turned skyward. Two ducks swam toward us from the far side. Bob and Ann cast their bread on the waters while the ducks quickly ate both cupfuls.

With nothing left to do, the children filled their cups with mud from the bank. Somehow a visit to the pond always got around to mud pies. While they played I strolled around under the trees thinking about my efforts to create space for God. I had been unable to make any headway. I wondered how God was going to answer my prayer.

Over me the blue sky shone through the burst of new green leaves. I needed some newness in my life—I would look for a sign. I am a believer in signs. I don't mean the sort of sign where you make a demand of God and expect Him to come through just as you envision. I'm talking about searching for spiritual significance cloistered in the world around you that connects to your own life.

Life speaks eloquently. God speaks eloquently through life. And if we seek the words it whispers and take time to decipher its secrets, we often have a sign. In fact, we have an uncanny ability to zero in on the very truth we most need to hear, as if a homing device planted in our subconscious flashes when we find something that represents the message we need. Leslie Weatherhead said that we ought to spend our lives watching for God's messages, even from trivial events and objects.[5]

As I turned back to the edge of the pond, I saw Ann's little cup sitting on a rock shimmering in the sunlight. It was packed full of mud to the very top—but the outside was washed as clean could be. And it was all the more obvious because Bob's cup, also full of mud, was grimy on the outside as well.

Something leaped in me, connecting with the words of Jesus I'd read many times. "You cleanse the outside of the cup and of the plate, but inside they are full of extortion and rapacity.... *First* cleanse the inside of the cup" (Matthew 23:25, italics mine).

The cup was my sign. The verse my answer. Here was the first step in making space for God. To cleanse my cup.

A Clean Cup

God showed me that afternoon that making space for Him begins with confession and forgiveness—inner cleansing. We are not able to let God's presence shine through fully until our own rock piles of guilt have been cleared away. Guilt obstructs. Without forgiveness it is very hard to let God's love in to re-create us. "When we are willing to confess our true condition," says Henri Nouwen, "God will embrace us with his love, a love so deep, intimate, and strong that it enables us to make all things new."[6]

I'd fallen into the habit of asking forgiveness in a general and haphazard way. Mostly I didn't name my sins. I would say, "Lord, forgive my sins." Half the time I didn't pause to figure out what they were, and worse, I didn't care. You don't have to confront what you don't name.

Over the years my sins grew into vague shadows. After a time I imagined that maybe my sins weren't so bad or numerous because they were so unfocused and distant. A large part of me didn't recognize my sins at all. I was an unwitting example of Karl Menninger's provocative question, "Whatever happened to sin?"[7]

I don't think we should beat ourselves over the head with our sins, but my attitude was so casual, I tended to perpetuate the same sins and ignore others. I had no specific guilt—just the diffused, vague, free-floating, unredemptive kind. There was also the false guilt I'd carried inside for years as I'd tried desperately to win God's approval with my religious doing, attending and rule-keeping. It was time to cleanse the cup.

I wanted cleansing and forgiveness to be an "event," a

moment that would capture the experience in my mind and heart and seal it in time. Surely now and then we should do something to make it real to us.

The following day the family went on a picnic in the mountains near our home. After we had eaten and waded in a little creek near a splashing waterfall, Sandy volunteered to lead Bob and Ann on a hike while I packed our gear. When I finished I sat down on a rock by the waterfall to watch the water pour clean over the rocks—and slowly an idea was born in me.

I pulled a pen and tablet from my purse and began to jot down all of my sins that I could possibly remember. Things came to me, popping almost magically into my head, while others appeared only after I dug painfully for them. I relived hatreds, resentments, caustic words, lies, self-seeking. I wrote about the day someone apologized to me and I smiled, accepting it, then walked away bitter as a winter night. I wrote about moments of pride, indifference, envy. The times I'd failed Sandy, Bob and Ann.

Most vivid was the time I'd promised to spend the evening playing Monopoly with the family. The children set out the game. Sandy was in place as the banker. But I was so busy preparing a speech to deliver to a church group the next day, that I begged off. "But you promised," Bob pleaded. All three of them gazed sadly at me. Feeling tired and torn, I shouted to them to leave me alone and stomped off to my speech. It was titled, "Families Are for Loving." Even now, years later, the guilt of that moment squeezed my insides. During those hurried, busy years, there had been lots of moments like that. Moments I'd never confessed.

I wrote for what seemed a long time, though only half an hour passed. Then holding my list, surrounded by the little chapel of trees and rocks and gurgling water, I read back my words, whispering them aloud. This was the "event" of cleansing God asked of me. It was not like opening old wounds, but healing those that had never closed.

"Lord, have mercy on me, a sinner," I said. I dropped the paper and let it flutter to the foot of a rock that stood nearby like the stone altars of old. I don't think I will ever forget the sight of it . . . the way it twisted and spiraled down to the ground like a dying leaf. From me to the ground was as far as east from west, and all the air between was forgiveness.

I retrieved the paper and tore it into shreds, feeling light and free. I was a clean paper cup. The very air of the woods looked brighter.

The hikers returned. As we walked out of the woods, I kept thinking that next to *Jesus, forgiveness* was the loveliest word of all. Or perhaps they are the same word.

Such an experience of cleansing can occur anywhere. For me it was on a rock in the mountains because that's where I happened to be. The important thing is that with everything spilled out, suddenly there seemed to be wide spaces within where I could invite God's love.

My Own Space

Now I had to discover how to keep those spaces open for God. In the past, I'd tended to stereotype a space as twenty minutes in the morning to read the Bible and pray. But I have learned that any time, any place, any event can become a space in our life for God. The spaces we create do not have to fit into a mold. They can be our own unique openings, individual and free.

This insight came to me that spring during a canoe trip Sandy and I made down a serene portion of the Chattooga River. Early in the morning we pushed off into a silky mist rising off the river. The water, nearly invisible beneath the vapor, moved in silence except for a trickle at the bow. Neither of us spoke. And slowly I began to sense the presence of God. Soon I felt His love splashing over the rocks, filling me with joy. I had made a space for Him with my paddle!

We are all wonderfully different. It's important for us to

open ourselves to God in our own special way. "God chooses one man with a shout, another with a song, another with a whisper."[8]

Remember the story in Mark about the paralytic who tried to find a way to Jesus (Mark 2:1-15)? Four men carried his pallet to the house where Jesus was staying, but the crowd was so packed they could find no way to reach Him. One of the men looked up at the roof, envisioning something no one else saw—a unique and uncommon way into His presence. The next moment, all of them were carrying the pallet up the outside stairs to the roof. They pulled up the tiles (removed the rocks!), clearing a way. One of them peered down through the space in the roof, perhaps seeing Jesus' face turned up to him. Down went the pallet and the man in need came dangling like a spider into the presence of the Lord.

The story holds a message for us. Make a space any way you can. Chapels and rivers. Front doors and rooftops. We shouldn't be rigid and unimaginative when it comes to a discipline of prayer. I decided I should not "fit" myself into someone else's idea of how to experience God. You and I can create spaces in our lives that are joyfully our own. We are confined only by our vision.

We can create a space for God with our Bible, our church, our silence. We can also create it by taking a walk or paddling a river, by painting a picture or playing a flute. We can do it by feeding the hungry and listening to a friend . . . by anything at all that bears the intent of coming quietly and deliberately into God's presence. All of it is prayer. Every time we make a way, He comes.

I am not much of a believer in "levels" of prayer. I don't think prayer is a ladder with rungs, or a beanstalk that disappears into heaven. It is a passing through into the center of the moment you are now in and meeting God there. It's true that gradually your sense of God's presence deepens with practice, and the veneer that coats the world, blotting Him out, grows thinner with time. But one discipline is not necessarily loftier and holier than another. Sometimes as we grow, old ways of making space will naturally fade and we will create new disciplines that are more fulfilling. This is a natural ebb and flow.

We only need to begin, starting where we are, not where we are not. As we begin to create spaces for Him, we will deepen the sense of God's presence that is struggling for life in us. God will enter our interior castle, and more and more we will find ourselves loved. "O taste and see that the Lord is good," wrote the Psalmist (Psalm 34:8).

I eventually found my own ways that I tried to blend into my life with consistency. I will describe some of them in the chapters to come.

A New Story

Weeks later Ann appeared beside my blue wing chair wanting a new story. As she climbed into my lap, I decided to retell the story of the castle. Once again I told about the damsel in the castle and how His majesty, the king arrived to find a pile of rocks against the door.

"You've already told this one," protested Ann.

I smiled. "But this time the damsel went upstairs to her tower, put on her blue jeans and got to work moving the rocks," I continued.

Ann giggled.

"When the king saw how willing the damsel was and how hard she was working, he climbed from his steed and helped her. Together they moved all the rocks. As the sun sank over the turrets, the damsel had blisters on her hands, but her heart sang with a brand new joy. For inside in the heart of her castle she entertained the king."

"I like this story better than the other one," Ann said.

"Me, too," I said. "Me, too."

Receive with meekness the implanted word.
JAMES 1:21 RSV

13

Living with God in the Scriptures

I USED TO have a Bible teacher who said that the Bible is not so much precepts as it is a person. She was speaking of the encounter with God that is possible through the Scriptures. During the following weeks, as I began creating space for God, I turned to the Bible in a brand new way, and discovered the truth of her words for myself.

I grew up reading the Bible, a practice encouraged by the Bible-centered environment of my Baptist upbringing. My first Bible was the predictable black leather book presented to me by my church on September 29, 1957. I sat down front among my friends on the right-hand side of the First Baptist Church of Sylvester, Georgia. We were all approximately nine years old. The picture is still vivid in my mind: the way mother had pin-curled my hair the night before so that I had an enormous mass of tight black curls . . . the way we lined up in alphabetical order before the service so that we walked to the front of the church to receive our Bible with smooth and solemn ceremony. I remember especially the way my heart beat when my name was called and the Bible was placed in my hands. I carried it back to the pew feeling I had crossed a bridge of some sort.

In a sense it was a rite of passage. Now I, too, was a keeper of the "word." A bearer of those splendid and terrible things written inside the Book.

The pastor stood before our little group as I stared conspicuously at my name embossed on the cover in gold. "Open your Bible to Isaiah 34:16," he told us. There was a swishing of paper that gradually died away as the slowest of us found the place. "Seek ye out of the book of the Lord, and read," the verse said.

I plucked the pencil out of the offering card holder and copied the verse inside the cover of my brand-new Bible. Those words, "Seek ye out of the book," would fashion the shape of my religious experience.

Along with my friends at church, I was encouraged by continual reminders to read "the book." Nobody ever asked what book. There was only one book. "The" book. Every Sunday you checked off on a slip of paper whether you had done your "daily Bible reading," as it was called. It was one of your eight points. And if your particular Sunday school group had the most points—well, that was something quite special. You got a gold star beside your class's name on the roster.

To show how serious we were about this, at our slumber parties, late in the night, before we giggled ourselves to sleep, someone would always say, "Hey, we almost forgot our daily Bible reading." And believe it or not, we would dredge up a Bible and someone, usually my cohort Connie would read from it.

But somewhere along the way I had turned Bible reading almost exclusively into an academic pursuit, a way of earning straight As and gold stars. When I read the Bible, I did not think of it as a time when God and I conversed and communed. For me it was always *study*. Get out the commentaries, the underlining pencils, the maps of Palestine! I was always straining to dig out the historical background, the cultural implications, the meaning of a Greek or Hebrew word. It was tough mental work.

I would never want to diminish this approach to the Bible. It certainly is important. In fact, I continue to attend and teach Bible studies that take the studious approach. But there is another way to approach the Scriptures, one just as important as the analysis and study we do; and that is "praying" the Scriptures—being with God as we read them.

We cannot disassociate our awareness and attentiveness to God's presence from our Scripture reading. Making a deeper space for Him in my life meant coming to the Scriptures not only as a matter of study but as a matter of prayer. The goal is ultimately an encounter with The Word, who is Christ.

It was St. Bernard who wrote, "Instruction makes learned men; contact makes wise men."[1] I believe the progression we are called upon to make in our relation to the Scriptures is to go from instruction to contact.

When we search the Scriptures, for what are we really searching? An insight, some advice, a guiding principle? On the surface, yes. But maybe beneath all of that we are searching for God, for intimate encounter, for His love and presence in the midst of our daily lives. We want to connect with a Person, to become more at home with Him.

How do we do that? How can we go beyond mere mental activity to personal encounter? The three R's have become the basis of my approach to reading the Bible: receive, reflect, respond.

Receive

A receptive attitude is extremely important when we come to the Bible. In addition to examining, exegeting and interpreting, we need to listen, receive and experience. Dietrich Bonhoeffer, who died as a martyr at the hands of the Nazis, encouraged the students in his underground seminary not only to study the Bible but to spend time with it daily in an attitude of receiving.

> And just as you do not analyze the words of someone you love, but accept them as they are said to you, accept the Word of Scripture and ponder it in your heart, as Mary did. That is all . . . Do not look for new thoughts and connections in the text, as you would if you were preaching! Do not ask, "How shall I pass this on?" but, "What does it say to me?"[2]

In other words, we are to come to the Scriptures to receive what God wants to give through them. In my own reading I start with a prayer of receiving. I ask God to come to me through my reading, and help me open a space to receive Him. As I read the passage I am listening to it with a quiet, restful, receptive mind. I am not feverishly trying to wring meaning out of the verses. Rather I am waiting for God and what He wants to bring to my attention.

We can enhance our attitude of receiving by recognizing that God is coming to us *here and now* through the passage. For most of my life the immediacy of the Scriptures was rather hidden. The biblical events were locked in a time warp of long-ago history. But there is a sense in which biblical accounts also describe events that are occurring in our own lives right now. That is what A. W. Tozer means when he talks about approaching the "Bible with the idea that it is not only a book which was once spoken, but a book which is *now speaking*. . . . We may use the past tense properly to indicate that at a certain time a certain word of God was spoken, but a word of God once spoken continues to be spoken, as a child once born continues to be alive."[3]

This is the quality of receptivity we must bring to our reading. This event *is* happening now. These things are being spoken to me by God right *now*. The parables are unfolding in my life *now*. The events of Christ's life are impinging upon my life *now*. I will listen and receive them as if God is speaking and touching me with His presence this very moment.

If we can come to the Scriptures with the thought that we are in God's presence and that He is speaking *now,* if we listen with our whole heart, we will hear. We will be in contact with Him and discover His love spilling into our lives from the Scriptures.

Like those two walking to Emmaus whose hearts burned within them as Christ opened the Scriptures to them along the road, we can also touch His presence and sense His word move like fire in us. As we take the words into our heart of hearts, into that place where Christ dwells within us, He will open the Scriptures to us, too. He will break open their light and warmth within us.

The Hasidic masters may have had something when they spoke of a certain light that shines within the Scriptures. "The sacred letters are the chambers into which God pours His flowing light. The lights within each letter, as they touch, ignite one another, and new lights are born," they believed.[4] When we come quietly and open ourselves to receive what is there, new lights are born in us.

Reflect

My second step after reading the Scripture with an attitude of receiving is to reflect on the words. By that I do not mean a relentless and tiring kind of "chewing" on the verses until you have devoured the meaning from them. Rather, as we reflect, we enter the passage in some way. We allow it to take on life in us, opening the way for the presence of God to enter. The words become a prayer.

The Jewish scholar Abraham Heschel wrote that in order "to sense the presence of God in the Bible, one must learn *to be present* to God in the Bible." And to do that, he said, one must be involved.[5] If we want to contact the Person of the Bible, we don't merely read stories. We experience them.

Using Imagination

The times I have heard God speak to me through the Scriptures most clearly have been times when I have used my imagination to put myself into the story. Our imaginations involve our emotions and feelings, even our five senses, as well as our minds, which means they are a far more potent avenue to God than intellectual concepts alone. The inner life responds to images and symbols, which are our inner emotional and spiritual language. "When prayer and meditation concentrate only on concepts," says Morton Kelsey, "they do not touch the most profound part of our being. . . . Conceptual thought does not have the same power as the ability to think in images."[6]

I have already recounted a number of my imaginative journeys into Gospel scenes, but I'd like to walk through another one here, one which remains particularly vivid. I was reading in Luke about Jesus healing the leper near the Sea of Galilee (5:12-14). I began to imagine a village street in Palestine bustling with people selling their wares. I saw baskets of olives and fruit, and crowds of sun-tanned men and dark-eyed children. I smelled fish drying in the sun and heard the noise of bartering and the clatter of donkey hooves.

Then, rising over all the other sounds came a plaintive cry, a voice calling rhythmically in the distance. It grew louder and louder until I could make out the words, "Unclean . . . unclean."

As a bent figure hobbled into view, supporting himself on two sticks, people began to grab children and wares and scurry away. The leper's wailing cry of "unclean" finally cleared the street—except for one white-robed man whom I noticed for the first time.

I watched the leper limp along the road on what I realized were toeless feet. Shrinking in the shadows, a handful of remaining persons stared at him as if frozen—a mother clasping her child's hand, a boy touching his dog's ear. The leper paused and looked at them with a yearning to be touched—to be touched like a child's hand or a dog's ear. The need blazed out of his eyes as he passed.

Then he moved on toward the man in white who seemed to be waiting for him. The leper threw himself at the feet of Jesus, who did not flinch, but bent toward him.

At that moment in my imaginative journey, tears began to form in my eyes, tears for the untouchable man who longed for a human embrace. Tears for everyone who, half-eaten by rejection, searched for a touch. I was crying, too, for the deep, painful parts of myself that needed to be embraced.

Jesus stretched out His hand. I saw it coming, slow and gentle like a bird that lights upon a rotting limb . . . but deliberate and strong too, with the press of firmness. He touched the man's head, then his hand. Lifting him up He held him like a lost brother who had been found. And when He let go, the longing was gone from the man's face—and the leprosy from his body.

In those moments Christ was the long reach of God's arm to me, too. He was touch. I found myself embraced, loved, and healed, like the leper.

Slowly the scene faded. Only ten minutes had passed. But the Gospel event had happened to me! I had internalized it, had participated in it on a level that was astonishingly real. And for the first time that particular passage of Scripture had an impact upon my life, though I'd read it countless times before.

As we journey into the Gospel scenes, we not only have a growing sense of contact with God's presence but through imagination we begin to penetrate truths hidden to us, see relationships we haven't seen before, actually find ourselves being changed by what we read.

The images that rise in these journeys often stay with us for a long time, maybe forever. Once in a while, when I am feeling rejected or eaten with loneliness, the picture of Christ's hand touching the leper returns to me exactly as it looked that day I saw it in my imagination, and I am comforted.

This way of interacting with Scripture need not be limited to the Gospels. I have sometimes entered events in the Old Testament, like Moses telling God he wasn't qualified to lead the people of Israel out of Egypt or poor Job bewailing his afflictions or little Samuel lying still on his bed hearing God call to him out of the night, thinking it was Eli.

Role-playing the Parables

Another way of reflecting on the Scriptures is what I call role-playing the parables. To do this, we imagine ourselves in the roles of the various characters in the parables. By acting out the parts in our imaginations, the most hidden insights about ourselves can be discovered, and God can talk to us inwardly about our lives.

One day while browsing through Luke I came upon the prodigal son parable (Luke 15:11-32). It had been a long while since I'd read it, yet as I began to read, it seemed terribly familiar. I was drawn to the events, almost as though I had been there before.

I read how a Father (God) had two sons. Only I found myself thinking of it as two daughters. One of the "daughters" took her inheritance from the Father and went away from him into a "far country." There she squandered her life. The word struck a chord in me. *Squander* meant fritter away, deplete, expend and exhaust. I wondered if it meant to divide up your life like an "algebra pie" and dish it up to the world. I thought about my life and how through those years of feverish activity, increasing stress and disintegration, I had been journeying to a "far country"—a spiritual terrain that was far from my Father's presence.

Of course! This story was familiar because in an off way I had lived it.

But there is more. I read how the "daughter" ended up in a pig sty feeding swine and growing more and more hungry until she feared she would perish from hunger. Yes, in that "far country" I had lived with a deep-down gnawing hunger, though I was not able to understand for a long while what I hungered for. Then I remembered how one day, just before my pivotal episode with the chest pains, we visited Monk Farm and I took the children to visit the pig pens. The hunger in my spirit that day was nearly as great as the stench of the pigs. Everything was converging in my life—the frenetic pace, the divisions, the compulsion to earn badges of love, the growing tensions of the "far country." I remember watching the pigs eat and feeling nearly sick with hunger myself.

I hadn't thought of that visit since then. And it was not long after that, like the prodigal in the story, I "came to myself." Later I learned that this phrase came from Greek medicine, where it was used to indicate someone waking up from a coma.

I read on. The "daughter" in the story said, "I will rise up and go to my father." Rise up! That was the very language I'd heard echoing inside myself that day under the reflection tree when I began this journey to God. It was a journey of "waking up." And I had heard Jesus saying to me as He said to Jairus' daughter, "*Talitha cumi* . . . Rise up, daughter."

Yet the strangest part is yet to come. I read how the "daughter" began her journey back, from the hunger and the pigs and the squandering of her life, back to the Father's presence. Back to wholeness and unity with Him. And what did the Father do? In His love, he went out to meet her while she was still at a distance, brought her a robe and *put a ring on her finger!*

At this point I was overcome. Because I was wearing that ring.

A few months after my chest pains and after I had begun my journey back to God, I had gone into the bedroom and opened the little case where I kept a few trinkets I'd brought back from the Holy Land—two tiny crosses, a mother of pearl Bible, an olive wood carving . . . and a *ring*.

I had bought the ring in Bethlehem, though at the time I couldn't imagine why. It is a slender band of silver-colored metal with some tiny carving around it, utterly simple, and cheap. (It cost three dollars, and when I wear it in the swimming pool it turns green.) But I was attracted to it as it lay in a basket of "junk" on the counter of the souvenir shop. I bought it on pure impulse and had kept it hidden away in the case.

That day I had put it on my finger and said to God, "Father, I will wear this ring as a symbol and celebration of my journey to You. It represents my new wholeness, my center, a reminder of Your love." And with a small ceremony I slipped it on my finger. I have worn it ever since, only removing it to wash away the "green" after I swim. My attachment to it is enormous.

As I finished reading and reflecting on the parable, I looked down at the ring on my finger with awe and amazement. What did all of this mean? I'm still not sure. But I do know that through that parable I began to have a profound sense of God's participation in my journey.

When we "enter" these universal stories that Jesus told, new worlds of insight and meaning open to us. We experience God's presence. Admittedly, I've never had another parable-experience quite like the "prodigal-daughter" one, but each of them in their own way has touched my life.

I have been the servant who buried the talent, I was the rocky soil where the sower threw his seeds, I was once the man who found the pearl of great price buried in a field. On another occasion I was the pearl and God was the man who found *me* and gave up all he had to purchase me.

I have been every one of the characters in the Good Samaritan story, from the robber to the innkeeper. I recall the time I role-played the part of the Levite who crossed to the other side of the road to avoid a wounded man. Only I saw myself ignoring the chatter of an old woman in a nursing home, wounded by years of loneliness, just as I had actually done on one occasion. I'd gone for a visit, but tuned her out, watching the clock and biding time until I could escape. In my own way I had "crossed to the other side." I'd forgotten that callous moment, but by entering that parable as the Levite I was able to ask forgiveness for that event and experience God's waking me to the need of the lonely for someone to listen.

Sometimes we can draw parallels from the parable to specific events in the past, seeing new meaning. Other times as we play out the different parts, we discover ways we are responding to something in the present, or are given clues as to how we ought to respond in the future.

When we begin to find ourselves in the Scriptures . . . when the "she" or "he" becomes "me," we invariably open a way for God to speak to us in His word. We commune with Him there. We "pray" the Scriptures.

Free-fall Meditation

A third way of reflecting on the Scriptures so that we experience God's presence in them is through what I call the "free-fall" meditation. This is a meditative approach in which we turn loose and fall freely, quietly, gently, into a passage, allowing it to speak and carry us wherever it will.

I select one verse, one sentence, or one word. After I read it, I close my eyes and "free fall" into the different levels of meaning that lie within it. *What is God saying to me right now through this piece of Scripture? What does it mean?*

Usually at this point I do not see beyond the obvious meaning that I've always attached to the verse. So after musing on this level awhile I try to free fall to another level . . . to break out of old thought patterns and let the Scripture evoke some new thought, image or idea inside me.

Sometimes it helps to think of the words as a statue that I have always looked at from the same angle. Now I walk around to the other side and view it from new angles, seeing how light falls on it in different ways. Or I think of the words as a stone lying in a creek, to be turned over so I can reflect on the underside. The Bible has infinite riches and beauties waiting to be discovered. God has much more to say to us than we have yet heard.

I was intrigued to read of a Baptist pastor's "free fall" into those words of Christ on the cross, "My God, why hast thou forsaken me." Carlyle Marney allowed the words to yield up their obvious meaning. Then he pondered the words on a new and different level. Focusing on the word "thou" in the sentence, it occurred to him to ask, "What if this cry . . . is not addressed to God at all? What if he is not talking to God but to us? What if the 'My God, my God, why hast thou forsaken me?' is addressed to us who 'sitting down watched him there'? What if this cry is an appeal to us, not a cry to God at all?"[7]

What if the "thou" in this sentence is "me"? Here suddenly we are face to face with something entirely different. Something personal and searching. Am I forsaking Him in any way in my life? How? God speaks to us now from the same Scripture, but with a new particle of truth.

Next, I free fall into prayer—into a dialogue with God. I converse with Him about the new meanings I am discovering, and most of all, about what it is invoking within me. I let Him talk back to me and imagine what He might be saying.

Praying the Psalms

There is at least one other way to enter or reflect on Scripture. It is praying the Psalms. The Psalms are essentially prayers, universal prayers that have the power to draw us into an experience of God's presence. I take a few moments just before going to bed or early in the morning, to pray through one of the Psalms, or, if it is lengthy, a portion of it. Then I try to live with it throughout the days ahead.

By that I mean that during the rest of the week I return to the Psalm every day, praying it as if it were my own prayer. I breathe its ejaculations of awe and praise or whisper its pleas for help. Slowly the prayer becomes my prayer. Usually as the week unfolds I can identify my own personal situation somewhere within it.

There are places in the Psalms where it can be difficult to identify with what is flowing from the psalmist's heart—for instance, when he writes with such vengeance against his enemies. But if we think of them as the "inner" personal enemies that seek to destroy us, the psalms can help us identify the enemies of the spiritual life: hate, lying, greed, fear, pride, lust, jealousy, and so on.

Once I tried to pray a section of Psalm 140 (v. 10 RSV)

> Let burning coals fall upon them!
> Let them be cast into pits, no more to rise!

I wasn't sure what to do with those words. The thought of such vengeance struck me as repulsive, until it dawned on me that the way into this prayer was to call down burning coals on one of my inner enemies. At the time I was wrestling with an irrational fear of breast lumps. I'd had two benign ones removed within a short space of time, going through the surgery, biopsy, waiting, and wondering. It had been a tormenting time and the thought of having to go through another such time left me weak with fear. Through the Psalm I was able to name my inner enemy and ask God to help me cast it into the pits, no more to rise. As I entered more deeply into the Psalm, I became drawn intimately into God's presence each time I prayed it. And gradually I found the strength to overcome the fear.

Where the Psalms burst open with praise, we can especially adopt the prayer as our own. I find the Psalms can put words to some of my deepest and most inexpressible emotions, especially the praise I feel but rarely express.

Sandy and I were cross-country skiing one morning in the shadow of Grandfather Mountain in North Carolina. Earlier that week, knowing we would be going to the mountains, I adopted this portion of Psalm 104 (vv. 31–33 RSV) to pray during the week:

> May the glory of the Lord endure for ever,
> may the Lord rejoice in his works,
> who looks on the earth and it trembles,
> who touches the mountains and they smoke!
> I will sing to the Lord as long as I live;
> I will sing praise to my God while I have being.

When we read the Psalms as if they were our own deepest prayers, they become carved on the walls of our soul. Through them we touch the springs of praise in our lives. We identify our specific needs and inner enemies. Most of all we open ourselves to another way of being in God's healing presence.

Respond

Our contact with Scripture is always incomplete unless we translate what we read into some concrete response or action. At the close of our time with God's word, we need to ask ourselves, "What must I now do? How must I change?" The answer should involve some specific response or change we will try to make in our lives. Then we need to speak with God about it. I often log my responses in my journal, simply because it makes it more concrete, more black and white, more unforgettable. Sometimes I read them back and evaluate how I've followed through over a long period of time.

While reflection on the Scripture involves internalizing it, responding to the Scripture means externalizing it. The passage we have "entered" must gradually "exit"—become action in our everyday life. This response phase might be termed, "making the word flesh." For we are bringing it into being in our everyday life. We attempt to flesh out through our behavior, relationships, work, play, conversation and attitudes the insights and meanings we have gained from our contact with God in the Scripture. We follow the admonition of the apostle James to be "doers of the word, and not hearers only" (James 1:22).

After reflecting one morning on John 15:11 where Jesus speaks about His joy being in us with fullness, I was reminded of what had happened when I picked up Ann at school one day. I saw a little fellow of six or seven walking across the school lawn toward his mother's car. About halfway there he stopped and began to toss his book satchel high in the air, trying to catch it. The joy in this free, childlike act was evident on his face. "Look!" he kept shouting to his mother, who sat impatiently in the car. After ten or so of his tosses, she got out and dragged him into the car, yelling at him for keeping her waiting. His face fell. She had extinguished something important in him—some important flame of joy.

It made me think of the times I'd done the same sort of thing to my own children, to Sandy, even to myself—puncturing the joy of others with my impatience or thoughtlessness. Jesus Christ desires my joy. He wants our joy to be full. I needed to change my attitude, to make a tangible response to these words.

That afternoon when Bob yanked off his shoes and waded gleefully through a mud puddle he'd created with the garden hose, I had to bite the insides of my cheeks, but I didn't say a discouraging or angry word. Instead, I peeled off my shoes and squished around in the mud with him. We laughed till the puddle dried. Our joy was full.

May my meditation be pleasing to him,
for I rejoice in the Lord.
PSALM 104:34 RSV

14

Focusing on God Through Prayer

ONCE AGAIN spring was stirring in South Carolina, and a little row of yellow tulips was pushing out of the dirt around the patio. One morning during my "quiet time," I found myself sitting and staring at the tulips instead of praying. Perhaps it was spring thumping in my spirit, or maybe it was the knock of God, but suddenly the need to move in a new direction, to venture out onto a brave new landscape of prayer pulsed in me with new strength.

All my life, praying had meant talking to God when I found the time. Often prayer was so automatic and rote that I experienced very little sense of contact with God. It was me chatting away. Now I needed a new wineskin of prayer for the awakening that trickled and at times poured into my life. I didn't know what sort of praying would lead me deeper into God's presence and open me more to His love. I only knew that the newly bloomed tulips somehow called me to search.

It was the books I was continuing to discover that introduced me to the kind of prayer I was looking for. In the classics of devotional literature I found a host of Christian thinkers and saints talking about a way of "being with" God—a way of meeting Him and experiencing Him in the depths of one's being—that opened the door to oneness with Him. They called it contemplation.

I was amazed to realize that I had known practically nothing about this ancient and powerful tradition of Christian meditation. Often I wondered, and sometimes aloud to Sandy, why I hadn't discovered it before. "When we're ready," Sandy said to me one day, "God meets us in our need to grow in Him." Yes, of course. I was ready.

When Dietrich Bonhoeffer was asked why he meditated he answered simply, "Because I am a Christian."[1] I began to understand his matter-of-fact answer as I discovered how deeply meditation is woven into our heritage, going back to both New and Old Testament times.

In the Old Testament I found the references numerous. We are told that Isaac went out to meditate in the fields (Genesis 24:63). The author of Joshua wrote of the need to meditate on "the book of the law" day and night. "I . . . meditate on thee in the night watches," wrote the Psalmist (Psalm 63:6).

> I will call to mind the deeds of the Lord;
>   yea, I will remember thy wonders of old.
> I will meditate on all thy work
>   and muse on thy mighty deeds.
>   PSALM 77:11–12 RSV

> I will meditate on thy precepts,
>   and fix my eyes on thy ways.
> I will delight in thy statutes;
>   I will not forget thy word.
>   PSALM 119:15–16 RSV

And what about Jesus? I wondered. Did He practice meditation? I had always seen Jesus' outgoing relationships with people, His outward acts, His words before the multitude. But now as I read the New Testament, I saw another side of Jesus. The Gospel writers show us a Jesus who was at home with solitude and the interior world where God dwells. He spent whole nights in prayer (Luke 6:12). The most significant events of His life were preceded by concentrated periods of time just being with the Father—His forty days in the wilderness before He entered His ministry, His time of prayer in Gethsemane before His crucifixion (Luke 4:1–14; 22:39–46). He communed with God in the hills and along the shore, on rooftops and hidden away on a boat. There He listened, becoming so united with the Father that we find God's presence breaking into the world wherever He went.

Jesus also guided His followers into a way of praying that does not use "many words" (Matthew 6:7). We are to pray to the Father in secret, He told us, in the silence of the heart-closet. The one prayer Christ *did* teach was very much like a contemplative or meditative prayer.

The prayer Jesus taught us, which we call "The Lord's Prayer," starts with "Our Father." Here is a new dimension of intimacy. Though we may have looked upon these words as a mere salutation, I believe Christ intended them to be the center pole of the prayer, around which the rest of it revolves. He is asking us to come to God as *abba,* an intimate daddy—to focus on His presence and become aware of Him who is also Father to every one around us. (The Hebrew and Aramaic word *abba* is what children in Jesus' time called their daddies. The Apostle Paul picks up the word in Romans 8:15.)

In meditative prayer, we begin with God as our intimate Abba-Father. We focus on Him, on His love, immersing ourselves in it. This "being-with" God in a close, daddy-child experience forms the very core of contemplative prayer. Everything else revolves around it.

Clearly, the tradition of Christian meditation was handed down from Christ and the early praying Christians[2] who tapped into some of the most amazing resources of God's power ever witnessed. The early church fathers knew and practiced the "prayer of the heart," which was the name they gave to this interior meditative experience.

Meditation is also being researched and written about by twentieth-century science. It has been found to enhance something called "right brain" activity. It seems the two hemispheres of the brain each control a different set of functions and "interpret the world through a different lens."[3] Most of us live predominantly out of the left side of the brain, which is our rational, objective, action-oriented side. We know or relate to things in a reasonable, analytical way. With left brain activity, we use words, analyze things into parts, and attend to details. If we act primarily from this side, we may tend to be busy, talkative, anxious, success-motivated, and to make decisions on the basis of facts and logic.

The right hemisphere, on the other hand, is our intuitive, visionary, creative and meditative side. When we respond from this part of our brain, we allow ourselves to be open to fresh insights, to ways of knowing other than mere critical or logical thinking. With right brain activity we may simply relax and "be." We see whole pictures instead of parts, use images more than words. We open ourselves to mystery, we imagine, dream and make decisions based on the still small voice inside us. We know things in our heart.

Today we are being told that a fulfilled, whole life is not possible without a balancing between the right brain and the left brain. For most of us, this means activating the use of our right brain, since from early childhood our culture generally encourages left brain activity and stifles the more creative use of the right.

Had I been praying out of the left side of my brain, I wondered? When I tried to approach God with words, concepts, logic, requests, information, lists and formulas, wasn't that my left brain working? Yet praying from the right side—the meditative, inner side—would let me encounter God in my "center," would help me create space for God.

God was calling me, I realized, to more balance in my praying.

What Happens When We Meditate?

Many things happen when we work at meditative prayer. The most important is that the presence and love of God is stirred to life within us.

When we grow still and meditate on God, *we activate His presence deep inside.* Now and then I have felt that a power was released within which I have dared to call God's Spirit. It seems to flow inside and infuse me with a deep awareness that God is there, and that I am loved by Him. I am helpless to explain it. I can only sit in awe of it like a child.

But I want to be careful not to fall into the trap of thinking meditation produces God in my life. It doesn't. It is simply a way of preparing to receive Him, of creating a climate in which the experience of God and His love can take place.

"The great gift of God in prayer is himself, and whatever else he gives is incidental and secondary."[4] God's presence is always a gift. I can't navigate myself to Him through meditative prayer. I am pulled. Pulled by grace. The best I can do is consciously cooperate by pulling up the stakes that keep me planted in unawareness.

I have to remind myself continually that meditative prayer is not only something I do but something God does in me. There is a dual activity. "God works in us while we rest in him."[5] Our part is to be still and alert in God, to focus, imagine, listen, receive and respond. God comes, speaks, gives, guides and loves. He plays directly on the soul. His presence is alive in us and we are aware of His love.

Through meditation *we can also receive guidance, insight and direction.* I had been meditating only a few weeks when one morning near the end of my prayer time I received a well-formed impression that I should remain home instead of going to a meeting scheduled at ten. The impression was so deep and solid that I called in my regrets and stayed home. By ten o'clock I was feeling foolish. Then at 10:15, when I would have been unreachable, the phone rang. Ann's teacher was calling to tell me Ann was sick, throwing up and crying for her mama. It was the first time she had become sick at school. "Can you come for her right away?" she asked. I was awed.

On several occasions, usually after my meditation time has ended, I have been given small flashes of wisdom about how to respond to some request or problem, though I hadn't been thinking about those things at all during the meditation. Mostly these small "breaking moments" of insight deal with very practical things I need to work on in my life. And sometimes— most of the time—I hear nothing. But that's fine. God's voice is not guaranteed. I would never suggest that because you meditate you will have transcendent breakthroughs all the time. That is pure delusion. Much of the time I haven't the foggiest notion what God is saying to me even though I have opened myself to Him.

A third thing that happens through the discipline of meditative prayer is that *inner storehouses of strength and ability to cope are laid up inside us.* John Killinger pointed out that Jesus had built up a reservoir of power during all those years He communed with God. When His dark moments came, He was able to tap into that storehouse and meet His crisis with serenity and faith.[6]

A woman I met on a plane once noticed a book I was reading on meditation, and we struck up a conversation. It turned out she was a Christian who had practiced meditative prayer for several years. She spoke of how it had helped her grow to "know" God intimately. Then she mentioned a curious thing. "It helped me enormously when my husband died."

"What do you mean?" I asked.

"Well, at first I sank down into a great blackness. But very soon it seemed I landed upon some bedrock inside myself, which I had not known existed. I found myself supported by it—held up by the most surprising foundation of strength and peace I had ever known." She paused and gazed past me through the little oval window. "You know," she continued, "I believe now that bedrock was the culmination of all those moments of prayer that I shoveled bit by bit into my life." I did not doubt that she was right.

Finally, we should be aware that *meditative prayer can bring about an inner realignment.* Meditation is centering, helping us to overcome anxiety and harmonize ourselves so we can know the peace of God.

One Sunday evening, seven or eight months after I had been practicing meditative prayer regularly, a psychologist friend of mine led the Church Training program. He showed us a small biofeedback device which fit neatly in the palm of one's hand. The device, he explained, picked up the amount of inner noise and tension inside a person as he or she held it in their hand, and would emit a sound to reflect that amount. A loud, high-pitched noise meant turmoil and tension inside. A low, humming sound pointed to a more relaxed state of inner peace.

I'd never seen anything like that before and was eager to try it. One by one, with lots of smiles between us, we passed the device around. As each of us wrapped our fingers around it, a shrill noise pierced the room. People tried to grow still and calm in order to diminish the sound. Some took a few slow, deep breaths, others closed their eyes. But it made very little difference in the noise level emitted by the device.

After class I decided to hold onto the biofeedback machine while I entered into the realm of meditative prayer that had become familiar to me. Within only a few minutes the shrill noise had dwindled to a low hum.

What had happened? What was the difference? I'm not sure I can tell you exactly. But I believe that in meditation you touch something secreted away inside yourself, something secreted at the heart of the universe—God's presence, power and love that flow through the world. For a space of time you allow yourself to flow with His life-giving Spirit. You move all the partitioned pieces of your life into the stream of God's presence, like a host of tributaries flowing in the vitality of the river, becoming one with it.

That's why the experience can be deeply healing and freeing.

Tension and anxiety drain away as we simply yield to God and become one with Him in His love.

But obviously these things don't occur with the whisk of a wand, or with one or two tries. Meditative prayer is fruitful, but it can also be difficult and demanding. We have to approach it with deep personal conviction and a certain steadfastness and enthusiasm.

We all have contemplative seeds sown in our hearts—a givenness to meditate that simply needs to be cultivated. "It is normal to be a contemplative," writes Thomas Keating.[7] But even though the instinct is there, we need practical help. We will likely have to make more than one start—to try and try again. But that's how it is when we're growing up, whether we're following the instinct to walk, or to pray inwardly.

Beginning

How do we begin to meditate? Here is a story that has helped me.

> There was a professor taking a sea voyage in a little boat and one night he goes up to an old sailor and says, "Hey, old man, what do you know about ocean-ography?" The old sailor didn't even know what the word meant. The Professor said, "You've wasted a quarter of your life! Here you are, sailing on the sea, and you don't even know any oceanography." . . . The next night the Professor goes up to the old man. "What do you know about astronomy?" "Nothing." "Here you are, out on the sea, and you need the stars to navigate, and you don't know anything about astronomy. You've wasted three-quarters of your life!" The next night the old sailor comes rushing up to the Professor and says, "Professor, what do you know about swimology?" The Professor says, "Oh,

nothing, I've never learned to swim." "Ah, too bad,
the boat is sinking. You've wasted all your life."

It is the swimology which is important.[8]
We can go on learning all there is to know about the
"ologies" of prayer and the meditative way of encountering
God. But the only way actually to encounter God is to meditate
and pray—to dive in and learn to swim. Otherwise we will
have wasted our life learning about things but never experiencing them. This is a great danger in the spiritual life, one I
am very prone to.

"If you want a life of prayer," wrote Thomas Merton not
long before he died, "the way to get it is by praying."[9]
So I began. My first step was to fashion a time and place to
be with God three or four times a week. Finding and protect-
ing that cubbyhole of time with God in a busy day is a
discipline I have grappled with a lot at various times in my life.
Inspirational writer Karen Burton Mains once noted concerning Moses and the burning bush that God revealed Himself only after Moses "turned aside" to see this unusual sight—
after he paid attention to it (Exodus 3:2-4)![10] The discipline of
"turning aside" is somehow necessary. I'd only loosely continued the quiet time I had begun at the start of my awakening
journey. Now, I returned to it with conviction but pushing it
forward to a time when I wasn't as likely to fall asleep in the
middle of my meditation (which I did on more than one
occasion). Now my time comes during the morning just after
the children hustle off to school and just before I settle down
to the day's work. That is when I am most receptive.

I am a person who has a strong sense of place. I need a
particular place, quiet and uninterrupted, in which to meditate.
Of course, my meditation isn't limited to that place, but when
I sit in the green leather chair at my desk and place the little
brass cross that sits upon it in front of me, I become aware of
a climate of prayer. Sometimes only to look across the room at
the green chair draws me to God.

The first time I sat there to meditate was not momentous.

But I broke ground, and that is often the hardest part. I started with a prayer that God would help me, then closed my eyes and tried to be still enough to focus. But I was too tense. I couldn't find a comfortable position in the chair. And my mind was just as tense.

I quickly discovered that *the first task in meditation is to relax the body*. Preparation for prayer is an area I'd never given much consideration. But it can make our prayer experience more vital and enriching. When our bodies are tense, fidgety and wound up like a ball of yarn, we will not pray as well. Have you seen someone who, even when she thinks she is sitting still, is actually shaking her foot or tapping a pencil? Most of us carry more physical and mental tension in us than we are aware of. This tension can clog our spirit and prevent a calm, receptive attitude.

One evening Ann, all red-faced and breathless, handed me a stubborn orange balloon and asked me to blow it up. I blew. And blew and blew. The taut little balloon was impossible to fill. So I took a few minutes to stretch and pull the elastic material gently until it was supple and "relaxed." Then the balloon gave way freely as I blew it up and was soon floating about the house.

The point was not lost on me. I was as tight as the orange balloon when I prayed. God was waiting to breathe His presence into my life, but I was so tense with the sound and fury of the world that He could not get through. I believe Harry Emerson Fosdick was right when he said that there are somethings God cannot give us until we are prepared. We must be ready and willing to receive them.[11] I needed a few moments to relax and "stretch out" spiritually before I could pray.

Sandy had started leading some stress seminars for ministers that spring, so I asked if he had a relaxation technique up his sleeve that would be appropriate to use before prayer. He took me by the shoulders and sat me down in a chair. "Try this," he said. "Sit comfortably and close your eyes. Now become aware of your toes."

I squinted up at him. "Toes?"

"Yes, toes," he said, grinning. "Tighten them, along with your feet and legs, contracting the muscles as hard as you can. Then quickly release all the tension."

I tried it, feeling a melting sensation through my muscles. Then he had me contract and release all my muscles, moving up my body until I came to the top of my head. By then I was feeling like a puddle of gelatin. "This little exercise siphons off tension in only a few minutes," he said.

But even with my body relaxed, I had a hard time focusing. There was so much inner noise inside myself I realized I needed an inner riot-control team to calm all the chaos. *The second task in meditation,* I learned, *is to still the mind,* or as some might say, to "center down." When the day's rush and confusion are still swirling in our thoughts, we are unable to focus on prayer. To help us find a state of mental relaxation, we must use our imaginations.

For instance, one morning, when my thoughts were particularly clamorous, I recalled the scripture of Jesus' calming the wind and waves on the Sea of Galilee. I closed my eyes and imagined the storm lashing inside my own head. I pictured Christ standing over me. He touched my forehead. "Peace be still," He said. Then I envisioned all the turmoil subsiding until the watery surface of my mind rocked serenely to a standstill and I heard the lap, lap, lapping of the waves grow quieter and quieter until there was only silence.

We can each call forth our own centering images from inside ourselves. Sometimes they simply come like a gift. One morning at my desk, a "circle-of-quiet" image rose up spontaneously in me, like a bubble floating to the top of the water. I suddenly imagined Christ drawing a circle around me. I sat in the middle of the circle, which was shining like a ring of light. Inside there was a hush, a deep still calmness. A Presence. Christ assured me nothing could penetrate the circle from the outside, but that I could send all my concerns, fears, frustrations and thoughts outside the circle. One by one I mentioned the things weighing on my mind, imagining them moving outside the circle: the anger I felt during breakfast . . . the clothes waiting to go in the washer . . . the cookies I had to bake for Ann's school . . . anxiety over a doctor's appointment. Gradually my mind was slowing down.

With body and mind relaxed and quiet, we are ready, then, for meditation.

Praying the Prayer of Presence

I call this time of meditation "the prayer of presence," because in it I simply try to be there for God, to be present in His presence with a kind of quiet and loving adoration. That is all.

"You mean that's it? That's the whole thing?" an incredulous friend asked me as I told him about this kind of prayer one day.

"That's the essence of it," I said. He could not get over the idea that he did not have to do anything, that he could leave it all to God. I suspect that like most of us he wanted to be in control instead of letting everything go and allowing himself to simply be there with God and let whatever happens happen.

But if getting to that quiet inner place within is difficult, staying there in the circle of quiet is even more so. We may find that our minds wander, distractions fly out of every crevice of our brains, diverting us from God's presence and love.

Teresa of Avila once remarked that we can make more spiritual progress contemplating God for five minutes than by contemplating ourselves for thirty. [12] If we will begin by trying to turn our entire being toward God for five minutes, perhaps gradually we can work up to ten and later to fifteen and twenty.

The way to stay in God's presence is not to do battle with each distraction as it comes. I tried to at first—struggling to force each wayward thought out of my mind. But that did not work. The distractions remained. It is truly amazing how undisciplined our minds can be, how unresponsive to our will.

Plato said that the mind was like a ship where the sailors had mutinied and locked the captain below. He wrote that the task of a human being is to quell the mutiny and regain control of the ship's wheel.[13]

I have found help in the book *Centering Prayer* by Basil Pennington.[14] He suggests using a "prayer word" drawn out of the Christian meditation tradition to help us remain in our center with God. Repeating the word does not "become" the prayer. Rather the word hangs quietly in our thoughts like the backdrop of a curtain. When you go to a play you don't go to focus on the backdrop. You go to experience the play itself. But if the backdrop were not there, you would be bombarded with the backstage confusion of lights, props, people, cue cards, etc. The curtain or the prayer word is there to block out all the rest so you can attend to the main event: your loving and receptive attention to God's presence.

In my prayer time, I use a word that casts a quiet, peaceful reflection within: *love, center, reverence* ... or one of the names of the Trinity: *Father, Holy Spirit, Jesus.* I repeat it in my thoughts without effort, like the slow dropping of the curtain. Then I allow it to "lie quietly in the consciousness," as Pennington puts it, until the need arises to return to the word and repeat it again. I use the word only to pull me deeper into prayer when things threaten to draw me away. Instead of fighting the distraction, I just allow it to float by like a puff of smoke.

I have found it true, as Pennington suggests, that it doesn't matter much which word we use as long as the word emits something positive and loving from us. Mostly I use the word *Jesus.* It is the most loving word for me. Sometimes, though, the word shifts spontaneously. Once as I began to let the word *Jesus* sound quietly in my thoughts, the first part of it fell away and the word became *us*, shining across my mind like a light. I was touched by a reality of togetherness with Him held somehow in that little word. There at my green chair there was only *us.*

Other Ways of Meditative Prayer

The prayer of presence is only one way of meditation—a rather formal, disciplined way that has become the bulwark of my daily work in expanding my awareness of God's loving presence with me. But I have come to recognize other, more casual, spontaneous, everyday ways of meditating.

Tucked into our days are ample moments to *"be still and know."* In the texture of an ordinary day, we can learn to meditate. Almost anything can become a prompter to point us to God, if we pause and let it draw our minds and hearts to Him.

I remember a "be still and know" moment that popped out of the unexpected blue. There is not a time at my house full of more fuss and bother than the children's bath time. They have always hated baths and I have done some ridiculous things to persuade them into the tub, including letting them bathe with goggles, snorkels and inner tubes! So it wasn't entirely strange that I bribed Ann into the tub one evening by suggesting a bubble bath and candles. When the tub was snowy with bubbles, I lit four candles around the bathroom and cut off the light.

Instantly Ann and I fell absolutely silent. The light was pink and golden and enchanted like a spell of magic let loose from a fairy tale. I sat down and watched her move in the little bubbles of light. As I began to be still and focus on one round bubble dancing around her head, spinning and shimmering in the candlelight, I was drawn to God . . . the God of little girls and bubbles and light reflecting around and through us. Sitting there in the bathroom I was surrounded by His love.

A raindrop winding across a window or a tear winding down a face can take on a holiness if we use them to focus our attention and interface our moment with God's. Charles Cummings tells of such a spontaneous moment of meditation. A woman who was eating a piece of bread noticed a half-circle of teeth marks left on the buttered slice in her hand. As she gazed, she become aware of all that had gone into the bread—sun, soil, seed, rain, sowers, harvesters, bakers. Suddenly she was overwhelmed by the nurturing of God for His children, the sustaining gifts that come from Him, the One who called Himself the Bread of Life.[15]

This is meditation springing up in our dailiness, when we become still and know Him through common sights and sounds. Allowing these real things to be vehicles of prayer keeps my spiritual journey rooted. I certainly don't want to become disengaged from the practical side of everyday life, but to meet God within it.

Any task can be meditative if we learn to do it meditatively— that is, with awareness and a still heart waiting for God. I have discovered that I can draw, jog, even cook meditatively, if I work at it. I have to begin by deciding that this task is the most important thing at the moment. It is not in the way of God's presence, but the way to it. If I concentrate gently but completely on it, it is possible to fall into a prayerful cadence simply through the movement and rhythm of my hands or body. Focusing on God in this way can be called a task-meditation. It blends into our mundane routine like music.

We can also meditate as we write. A friend of mine who was forever saying she hated to write went to a conference where she was asked to retire to a quiet place and write whatever came to her. As she began to scribble words on the paper, something beautiful occurred. "It was like a wall gave way inside," she said. "The words began to pour out. The meditation nearly wrote itself." Spontaneously she was "with God," meditating as she wrote down the things in her heart. Now she often keeps a little notebook handy during her day, moving into meditative prayer as she pauses now and then to write what her heart is saying.

Moving to the Grateful Center

Teresa of Avila said that prayer is not meant simply for our own enjoyment but for the effect it has on our lives.[16] The prayer of presence, everyday meditations, or any ongoing experience of contemplative prayer, reshapes our lives. It can change our inner geography. But the most profound relandscaping of the spirit takes place as we are moved to a new spirit of gratitude. "Prayer reaches its highest nature, its finest meaning, as gratitude."[17]

Inside each one of us there is a place I call "the grateful center." To find it, use your imagination, that wonderful "right brain" activity, to picture a place where you are free from all your compulsions of wanting and grasping, your preoccupation with the needs and negatives in your life, a place where you celebrate what you already have. It is a golden place where you are able to see all the gifts that are here, and simply to open your hands to receive them.

Whenever I picture such a place, I always come up with the image of a Georgia watermelon field running over with ripe green fruit. I grew up loving watermelon as much as anything in life. When I was still small enough to ride my daddy's shoulders through the watermelon field on Monk Farm, he taught me a song that went:

> Plant a watermelon upon my grave
> And let the juice run through.
> Plant a watermelon upon my grave,
> That's all I ask of you.
> Now chicken and dumplings taste mighty fine,
> But there ain't nothing better than a watermelon vine.[18]

We stomped through the summer, laughing and singing our song, bursting open the hot pink fruit right in the field and eating it on the spot. It was all gift and miracle. And it was enough.

In the watermelon field I never wanted or needed anything. I quit demanding, whining about whatever problems life had dealt me, and turned to celebrating what was there. Life was just too good to waste on doing anything else! The moments in the watermelon field were always a festival of gratitude. I was in my grateful center.

Meditative praying, more than anything I know, moves us toward our grateful center—to the place within where we see life with a sense of miracle, gift, abundance. We begin to experience it as a banquet in which we grow sensitive to what God has already given instead of always thinking about what we need and want, and cajoling Him into giving more . . . more . . . more.

Thomas Merton spoke of this transformation to the grateful center when he said,

> In prayer we discover what we already have. . . . We already have everything, but we don't know it and don't experience it. Everything has been given to us in Christ. All we need is to experience what we already possess.[19]

When we pray meditatively, in touch with the nurturing presence of God, we eventually come to see God giving Himself in all things. This vision lets us shift from the stance of wanting, demanding, whining, to the place of receiving and celebrating.

Jesus, who made time to meditate and commune with God, was the ultimate thankful person. He gave thanks for what was here. In the midst of a vast, hungry crowd, He didn't ask for five thousand dinners, or wring His hands over what was lacking. He picked up five loaves of bread and two fish and simply gave thanks for what He had (Luke 9:10–17). Suddenly the moment broke into plenitude.

On another occasion He told us not to spend all our time fretting and grasping after food, clothes, or all the things we and the rest of the world think we need and must have. God is a good parent, He told us, who gives to us abundantly. We are to seek first His kingdom, His goodness. And His Kingdom is within us (Matthew 5:24-34; Luke 17:21).

As I have prayed the prayer of presence in my green leather chair and meditated in everyday moments, I have found the most remarkable transformation beginning in me. Ever so slowly, I am looking at things differently, delighting in what is there. Prayer awakens me more and more to the ripe, sweet, dripping goodness of God's gifts. Life and God's loving presence—what more is there! It is as if sometimes I am back in the watermelon field with my father singing over God's gifts and celebrating the deliciousness of being part of the kingdom. And when I neglect these prayers of encounter, I grow restless, acquisitive and greedy.

In fact, the more I respond to life from the grateful center, the happier I become. The reason for this was confirmed to me recently at a conference where Dr. Scott Peck, a psychiatrist and author, was speaking. People who are depressed, he told us, think differently. The new way of treating depressed people is to help them stop picking out only the negative things in their lives and begin to perceive the positive aspects. When we are down, blue and miserable, he went on to say, it is mostly because of our refusal to praise and be grateful.[20]

We may be able to offer gratitude now and then, but to live with a deeply underlying orientation of gratitude—to look at life from this basic stance even in painful circumstances or when our agony is very great—requires a great transformation of our inner spirit. As I pondered the psychiatrist's words, I understood that contemplative prayer does this work in us. It helps us think differently. It opens us to transformation. We will be putting into practice the biblical command, "In everything give thanks, for this is the will of God concerning you" (1 Thessalonians 5:18). Indeed, as we taste the love of God in prayer and get in touch with His presence in our own inner life, we may be surprised at the fruits that blossom. With love and commitment, the prayer of presence will pry open our arms to receive and celebrate what is here. Meditation eventually enables us to walk through this world saying, "Oh, yes! For this moment, Lord, thank You. Thank You."

We will give ourselves continually to prayer.
ACTS 6:4

15

Keeping a Running Conversation with God

"WHEN SHE PRAYS, God listens."

I overheard that comment one Sunday morning when I was a child. The two ladies were talking about a third woman, whom I had always admired. She prayed the kind of prayers I knew pleased God, full of beautiful, holy words. And sometimes, when I would peek at her through my lashes, her face seemed full of light.

I wanted very much to be like her and I hoped she would take a special liking to me. So in true childlike fashion I decided I would make my way into her heart and ask what her favorite Bible verse was. But every time I saw her at church I choked on the question.

One Saturday, as if fate had arranged it, I rode past her house on my bike and saw her outside watering her flowers. With my stomach fluttering, I got off my bike and cut across her yard to ask my brave question. Before I could get close enough to blurt it out, she stopped watering and turned toward me, drawing her face into a pointed, angry frown.

"Get off the grass!" she shouted. "Can't you see it has just been planted?"

I stood there frozen while something shattered in me like a crashing teacup. I'm not sure what I expected—probably that her prayers, which seemed to sweep up to God, were just as vibrant in her garden as they were in church.

Maybe she was having a bad day. Maybe she was not feeling well. I have those days, too. Or maybe she confined her praying to certain special times. I would never know. But there was a lesson there nevertheless, a seed of truth that a little girl of nine buried away in her heart. Our praying must not stop when we water the flowers. It must somehow keep going.

I hadn't thought of that woman for years, but one spring day, while watering the newly planted grass in our backyard, I found myself seeing her picture in my mind. And I knew why. I *had* become that woman—watering her garden, but unable to keep her prayers flowing. How, I wondered, could my special times of prayer melt into the rest of the day and soak the ground?

Brother Lawrence said, "I made this [practicing the presence of God] as much my business all the day long as at the appointed times of prayer."[1] Praying on his knees at the altar or scrubbing a pot in the kitchen . . . saying a prayer in church or hosing your garden . . . the prayer goes on.

Brother Lawrence had come upon a great secret in the spiritual life: praying always. I began to desire this secret, a pattern of living in which I was in touch with God all through the day.

Unceasing prayer is planted firmly in the New Testament and the writings of the church. Jesus "told a parable to the effect that they ought *always* to pray" (Luke 18:1 RSV). He seemed convinced that one of the more significant aspects of prayer was staying with it. Prayer for Jesus was like the inner layer of His skin. If you scratched Him any time at all you would find it there, wrapping Him in constant awareness of God. The apostle Paul does not tell us to take time out every day to pray regularly. No, he goes far beyond that. Do not stop praying at all, he says. "Pray without ceasing" (1 Thessalonians 5:17). Origen, one of the early leaders in the church, said that life is "one great continuous prayer."[2]

We do not easily grasp to what extent prayer is meant to have a dynamic, ongoing quality. Yet God desires intimacy with us every minute. "Abide in me, and I in you," Jesus told us (John 15:4). *Abide* means "to stay with" or "live with." We are asked to "stay with" God in prayer. O. Hallesby, a Norwegian theologian, compared prayer to something as vital and continuous as breathing.[3] We don't take one breath and hold it all day long, he reminded us. We continually exercise our lungs so the air can perform its life-giving functions. Prayer is the breath of the soul. We must "breathe" prayer continuously so God can continually give us the life of His Spirit.

Augustine used another image. The soul needs prayer, he wrote, just as a fish needs water.[4] As I girl I did some fishing on Monk Farm and I knew well how long a fish would last once it had been yanked from the pond. Without continuous prayer our sense of God's presence and our openness to Him suffocates.

Most of us, I suspect, carry around the notion that praying always is meant probably only for super-Christians—which eliminates us right away. This idea was a real stumbling block to me. But as it began to dawn on me what "praying always" actually means, I discovered that this call is for me, too—for every Christian. Ordinary people. Contrary people. People who dress children for nursery school, rush to work, stare at televisions, forget dentist appointments. People in busy offices. People in nursing homes. People like us. Praying an unbroken prayer is not something to struggle and perspire over. It springs up inside us and becomes a way of life, as natural as breathing.

What Is Praying Always?

In a religious bookstore in Indiana one day I began to talk with Samuel, a wise, spiritual man who managed the store. As our conversation spread from books to the spiritual life, I asked, "What do you think it means to pray without ceasing? It sounds like such an impossible undertaking. Do you think the command is just a hyperbole, an exaggeration to make a point?"

"When you pray always, you don't pray exclusively. You pray simultaneously," he said, gazing at me with dark smiling eyes. "It is to pray when I catalog these books and eat lunch and make change. It is to keep up prayer beneath the surface, lifting my heart to God during all my daily activities."

As I watched Samuel shelving books, smiling and talking with those who entered the store, I could see prayer in his face. I could see that to pray without ceasing is an attitude of prayer. It is not moving one's lips, muttering prayers around the clock, or stopping everything else to pray formal prayers. It is praying "simultaneously."

It we define prayer strictly as our talking to God, it will be difficult to come up with a way to pray always while we are concentrating on baby formulas or chemical formulas or driving home in rush hour traffic. Thomas Kelly, however, defined prayer as living concurrently in the level of the world and in the level of God's presence. And when Douglas Steere, a friend of Kelly's, was asked whether it was possible to carry out his friend's call to live in the awareness both of the world and of God's presence, he wrote:

> An old Indian saint gives the identical counsel: "Do all your work then, but keep your mind on God. . . . The tortoise swims about in the waters of the lake, but her mind is fixed to where her eggs are laid on the bank. So, do all the work of the world, but keep your mind in God."[5]

If we can think of prayer like that, as an attitude and attentiveness that permeates our lives, then praying always becomes a possibility. Not a simple, overnight possibility. But possible nonetheless. It is a discipline that can be realized.

Stages of Growth

It takes years of growth to keep our mind in God as we go about other activities. It requires a certain maturing of our praying. I believe it involves growing from praying as a child—the stage of "saying" prayer—to praying as an adult—the stage of "being" prayer.

In childhood we "say" our prayers. As a young girl I repeated lots of prayers that I memorized. In adolescence I learned how to speak my own prayers before God. We were taught a little formula in Sunday school: Prayer was praise, thanksgiving, confession, intercession and petition. I have warm memories of going through that list while lying on the blue polka dot bedspread in my room. That is still a fine way to pray, but there are deeper dimensions to prayer than that. I have to move on, not discarding the "saying" of my prayers, but cultivating the other as well.

A friend recounted to me that one of her most persistent memories of her mother was hearing her call out as she climbed the stairs to bed, "Remember to say your prayers." She would kneel by her bed dutifully and say, "Now I lay me down to sleep . . . "

"Do you know I still kneel beside my bed and say that same childhood prayer even though I am all grown up," this woman told me. She seemed to have gotten stuck at a stage of development in her praying and was still relating to God the same way she did as a child. In speaking about the spiritual life, Paul wrote, "When I was a child, I spake as a child, I understood as a child, I thought as a child: but when I became a man, I put away childish things" (1 Corinthians 13:11).

Now of course we must continue to "say" prayers. Verbalizing them helps us understand our needs so that we can not only ask intelligently (Luke 11:9-10), but also tell God everything in our hearts. But we also need to "become" prayer. This involves a changing of our consciousness—the way we think about ourselves and our relationship to God.

In the childhood level we think of God outside of ourselves.

We talk "to" Him. But as we grow up in the spiritual life, we come to think of Him as deep within us, in our thoughts, moods, feelings, aspirations. God flows inside us. He is our center. As we come to perceive God in this more intimate way, we are filled with a growing sensitivity to Him. We cannot separate ourselves from Him. When it is my carpool day it is His carpool day. When I laugh, He laughs. When He hurts, I hurt. "Christ in you," Paul says, is the secret he was commissioned to reveal and preach (Colossians 1:23).

To become prayer is to so unite ourselves with Him in our thinking and our hearts that daily practices are touched and transformed. To walk, sit, snap beans, dust furniture, rake leaves, wipe tears, is prayer. It is God within doing these things along with us.

I remember the shock I first felt when I discovered this line in Frank Laubach's prayer diary: "God, I want to give you every minute of this year. I shall try to keep you in mind every moment of my waking hours."[6] *That's preposterous,* I thought.

But Dr. Laubach had been learning to live with God for years. He had come to think of God as living so closely in him that they shared the same thoughts. Frank Laubach *was* praying in the sense that what he said, did and thought were done consciously in the presence of God. He prayed without ceasing.

Such a transformation comes slowly, but it comes. Especially if we stay in touch with our center—that deep place in us where God and the soul are eternally at play, where "God laughs into [the soul] and [the soul] laughs back to him," as Eckhart said.[7]

One hot July day, with the sun beating down, and my shirt drenched with perspiration, I stooped over my tiny tomato garden and picked a tomato. Prayer was the last thing on my mind. But as I held it in my hands, I was struck by how beautiful and red it was. Suddenly I was overwhelmed with the simple joy of being alive. I wanted to share the moment with God, to lift the tomato up into His face and laugh with delight over it. It even seemed that God, deep within me, was as delighted at this moment as I was. We were suddenly together in the garden. Together at the center.

For nearly an hour I went right on with my work in the garden, pulling weeds, hoeing around plants, picking tomatoes. But inside, in a channel just beneath the surface, a stream of communion flowed silently between God and me. I never actually spoke words to God. I was utterly aware of my business in the garden. But I was somehow praying.

This was the discipline of unceasing prayer, I decided—to be busily engaged in other things and abide consciously in Him. To pray as I lived my life. But also to live my life as I prayed. It meant to enter life fully—but behind the scenes to pray as I lived.

Mindfulness vs Forgetfulness

The sense of attentiveness to God I'd found in the tomato garden soon vanished—the stream dried up. I simply forgot Him. I walked into the house to wash the tomatoes and it was over. "The primary enemy of prayer is forgetfulness."[8] It's not that I have no interest in praying always, or that my commitment lags, or that I love everything else more than God (though each of these is sometimes the case). Mostly I forget to remember Him. I have not trained myself to remember Him.

When Bob was a few weeks old, Sandy and I took him to church for the first time. It was strange to be taking along someone else after years of just the two of us going to church. The next week, Sandy went to church early for a prayer breakfast, and I brought Bob later. After church, with my mind still on the service and conversing with friends, I walked out of the sanctuary through the same door I always used, into the parking lot, got in my car and drove three blocks before I realized I had left Bob in the nursery! Taking the opposite door to the nursery had not yet become routine.

It was the most embarrassing moment of my life—shuffling up to the nursery door to find one dear lady holding Bob, wondering aloud where his mother might be. It was so unmotherly that for a while I could not tell Sandy what I had done—forgotten I had a child! Believe it or not, the same thing happened to me again years later, only I was the nursery worker this time, and a red-faced mother showed up saying she had gotten to the parking lot before remembering. (God is very good about assuring us that we are not the only ones who do dumb things.)

It is the same way with our remembrance of God. If we do not train ourselves to remember Him, we forget Him.

Perhaps we could say that praying always is simply being mindful of God—our minds full of Him, our minds "in" Him. The early church had a term for this. *Memoria Dei* they called it, the memory of God. "We are to remember Jesus Christ" (2 Timothy 2:8). As we grow in Christ we must make recurring efforts of the heart to be aware of Him. There is nothing particularly mystical about it. We simply turn to God with an inward embrace as we shelve books, pluck tomatoes, hoe a garden or turn to use a typewriter. As we deliberately turn to Him, remembering Him along with our other activities, we attain a disposition for unceasing prayer. The channel is cut deeper and deeper. It has the power to transform us so that we become prayer.

In the beginning, unceasing prayer is only possible if we fashion a way to practice it. "Multiply as much as ever you can the turning of your spirit to God."[9] Of course, we don't want our ways of keeping attuned to God to deteriorate into rote, empty forms or compulsive practices. There is always that danger. Everything good and worthwhile has a dark side. Our ways of practicing unceasing prayer are meant to be done in love and freedom—and never as ends unto themselves.

Gradually I have formed some loosely woven ways of unceasing prayer that help me remember God.

Loving Glances

There is a frequently told tale of a peasant woman who stole into the village church each day, sat on the back pew for several moments, then left. She did not kneel, or use the prayer book, or even close her eyes. One day, perplexed by her habit, the pastor asked her what she was doing there each day. She replied, "Oh, I look at Him and He looks at me. And it is enough."

During the day I try as often as I can to cast God a loving gaze. No words are needed, only a gathering up of my loving concentration and turning it toward God. It began one day when Ann burst into the house from playing outside. She was going through a short-lived phase that children sometimes have in which they don't want Mama out of sight for very long.

"Mama!" I heard her shouting as she raced through the house looking for me. She found me standing on a chair in the closet, trying to find a bud vase. "What do you want?" I asked.

"Nothing. I just wanted to see you." Her blue eyes swept over my face with intensity, as if she was drawing out strength and love from the sight of me. Then she was gone, fortified with my presence. That was enough.

Standing on the chair, I had the sudden insight that here was a means of keeping my mind steadied on God . . . brief, repeated "glances" during the day in which my mind and heart were turned Godward, fortifying me with His presence until I could return.

We have an old schoolhouse clock with a swinging pendulum that chimes out the hours. I decided that its bong would become a reminder to cast an inner gaze at God. When the clock strikes, I center myself into a moment of inner stillness, letting my eyes sweep over the nearness and beauty of God's presence within me. Sometimes that one brief gaze is enough to last the rest of the hour.

It takes effort to make such loving glances part of one's life, as it does to establish any worthwhile behavior. The stones which block our doorways, preventing God's loving presence from getting through, will not move by themselves. We must move them, at times with sheer strength and endurance. So in the beginning our efforts may seem to be forced, but eventually they emerge as a dominant and spontaneous attitude.

I have a friend who has conditioned herself to focus on God whenever she climbs steps. She has a flight of stairs in her house and was always running up and down them, despising the trouble. Now she looks forward to being on those stairs, any stairs. Like my schoolhouse clock, it is her way of reminding herself to turn her spirit to Him. Anything can be a reminder, especially if it recurs during the day.

These quick and burning glances hollow out a place for His presence to remain. They nourish our lives in a real way. For while we are glancing toward God, He is gazing back at us. Once in Bermuda, as I walked along Horseshoe Beach, for a moment I turned my gaze on God and felt warmth spread through me. It was as if I could sense Him gazing back at me, warming me with His stare. As His nearness poured through me, I suddenly found new strength to serve Him in a particular way that had recently been proposed to me, but which I had avoided.

Glances Godward are not mere sentimentalism. We express our love and desire to be attentive to Him. And He fills us quietly. We don't have to "feel" anything when we glance at Him. We glance toward Him in faith.

Interior Conversation

There are other ways to open ourselves to unceasing prayer. Perhaps the most demanding and also the most rewarding is the interior conversation with God which we carry on throughout the day. A continuing flow of dialogue with God is difficult in the beginning, but not impossible. In his journal, Frank Laubach once penciled, "The habit of constant conversation grows easier each day. I really do believe all thought can be conversations with Thee."[10] If we begin and keep at it, to our astonishment we will find ourselves one day turning naturally to Him in inner dialogue.

In this ongoing conversation with God, we do not go about thinking of Him and Him alone or spending time talking to Him instead of with others. That strikes me as dangerous for our mental health. No, the secret of constant conversation with God is to dwell so closely with Him in the midst of our ordinary thinking and speaking and doing that they overflow almost spontaneously into conversation with Him.

Henri Nouwen points out that there is not a single waking moment when we are not thinking.[11] Whether we are willing or unwilling, our minds rattle on in an incredible parade of good, bad, important, trivial, wandering and focused thoughts. This came home to me one day as I worked at my desk. After a couple of hours, I got up and walked around the room to "clear my mind." My mind did not clear. Rather, I began thinking of the two little turtles my son had caught in the lake and how I was going to convince him to turn them loose so we would not have to keep swatting flies to feed them. My mind had merely shifted to another flow of thought. More often I notice that my thoughts just go on and on.

What might happen if all that unending flow can somehow be turned into prayer? In his little book *Clowning in Rome,* Nouwen put forth the idea that this is exactly what praying always means: "converting our unceasing thinking into unceasing prayer."[12] We do this by sharing our thoughts with God, presenting them to Him so that they take on the essence of a conversation. We begin to "think" them consciously in His presence, allowing God to "listen in" and be part of it all.

Even the small, insignificant thoughts?

Yes. I happen to believe we should not even keep thoughts of turtles hidden from God. The whole steady parade of minutiae that wanders through our minds should be lifted to Him. The question is not whether God is interested in all that trivia. He is, because He is interested in us. The question is how much do we choose to share? How far will we invite God in? How intimately will we draw Him into the daily stuff of our lives?

More than anything else, our lives are a collection of little thoughts and moments. To live them apart from God is to eclipse Him from a major part.

I remembering hearing a young man pronounce talking with God about little subjects "a waste of God's time." God, however, does not experience time as we do. He dwells beyond time. But more important, He wants us to become so intimate with Him that we share *all* our lives with Him, even the small stuff. No, *especially* the small stuff. Weaving the ordinary thoughts of daily experience into something holy is never a waste when it furthers God's creative purposes within us and draws us deeper into oneness with Him.

The aim is to carry on this conversation amid everything going on about us. Before my mother-in-law retired, she would carry on a conversation with God as she drove to work. She would mention the people to Him that came to mind, along with various problems as diverse as stopped-up water pipes and how to deal with a student in her class. Whatever passed through her mind became conversation with Him. It goes on too, I suspect, throughout her whole day. I once overheard her open a kitchen cabinet and whisper, "Now, Lord, what are we going to fix the grandchildren for breakfast?"

When I first started trying to carry on this kind of conversation with God, I would usually be halfway through the morning before I remembered to begin. But as I persisted, I gradually began waking up with Him on my mind. One morning while light filtered through the bedroom shutters, my eyes fluttered open and His name rose to my lips. I wasn't even fully awake, but for a few moments I was with Him in the silence of my soul, sharing my early morning thoughts with Him.

Dashing through the day, I can easily forget my interior conversation with God and have to call myself gently back to it. One way I have found to do this is to consciously walk about, thanking God for the things around me. For crayon pictures hung on the refrigerator, food on the shelves, plants, music, baseball bats, books, quilts, grapevine wreaths, windows, paper, firewood, dolls. . . . This places my mind back on the track of dialogue and soon I am sharing my thoughts with Him again.

Through our running conversation with Him we will be able to talk with Him about each worry and problem that intrudes upon our day. When I discovered a lump in my breast (which later turned out to be benign) I felt my interior conversation begin inside, in that place beneath words . . . "Another lump . . . O Father, not again . . . You know how frightening this is for me . . . this flood of fear . . . remember the last time we went through this, how scared I became? But You were there—I'm trying to remember that . . . I must call the doctor right away."

The conversation that ran on during the next few days brought me enormous peace through the surgery, the biopsy, the waiting, turning what might have been dark thoughts into an honest dialogue with God instead of a lonely monologue with myself.

The inner conversation can go on, too, while we play. One of the most delightful experiences I had was the day I went swimming with God in the Olympic indoor pool near my house. All alone in my little roped off lane, the water was like a world all its own. There was something about the buoyancy and silkiness of the water that opened me to commune with Him. I found I could move through the water with the rhythm of prayer, talking with God in the silence that lapped around me. "Oh, this cold water, Lord . . . the joy of being alive right now . . . Thank you for sharing Your aliveness with me . . . I am filled up with it . . . movement, play, energy, regeneration . . . I celebrate these moments with You . . . How present You are in the water with me." The random thoughts bubbled up between the silences and were lifted up to Him.

When I first began to learn about inner conversation, I was spending lots of hours sitting on bleachers—baseball, soccer, then basketball—watching my children play. One day in the gymnasium, a father sitting along my row was shouting all sorts of negative things to his son out on the court. "For heaven's sake, can't you get the ball through the hoop?" he yelled every time the boy missed. "Get in the game, son! Quit goofing off!" The little fellow kept glancing over at his dad, trying so hard he was falling over his feet.

I was getting more and more annoyed with the man and my thoughts ran along the line that somebody ought to stuff something in his mouth. Then came the impression "offer these thoughts to Me."

I'd not carried on any interior dialogue that day, but in the middle of the noisy gym I began to talk with God inwardly. 'Why is this parent yelling like this at his child? . . . He makes me angry, humiliating his son . . . Why I'd like to—I'd like to . . . " I glanced over at the man, with the sudden realization that what he needed was not my anger but my prayer. "Okay, Lord. You're right . . . Touch him with Your presence . . . I'm trying to visualize You sitting beside him . . . " My thoughts ran on in this manner through the game.

By the third quarter the father's shouting had stopped. The most astounding thing, however, came after the game, when I heard him apologize to his son for yelling at him. I can't say that the difference was the disjointed, behind-the-scenes conversation that I had carried on. But I do know the thoughts I had during the game changed me, making me aware of God once more.

Work as Prayer

We can also carry on our interior conversation at work. "Then is our life whole when contemplation and work dwell in us side by side and we are perfectly in both of them at once."[13]

There is a saying to the effect that work is prayer and prayer is work. How wonderful when we can blend them, giving our work a sense of holiness!

The best place to begin the blending of prayer and work is to form a clear vision of God with us in our work. Our work is God's work. It isn't the type of work we do that makes it holy, but how we do it. "Whatever you do, do all to the glory of God," wrote Paul (1 Corinthians 10:31 RSV).

"My job contributes nothing to the kingdom of God," a high school graduate told me one day.

"What do you do?" I asked.

"I work on a piece of tractor machinery as it passes on an assembly line," she said. At first I couldn't think of any response that could help her. Then suddenly it popped into my head.

"You aren't just working on a machine. You're helping to make a tractor that will harvest a field that will help feed the world!"

"Yes, I suppose I am," she said. "I am helping feed the world. I believe I can give myself to that."

Every task, no matter how menial, helps further God's creation. "We may . . . imagine that the creation was finished long ago. But that would be quite wrong. It continues still more magnificently and we serve to complete it by the humblest work of our hands."[14]

This is a very high vision—seeing ourselves as co-creators with God, helping by our labor to transform bit by bit God's creation into His kingdom. At a writers' conference a woman told our group that in some way God was at the tip of her pen. That thought stunned me. I began to view what I was doing very differently. I saw a sacredness in it I'd never glimpsed before.

God is at the tip of our scalpels, our screwdrivers, our computer terminals, our dust rags, our pencils and pens. He is with us in our wheelchairs, or on our hospital beds, when all we can do is sit or lie flat. When we envision Him and His purpose in what we do, then we begin to grow aware of His presence in the midst of it. We are able to engage in our inward conversation with Him as we work, naturally, without strain. He becomes our partner, our collaborator.

This secret conversation is fueled by offering our work to God, task by task, moment by moment. We not only do it *with* God, we do it *for* God. At the beginning of each new endeavor, whether it is typing a letter, giving a seminar, or preparing a meal, we might think, "I do this for You." We can refer the least thing to Him. Not only does this sort of dialogue keep us tuned into His presence as we work, it does wonders for the quality of our work and our own peace of mind.

When I first began writing, more than anything I wrote for myself, for my own success and personal enhancement. The first story I ever wrote started as a terrible flop. I had hoped it would draw favorable comments from my writing class. But they said, "There is not much here for a story. It needs lots of work and even then it is doubtful it will ever get published." Being thoroughly stubborn, I refused to give up. One night after rewriting it for the eleventh time, I laid the manuscript on my desk in exhaustion. "God," I prayed, "I give You this story. I will do it for You, not myself."

That was a turning point for me. I discovered that doing my work first and foremost for God was far more satisfying. It lost its compulsive, greedy edge. My writing became more of a source of peace and intimacy with God's presence.

When we raise children for God, teach school for God or sell groceries for God, our work draws us to Him. It is not a boring necessity, but a doorway to His presence. I heard Mother Teresa say once in a television interview, "Everything, in that it is for God, becomes beautiful, whatever it may be." Even if we cannot *do* anything—if we are confined to a wheelchair or a bed—we can offer that immobility to God as something for Him to make beautiful.

I try to keep this in mind when I'm doing housework. I am always thinking of something "more important" I could be doing. But of course the stuff has to be done. So I am learning to offer continually even the most menial parts of it to God. *Father, I offer You the task of cleaning this sink.* The truth is, when I clean my sink for God, it sparkles, and I take pleasure in Him as I work. When I clean the sink for myself, I grumble, cut corners and experience the work as drudgery.

A secret dialogue with God—which is nothing more than the lifting and sharing of our thoughts with Him as we work, play, suffer, laugh, rise up, lie down—can envelop our whole day with a pervading sense of God's love and presence. "There is not in the world a kind of life more sweet and delightful than that of a continual conversation with God," wrote Brother Lawrence.[15]

The Jesus Prayer

The ways of unceasing prayer are about as numerous and unique as the people who practice it. But there is one time-honored way, virtually unknown to lots of Christians, which is becoming, I've discovered, more widespread. I am speaking of the Jesus Prayer.

My introduction to it began on a summer morning on the campus of a seminary. Sandy and I were spending several weeks there while he did some post-graduate study. I had fallen into the habit of taking a walk across the steep green hills on the campus. That morning the sun was beginning to warm the grass, when I came upon an acquaintance of ours sitting cross-legged under a tree, gazing down the hill, apparently deep in thought, a slim paperback book in her lap.

"What are you reading that is so engrossing?" I asked.

She looked up and smiled a greeting. "I'm reading about the Jesus Prayer," she said, "even trying to practice it."

"Oh," I muttered, having no idea what she was talking about. I tilted my head to see the book title and said good-bye. Then I walked down the knoll to the seminary bookstore, where I found a copy of *The Way of a Pilgrim.*

That night, while Sandy studied, I sat in bed, reading. The book was the charming narrative of an anonymous Russian peasant in the nineteenth century, who went to church one Sunday and heard a Bible passage urging him to pray constantly. He was overcome with the thought. Pray constantly? Did he hear correctly? He checked his Bible and saw with his own eyes that it is necessary to pray continuously (1 Thessalonians 5:17), to pray in the Spirit on *every* possible occasion (Ephesians 6:18) and in *every* place to lift hands in prayer (1 Timothy 2:8). A strong and compelling desire took hold of him to discover how to pray always. Since he was a pilgrim, wandering across the steppes of Russia without family and with all his possessions in a small knapsack, he sought someone who could explain this mystery to him.

Finally he met someone along the road who taught him the prayer used by the early church, known as the Jesus Prayer: "Lord Jesus Christ, have mercy on me." He was to pray the prayer as many times as he could during the day, all through his waking moments. The pilgrim acted on the teaching and traveled with the prayer as if it was his friend.

As I read, I found the humble little pilgrim's burning desire for unceasing prayer was rubbing off on me. But how could praying this lovely prayer, taken from Luke's Gospel, lead one to uninterrupted communion with God?

For the pilgrim the transformation came gradually. He learned to correlate the prayer with his breathing, envisioning the prayer entering his heart as he inhaled. The prayer came to life inside of him, like yeast rising slowly and invisibly in the warmth of the dough. It became a self-activating prayer, working itself deeper and deeper into his thoughts until one day he was aware that the prayer had spontaneously moved from his head down into his heart and had begun to pray itself. It prayed in the rhythm of his breathing, in the beating of his heart. "I felt the Prayer, of itself, without any effort on my part, began to function both in my mind and heart; it was active both day and night without the slightest interruption, regardless of what I was doing."[16] He stopped vocalizing the prayer and began to listen to it.

The next morning I sat in the tiny apartment on campus and stared through the window, wondering about the prayer. Was God opening the riches of the prayer to me? How odd that I should come upon the girl cross-legged on the grass and then find this book! Should I try it?

The Jesus Prayer was foreign to me. But so what? Just because something was foreign and beyond my typical way of going about the spiritual life didn't necessarily mean it was wrong. Only that it was new. (What joys in growth I'd missed because of narrow thinking!) "Lord Jesus Christ, have mercy on me," I said a little shyly. Then I said it again. I said it for nearly five minutes, just letting the words happen to me. Below the window I watched the traffic, the squirrels jumping under a tree, students hurrying to class, and I said the prayer blending it with my breathing as the pilgrim had done. "Lord Jesus Christ," on the in-breath . . . "have mercy on me," on the out-breath. I said it slowly, silently finding a rhythm that seemed to slow everything down and focus naturally on Christ.

I have held onto the Jesus Prayer ever since. During those weeks at the seminary I breathed it as much as possible. Of course it was easier there. Bob and Ann were visiting their grandmother, and my typical busy life-style was left back home. There was nothing to do but pray the Jesus Prayer. I walked the hills and prayed it. It was with me so much that if I woke in the night I could reach across the bed and touch it. Oh, the peace of those days!

As the prayer sinks down into one's heart it takes on a life of its own, continuing in the subconscious when one is doing other things, like carrying on a conversation with a friend, washing the car or even sleeping—"I slept, but my heart was awake" (Song of Solomon 5:2 RSV).

"After the words appear to have 'set' in you, then they can

be continued behind and between everything else you do during the day," wrote Tilden Edwards.[17] With practice the Jesus Prayer comes to be rooted in your heart and is activated during the day as a living and conscious awareness of Christ.

The words of the prayer are said to hold the gospel within them. "Lord" is a recognition of who rules our lives. It puts everything in the right order. "Jesus Christ" draws before us His presence and His example. Bernard of Clairvaux wrote:

> When I name Jesus, I set before me a man who is meek and humble of heart, kind, prudent, chaste, merciful, flawlessly upright and holy . . . the all-powerful God whose way of life heals me, whose support is my strength. All these re-echo for me at the hearing of Jesus' name.[18]

"Have mercy on me" reminds us of our need for God's grace, and the revelation of that grace in the life and death of Jesus for us. It opens us to receive that grace in ever-widening circles. It even helps us direct that grace outward to others.

Sometimes the prayer becomes other-directed. It draws up the love in us and directs it toward other people. When passing a stranger on the road one day, I felt the prayer "activate" spontaneously in my heart. "Lord Jesus Christ, have mercy on *him*," I said, breathing the prayer for several blocks.

It can happen, too, with situations. In the midst of talking to a friend who was going through the pain of a rebellious teenage son, the prayer leaped to life. "Lord Jesus Christ, have mercy on this situation." It comes when there are no other words, when you don't know how to pray or what to say.

I have come to think of this prayer as living within me, beating like a heart. It is not in my thoughts all the time. That would be an utter distraction to have it constantly recited in my head. Rather I believe it recites soundlessly in my heart even when I am unaware of it. It returns during the day, sometimes rising up spontaneously. Other times I call it up when I dress or sit at a stop sign, or wait at the hairdresser. Any place at all we can breathe it in and out, always with gentleness.

When we enter unceasing prayer, we experience God becoming more our center. But the moment we think of ourselves as holier than someone else, more prayerful, more "piped into" God, we have defeated everything. As we attempt to turn to God with an unceasing movement, we do so with all our humanness and fallibility. I imagine with time unceasing prayer can slowly spread before us, becoming the water we walk on day and night. But for most of us, for myself, it is still mostly a trickle I wade about in when I can. But how wondrous even that is!

Beloved, let us love one another: for love is of God;
and every one that loveth is born of God,
and knoweth God.

1 JOHN 4:7

16

Meeting God in Others

IN A *Peanuts* cartoon Charlie Brown says, "I love humanity. It's just people I can't stand." I know how he felt. Throughout my life it seems I have been adept at caring about humanity on a broad, global scale, while having trouble loving the annoying person who goes to my church, the disagreeable person who lives down the street, or the frustrating member of my own family.

Once during those busy, stressful years when I was racing around trying to do everything, I came home from a church meeting very angry. The group had needed someone to organize a Sunday school social. "Sue, how about you doing it?" one member had said. "The rest of us work."

"Sometimes I hate people," I announced to Sandy as I came through the door. As I'd grown more overloaded and fragmented, drifting away from God as my center, cynicism had crept into my relationship with people. I saw them ready to take advantage of me, give me another job or generally make life more complicated than it already was. I'd been struggling so hard to be loved myself and just get through each day, it had become harder and harder to invest energy in loving others.

When I first found that Peanuts cartoon, I taped it on the refrigerator door, thinking about the spiritual journey that was now unfolding in my life. I began then to pay attention to how my new life was affecting the way I related to people. Was it drawing me to others? How did people enter into the experience of creating an everyday intimacy with God? I had been waking to God mostly through the realms of silence, solitude, scripture and prayer. Could I also find Him through the people around me?

The Loving Expansion

One of the misconceptions about journeying to a deeper intimacy with God is that we don't need other people. We may want to get wrapped up in the coziness of "me and God." But of course this is a perverted spirituality and doomed from the outset. "One of the worst illusions . . . would be to try to find God by barricading yourself inside your own soul."[1]

I knew that people did not enter nearly enough into my experience of prayer. Yet something had been happening to my fundamental way of thinking and feeling about them. A strange ache had been coming to life in me, some fresh new compassion shaping out of the dust that had settled from the upheaval of awakening. Perhaps I could only hold onto it for short spaces of time, but it was there—a desire to turn loose and follow after love.

I no longer saw people merely as an inconvenience. More often I was looking deeper into their faces, when before I never bothered very much. More frequently I was able to be "all there" with them. I was more haunted by the suffering I saw, more thrilled by their joy. I had a long way to go, but I sensed that my thick crust of apathy and selfishness was breaking up.

As we wake to God's love and presence in our lives, we

actually become more capable of loving others. It's as if our hearts are somehow being enlarged. We might call this transformation the "loving expansion," to borrow a term from Evelyn Underhill.[2] It simply means that as we open ourselves to God's love, journeying deeper into intimacy, we become more able to love ourselves. And when we love ourselves, we are finally able (sometimes for the first time in our lives) to love others—not with a what's-in-it-for-me love, but with the strong authentic, "wear and tear" love Christ showed us.

Gradually the journey brings us to the place where God has beckoned us from the very beginning, to a hidden country that can only be found in the heart, the place where we begin to love as we are loved. In this region we open ourselves outward as well as inward, and experience God through Charlie Brown's ordinary, down-the-street people.

Seeing God in Others

Can God really and truly be discovered through the ordinary people in my life? If someone had asked me that in the past, I might have scratched my head and said, "Well, now that I think of it, I suppose He can." But I didn't think in those terms. And for the most part I didn't relate to people in that way.

One Sunday evening in church we sang a hymn with the line, "Let others see Jesus in you."[3] I'd sung it hundreds of times. But that night I stared at the words as though I'd never seen them before, struck by their enormous possibility. What did they really mean? Be a good Christian? Do nice, loving things so folks will see your Christlikeness? Well, sure, it meant that. But I seemed to be taking it in from a new angle. I found the words shifting in my thoughts, from "Let *others* see Jesus in you" to "Let *you* see Jesus in others."

Did the words also mean we could commune with the Spirit of God dwelling not only within our own selves, but commune with His Spirit dwelling in one another? Dear God . . . !

The song ended and by some tiny miracle, as we placed our

hymnbooks in the racks the minister initiated something we did very rarely. He said, "Everyone turn around and shake your neighbor's hand." Usually this made me groan inside. But that evening because of the song, because of the pure grace of God, I turned around to shake hands invaded by a sense of love, awe and expectation.

In the pew behind me was an old woman whom everyone called Miss Liza. She had on a pink dress with a tissue thin handkerchief pinned to her collar like a rose bud. Miss Liza did not quite have all her teeth anymore and her gray hair was a bit askew that night. But as I touched her hand an astonishing thing happened. I saw Christ. For a split second the image of His face was where her face should have been. And then it was gone. Yet His presence was burning in her watery blue eyes like two candles. I was seeing the core of beauty hidden away at the heart of her—that spark that belongs to God and no one else.

In that deep moment of recognition, my spirit leaped to greet the Spirit of God within her. Our centers met. And I did not want to let go her hand.

Through Miss Liza I experienced God's presence. She had mediated the presence of Christ to me in a real and visible way. For the first time I comprehended that God is present among us in a more compelling way than we have imagined. Not only are we created in His image, but we can be crucibles of his immediate presence.

Jesus indicated that if we do something for another human being we are actually doing it for Him (Matthew 25:35-45). He asked us to respond to others as if we were responding to Him.

But we never seem to take this in. When we encounter another person, no matter how askew their hair or disagreeable their countenance, we should walk as if we were upon holy ground. We should respond as if God dwells there.

I once heard Dr. Paul Brand speak of his years working with the lepers in India. There is a common Indian greeting in which the hands are folded under the chin and one bows respectfully as an ancient Hindu sign which means, "I worship the God I see in you." Dr. Brand suggested we not reject it as a Hindu sign, but embrace it as a Christian sign.

But cultivating the ability to see God in other persons asks much. You have to look very deeply. It means voluntarily giving up superficial judgments about them and looking with love and acceptance at their lives. And that isn't easy. Of all the disciplines this one takes lots of time and growing. But this sort of vision will begin to teach us love. For when I truly respond to others as if they are Christ, then I have to admit them as my brother and sister.

That evening in church my heart seemed full of new light. We are Christ-bearers for one another. Miss Liza had borne Him to me. And I wondered if she had sensed Christ within me as I had sensed Him in her.

In the weeks afterwards almost every time I saw Miss Liza she grasped my hand, smiling at me as if we shared some secret bond that neither of us could figure out, whereas before we had passed with perfunctory greetings. Once in the ladies room, of all places, we found ourselves alone, washing our hands from the same sink. Neither of us spoke, but when we'd dried our hands, she laid her head momentarily against my shoulder and her eyes filled with tears, as did mine. Inexplicable? I imagine so.

Sometimes you may feel foolish looking at people in this way. I was walking through the mall one afternoon with the children when I began to notice the people. So many people. We sat on a bench while Bob and Ann licked ice cream cones and I watched the crowd passing by. Before my eyes these people—fat, thin, old, young, tired, energetic—spoke to me of God. He seemed written in their very faces, in the wounded lines and in the smiles. Here came a middle-aged man with steel braces on his legs, twisting himself along. His face was long and tired, yet God seemed present to me in his slow, difficult gait. For a one swift instant I remembered Christ lumbering through the streets of Jerusalem on badly scourged legs, a cross pressed on his back. A desire to visit the man with kindness welled up in me.

He looked my way and spontaneously I flashed him the "thumbs up" sign. It wasn't much, but it was all I had to offer at the moment. The man stopped, a grin breaking through. Balancing himself, he jabbed his thumb into the air, too.

"As you did it to one of the least of these, you did it to me," Christ said. Suddenly right there in the mall tears of love splashed down my face.

"Why are you crying in the mall?" Bob asked, embarrassed.

We may risk playing the fool when we turn loose to this kind of vision. We may open ourselves to vulnerability. Perhaps it is in some way crazy to smile and cry over a group of strangers in a mall. But what joy to see God in them for a few uninhibited moments!

When we engage in this deeper way of encountering people, we will be compelled to handle their lives with holiness, to understand, to reach out, to give or respond in some way to them. And when we do, we make the God in our own lives more visible to them. They glimpse His Presence in our manner whether they can name it or not.

Loving the Family

Sometimes it seems easier to love those whose lives only sometimes touch our own than to love our own families. We often vent our frustrations on those closest to us, and tend to focus on their faults. How was I doing with my family?

The question materialized one morning as the children were bickering over who would get the Garfield bicycle reflector that was inside the cereal box. "You got the last prize," cried Ann.

"Did not!"

"Did too!"

They both grabbed for the box and in the tug of war, tipped

a cup of coffee across the clean pages of a manuscript I had just finished typing. They froze, waiting for the explosion they knew was coming. But seconds before I boiled over, a thought danced quietly through my head. *They are a lot like you, aren't they? Imperfect, making messes out of things. Yet in the midst of your messes, I have loved you.*

I leaned back in my chair, my anger simmering down, and I looked at my children. Really looked at them. Yes, God was present in their faces, in the way they stared up at me with large, uncertain eyes. I felt a surge of love for them, so much I thought it would topple me over. I only wanted to try and understand, to hug them and show them a better way to solve things. Which is exactly what I did.

As I calmly mopped the mess and began to retype the article, the children kept looking at one another with such puzzlement I stopped typing and started to laugh. I had caught them off guard with my love. No, not my love. But God's love within me. One thing about it, God's love never seems to lose the element of surprise.

In that moment I saw clearly how I had been loving my family in the same way I once believed God loved me—conditionally. If they were good, they got my approval. If they were bad, my wrath. I had been demanding perfection, holding my love out like a carrot on a stick until they crossed some invisible line of behavior or met certain expectations. Yet what my children and husband needed was the thing I needed myself—to be loved right in the midst of their imperfections, to be accepted just as they are.

Ann's favorite fairy tale is *Beauty and the Beast*. The part she likes best is the magical moment when Beauty bends down to kiss the unlovable Beast and transforms him into a prince! Beauty did not wait until he became a prince in order to love him. She loved him in spite of his imperfections. And her love became the very catalyst that created the transformation.

As I thought about Ann's favorite tale, I couldn't help but notice the parallel. For hadn't God bent down to me, and kissed the "beast"? Hadn't His love been the very thing that tugged and pulled me toward transformation? Wasn't He asking me now to offer this same kind of love to my family?

What sort of magical transformations could occur if I stopped demanding perfection of Sandy, Bob and Ann and simply started loving them as they were? Loving them in the nitty-gritty moments of bike reflectors and spilled coffee, arguments and broken promises? What could happen if I loved them as God loved me?

Slowly I've worked at it. I don't always succeed. But something has changed. There was Sandy's comment to me one day after we'd quarreled and exchanged bitter words: "Boy, you sure are more forgiving than you used to be." Before I'd had an elephant's memory about our disagreements. And when I have changed, so has the family. The moments when we come closest are those filled with small miracles. For instance, the next time I put a box of cereal containing a prize on the breakfast table, here is what happened.

"Bob, do you want the whistle in here?"

"Yeah, but you can have it. I'll wait for the next box."

"Gee, thanks."

And there was no spilled coffee.

Listening to God Through Others

I had discovered during my journey that God's is the language of silence. Now I was also learning that His is the language of people. God's presence can come to us through the words of others . . . through the way they move, laugh, touch and see life. And if we are tuned into people, we can sometimes catch His voice speaking to us.

A friend told me about the time she took her little girl to visit relatives several months after the child's grandfather died. They stopped en route and bought her a helium-filled balloon, in which she delighted throughout the trip. When they arrived they found the girl's aunt still anguished with a heavy grief that nothing had been able to break through. As they all stood on the front lawn, the child suddenly let go of her balloon, allowing it to sail toward the heavens.

"Why did you let it go?" asked her aunt.

"I'm sending it to Grandpa," she announced.

They stood there watching the balloon until it disappeared. That was the moment the aunt began to find her way through the pain. God spoke to her through the unselfishness, the faith and the spontaneous movement of the little girl. That was this woman's "healing word."

God sends all of us healing words—words of hope, clarification, comfort, joy, meaning. Whatever word we are in most need of, that is the very word He is sending. And often He speaks that word through others. As we listen for it, we are able to commune with God, through these persons, as well as tune into them more lovingly.

Becoming One with Others

Have you ever tried looking at another person and seeing your own self within him or her? I don't mean projecting onto another person all our miserable traits. I am speaking of recognizing the hidden truth that we are one with all people. We are part of them and they are part of us.

Frederick Buechner spoke of growing to a point where "selfhood, in the sense that you are one self and I am another self, begins to fade. You begin to understand that in some way your deepest self is the self of all men—that you are in them and they are in you."[4]

Finding this sense of oneness is a natural part of the intimate journey with God. "The more we are one with God the more we are united with one another."[5] We begin to feel a new and deeper identification with people. We come to see that we are all truly related, that what happens to them happens to us.

I heard Scott Peck tell of a fascinating experience in which he was working with a group of people in a community-building session. One cigar-smoking man in the group was making a nuisance of himself in nearly every way possible and Dr. Peck was taking a dislike to him. Finally as the hour grew late, the man fell asleep and began to snore, proving himself as disruptive in sleep as when awake. Then as Dr. Peck looked over at him, he saw not the cigar-smoking man, but himself. *He* was sleeping and snoring. "I suddenly realized I felt very tired," said Dr. Peck. "I knew this man was the sleeping part of me and I was the waking part of him." After that the two men went on to become friends.[6]

It's not easy to despise or be apathetic toward someone when we perceive our own self bonded to them. Seeing ourselves in others means putting ourselves in their place and empathizing as deeply as we can. Whenever we do this we will feel new love and understanding for them seep in, as well as an awareness of the God who loves us all. We begin to grasp what Jesus meant when He prayed that we would all be one just as He was in the Father and the Father in Him (John 17).

John Youngblut, the spiritual writer, captured it eloquently when he said, "I am not just my brother's keeper; I am my brother."[7]

One of my favorite sermon stories is about a little girl who went to play with her friend Marcy. She was late returning home and her mother met her at the door. "Why are you late?" she asked.

"Marcy's puppy got lost," the little girl replied.

"Did you stay to help her find it?" the mother asked.

"Oh, no," she said. "I stayed to help her cry."

When we identify with others, discovering the hidden ties that bind us all together, our love begins to touch the painful edge. This is when many of us stick our toe in and run away because of the feel of the water.

I've run away many times. One day while visiting New York City, I walked along Second Avenue during the congested lunch hour and came upon a homeless man lying asleep or perhaps unconscious across the middle of the sidewalk. It was my first encounter with a homeless person, and my initial thought was to see if he was all right, call for help . . . something. The busy crowd walked on by. I hesitated. Then I stepped over his feet and kept walking.

Back home I faced the fact that I'd stepped over a human being, a child of God, as if he were a hot dog wrapper or a newspaper that had blown out of the corner trash can!

I began to think: If I'm serious about this journey leading me to greater depths of love, then I will do something to redeem that dark episode on Second Avenue. I'll learn to love the homeless as individual people, to try and bear their burdens. It took me six months to muster the courage.

Finally on a Friday afternoon, as a cold November wind blew through the streets, Sandy and I drove to a homeless shelter in Atlanta to spend several days. I watched the men as they wandered in from the streets, many clutching paper bags containing everything they owned in the world, some smelling of alcohol, others sick and coughing. Inwardly I recoiled. They eyed me suspiciously, too. "Another do-gooder, who drops off a hot meal, then cuts out," one of them said loud enough for me to overhear.

But when they discovered we were staying . . . sleeping on cots as they did and eating with them, the wall began to crumble.

The second night an old man named Al sat beside me during dinner. He'd spent most of the time brooding alone on his cot. On his right hand I noticed a tattoo, a little red heart with a crack through the center. I gazed at it thinking of the broken hearts and broken lives gathered around me. Suddenly the old man's anguish began to creep into the pit of my stomach. I felt what it must be like to have no home, no job, no family, no hope.

I poured a glass of tea and handed it to him. At the same time he offered me a basket of biscuits. I smiled at him, realizing how unlikely it was—the two of us here, sharing the same bread and cup. We were sitting at God's table, no longer strangers, but brother and sister.

During the rest of my stay Al opened his life to me, sharing the weight of his disappointments and broken dreams. We cried a lot together. But in that sharing I met the presence of Christ. On the day I left, I clasped Al's hand in both of mine, thinking of the fractured little heart imprinted there. I had not been able to mend Al's pain. But for a time I had at least been able to cup my hands about it with love.

So often there is nothing we can give someone but our presence and the willingness to share whatever heartache he or she is experiencing. Our first inclination is to think in terms of *curing* what causes the suffering, and curing is immensely important. (It's why I work when I can with Habitat for Humanity, a group building homes for those without adequate housing.) But God showed me there is something else we can do just as loving. We can step into the pain of another, simply helping him bear it. We are to carry "one another's burdens, and so fulfill the law of Christ" (Galatians 6:2).

Sometimes the act of sharing a burden creates a response from the person at which we can only marvel. Once I visited with a woman whose child had been diagnosed with a terminal disease. As she spoke tearfully of it, I thought of my oneness with her. Her pain began to fill me up. That's when I wanted to flee, to back away and say, "Gee, it's a terrible thing. But you have your pain and I have mine." But I made myself stay with it. I could actually feel the ache embracing me. I moved near her so I could hold her hand. It was probably more an act of need than giving. I think I wanted to be comforted as much as she did. I began to get an image of Christ holding each of our hands, completing the little circle. Slowly the pain diminished as His presence grew up around us.

As I left, she commented how much lighter and relieved she felt inside. She seemed puzzled by it. But I know it had something to do with the old adage that when pain is shared (really shared), it is halved.

Sometimes Christian love is quiet and tender like petting a lamb, but it is also a blood-stained, anguished, awesome affair.

That is what it was for Christ. He identified so profoundly with us, He saw Himself in each of us and carried our suffering as His own.

Perhaps it isn't possible to bear the burdens of every person we meet. But when we *are* able to love others in this way we will find a unique and powerful experience of the presence of God.

The Experience of Community

When we find ourselves loved, we begin to lose our sense of alienation. God's love, and the self-love that it breeds within us, restores to us a sense of real belonging in the world. We stop seeing the world as a place of strangers. We begin to find community—one of the most joyous ways of experiencing God. By community I mean a coming together that puts us in touch with ourselves, with others and with God's presence.

One way we can nourish community in our lives is by gathering together with a small group in order to share our spiritual journeys. The promise of God's presence in community is in these words of Jesus, "Where two or three are gathered together in my name, there am I in the midst of them." Commenting on this verse, Bruce Larson wrote:

> I don't happen to think this means that the Risen Christ has promised to be quantitatively more present with two or three people than with one—or that He is present in a special way. But I am convinced He means that if I choose to live out my Christian life alone, there are great limitations to what God can say or do or be in my life. . . . But if I have chosen to be accountable to a few people, to meet with them and to talk about life as I see God unfolding it to me, then God has a chance to hold up a mirror and show me who I am.[8]

The need for a small community soon emerged in my life. I

began to know how much I needed other people to find my way. I recall one day raking leaves in the backyard and praying about it. "God, please send me two or three with whom I can share and experience you more deeply," I asked.

There is a saying that when you are ready for a spiritual community, the spiritual community appears. There are always those around who are experiencing a new journey of the spirit and are ready to share it. And one day unexpectedly my community "appeared."

I was invited to join three other persons who were meeting weekly for an hour to share, pray and nurture one another's spiritual journeys. We usually began our sessions by reading Scripture and trying to relate it to our lives. Next we shared our journeys, being honest about our struggles and our growth. I found it difficult at first to admit my weaknesses and failings before others. But the more I opened up to God's love, and the love of those around me, the more trusting I became.

Finally we prayed together, sometimes conversationally, sometimes in shared silence. One day after many months of meeting together, I looked at this little community and felt an overpowering sense of love for them. Through them God taught me about listening, caring and forgiving. We met for more than three years, and then, when the time seemed right, we stopped meeting, finding new ways of community and moving on with our own journeys on new paths.

But we don't have to create a group. Some of the most vivid experiences of community spring to life in ordinary, unplanned encounters with others. On my first visit to New York's Metropolitan Museum of Art I wandered the endless wings oblivious to the people moving about me. In fact after three hours everything was starting to look alike, pictures and people. Then I turned a corner and found myself before Manet's "The Dead Christ with Angels."

One elderly man stood before it lost in thought. I joined him, studying the angel that lifted the head and shoulders of the lifeless Christ. But it was Christ's eyes that struck me. Open and staring, they had a life in them that the rest of his body did not. I had the feeling the artist had captured the first split second of the Resurrection . . . as if in the dark tomb Christ's eyes had just flickered open and focused.

"Do you see His eyes?" the stranger beside me said.

"Yes," I answered. "His gaze is so real . . . like He's actually here."

There in the middle of the museum we looked at one another, both of us seeming to sense the presence of Christ that suddenly filled the space around us. "Where two or three are gathered, He *is* present," the man replied. And with a nod, he disappeared into the moving crowds.

That moment of spontaneous community that I stumbled upon has lived with me ever since. These casual encounters that mysteriously bloom into community can occur anywhere. Before a painting, a tree in the park, on an elevator or a bus seat. Wherever there is a moment of heart speaking to heart, of gazing together toward Christ, He is there.

One of the more profound experiences of spontaneous community came when I visited the intensive care waiting room of Egleston Hospital in Atlanta. My little newborn niece was inside, struggling for her life. As I wandered about, a stranger invited me to sit down beside her and asked about Laura. I was surprised she knew about my niece. "Oh, we keep up with one another here," she explained. "I've been praying for Laura."

Then another stranger, a father whose son was in a coma, joined us, asking about Laura, saying he was praying for her, too. The woman patted his shoulder. "You look tired," she said, handing him a pillow. "Why don't you take a rest. I'll watch for the doctor for you."

The people there brought one another food, listened to each other's fears and passed on words of hope. As I sat among them, I felt strangely drawn into the strength of an unusual community where people nourished one another. Later when Laura died, the memory of that "community" and the Presence that dwelled within it helped heal the tears.

Sometimes a mere touch can be the spark that ignites community and a sense of God. My grandmother said that when my grandfather died lots of people came by and tried to console her. But what she remembers is the minister who reached over and held her hand without saying a word. "That was the most comforting thing that happened to me," she said. "I knew then God was there."

To experience God in spontaneous community merely requires that we become willing to allow people, even strangers, to gain access into our lives as we go through our days. As we shed our sense of alienation and the fear of honest encounter, we can begin to know small moments of intimacy that are touched with Presence and love.

Intercession

We can deepen our love for others by praying for them. Evelyn Underhill referred to intercession as loving cooperation with God.[9] In it we offer God another channel to bring about His creative activity in the world. But we are also offering Him another way of coming to us. Every prayer is important, primarily to the one for whom we pray, but it's important for us, too. For in intercession we yield ourselves to God, sharing in His compassion and opening ourselves to His presence.

As I indicated earlier, I have been challenged by Frank Laubach, who in trying to practice God's presence, made nearly every occasion an expression of prayer. Most of the time these prayers were for others.

He would say "flash" prayers for strangers he passed. He prayed as he read the newspaper, mentioning names and situations to God. He made an effort to pray for each person he spoke with, for the sender of each letter he opened. In his prayer diary he recorded God saying to him, "Make your whole day a prayer for others."[10] Because of his continuing prayers for them, his days became an unselfish communion with God.

As I have tried to sprinkle my days with prayers for others, I found special meaning in the Quaker practice of "holding the other in the light." To practice it one simply visualizes a person or group penetrated and surrounded with the light of God. I often visualize my children's classrooms bathed in the light of Christ. In this way I feel I am praying for each of them, their teachers and the other children in their rooms.

After a stormy day during which lightning struck the house, destroying the dishwasher, the stove and the television, Sandy took the family out to dinner. I was preoccupied with the frustrations of the day, impatient with the children and generally out of sorts. Then I noticed a table of people beside us. All at once I began to hold them in the light of Christ. Each time I glanced over I envisioned it encircling them. I asked God to let it sink down into their lives.

I don't know what effect it had on them, but it made my evening radiant with God. I became a better dinner companion to Sandy and the children as well, for there is something about praying for others that makes it impossible to be insensitive to those around us.

Another way of intercession is taking others into our center and allowing them to meet God there. Intercessory prayer is not so much calling out names while we pray, as it is taking these persons into ourselves, our center, where we encounter God. There we are able to bring them into the presence of God with us.

It is like having a room in the very core of your heart where all the people you pray for gather with you before God. This simple way of praying for others seems to bring me closer to the cutting edge of intercession. I do not mean that prayers prayed in this way are more readily answered, only that this way seems to draw me into a fuller love.

Taking other persons into this "compassionate space" simply means I turn to God, saying, "Lord, as I enter Your presence I am bringing these persons with me." Then by an act of will and creative imagination I open my center to them.

They descend from my mind into my heart. I do not even need to list their needs. I am in the place where God's Spirit prays within me for them. I simply offer a place where God can embrace them with His presence, opening my own reservoir of spiritual energy to God to use in their behalf.

We might think that bringing so many people into our center would make it very crowded. But our compassionate space is ever expandable. There is no limit to the persons who can dwell with us there. God's love has no boundaries. He is able to take them all into Himself within us. We do not keep their burdens, pains and needs inside us. We release them into the presence of God. Only the memory and joy of the encounter remains.

Rabbi Mendel used to say that while he silently prayed the Eighteen Benedictions, all the people who had ever asked him to pray to God in their behalf would pass through his mind. Someone asked him how that was possible since there was surely not enough time. The rabbi replied, "The need of every single one leaves a trace in my heart. In the hour of prayer I open my heart and say: 'Lord of the world, read what is written there.' "[11]

The joyful experience of being loved by God makes it impossible for us to separate loving God from loving others. No matter how we express our love for one another, we may be sure that God will multiply His presence to us. For we are nearest God when we love.

Epilogue

ANOTHER SPRING HAS come. I am sitting in the blue wing chair in my den, at the other end of the room from my desk, watching the crabapple tree in the backyard turn pink. It seems only days ago that the little tree was brown and bare. Now soon it will be a canopy of green leaves and red fruit. The metamorphosis of the tree reminds me of how spiritually bare I was not so long ago. In these past four years I have been changing, growing. And tomorrow? Where will this journey take me?

To understand where we are going, we must know where we've been and where we stand at the moment. So, where have I been on this journey? These years have been years of waking to God's love and a life of intimacy with Him. Through the stress and turmoil in my life, somehow I heard God's knock and managed to confront myself, discovering how fragmented and empty I was within, how needful of wholeness.

How difficult it was to learn to listen, to be alone, to leave old lands for new, to wait. I smile as I remember my encounter with God in the little Oratory chapel, and then the discovery that in the end there is no realm where God is not.

I have been learning how to be present to God, to see Him everywhere. I am constantly being surprised by His love in the most unlikely places. There has been also the toil of incorporating disciplines into my life, learning to be patient, to pray, to love. It has been glorious and painful both.

And now? I could not have imagined four years ago where it would lead, or how my life and the way I relate to God and nearly everything around me would change. Today I am a long way from the busy, stress-filled woman, striving and doing in order to be loved, hungry for a God she hardly knew. Sandy and even the children sense how different life is for me now. Merely sitting here content to watch a crabapple tree bloom pink is a long way from my old self.

There are no more tranquilizers in the medicine cabinet. No more rushing from one task to another. I am stepping more slowly through the world these days, doing one thing at a time, learning to savor the sacredness in common things. God is teaching me the joys of finding His love in everyday moments.

Even the perfectionist attitude, the driven need to earn badges of love and approval, has diminished. I no longer feel obligated to do everything everyone asks me to do. I am discovering how to order my life, to choose those things that are meaningful and to find a rhythm to them that seems to flow from a much deeper source. When calls come for me to be involved, I do not hesitate to say, "I'm sorry, but no thank you." That is a long way from the woman who had once stayed up past 1:00 A.M. painting life-sized witches for the school carnival. I am learning to create my life along with God instead of just reacting to whatever happens to me.

Of course, life still gets hectic. There are harried moments, stresses, demands, too much to do and too little time. Yet I marvel at the measure of wholeness I have found . . . the deep, still center from which my life flows when I take the time to nurture it and make space for God's love. Yes, slowly, quietly, my torn-to-pieces-ness has been healed.

I can remember the very day I realized it was true. I had walked outside and nearly run into a dragonfly. For a moment it flitted about my head, back and forth with an odd movement, as though it were stitching the air around me all together. I laughed at him, with a sudden feeling of being stitched together on the inside too. And my heart filled with gratitude as the awareness came. God had knitted me together with loving hands into someone stronger, someone new.

And the future? Where will the journey take me? I suppose one never knows for sure where God's journeys will lead. That's part of the joy of it. As John Claypool once remarked, God's "other name is always Surprise."[1] But because of where I have been on this journey, one thing I know. No matter what happens, all will be well. That is the destination toward which we travel, and it is borne out by where we have been. This journey of being loved takes us to a deep inner sense of "all-rightness" in ourselves, in God, in the world.

"All shall be well and all shall be well and all manner of things shall be well," wrote Julian of Norwich. Madeleine L'Engle points out that it is important to add the words, "No matter what."[2]

Owning such a truth does not come easily. Not long ago I was hospitalized with a "mass" in my abdomen. "Probably an ovarian tumor," the surgeon said. "Of course, we don't know whether it's benign or malignant, so we need to operate right away. I've scheduled your surgery in the morning." Beside the hospital bed Sandy reached for my right hand. I held out my left one, too, and he squeezed them both.

I never realized how lonely a hospital room can be late at night when all the visitors have gone and the nurses dim the lights. Darkness pressed against the window with a tightness I could almost feel against my skin. I sucked the air deeply like a child with a straw who tries to get the very last drop of goodness from the bottom of a glass. I thought about the surgery, about what they might find and what it would mean. What about my future? Would I even have one? I was alone with the most awful reality, and I knew that fear—the kind that roars up out of your belly like a lion and tears you into tiny pieces—was very near.

Then I thought about my journey with God during the past years . . . the spiritual wanderings that had taken me into the surprising joys of His love. It had brought me wholeness and new life. But would it make any real difference in how I was able to deal with *this* moment? Would this journey sustain me now when darkness closed in all around?

"God," I whispered into the silence. The name pushed up from deep inside of me. And with it came the Presence of love I'd come to know. "What happens to you happens to Me," God seemed to say to me. "We are in this *together*. Hold onto My love. It will see you through anything." The fear I'd sensed clawing nearby was swallowed up in His love. I felt myself immersed in it, borne up by an unfathomable peace. Sweet suffering peace.

Whatever happens, I will be all right, even if the worst possible thing comes to pass. The awareness startled me so I reached for my Bible and found Paul's passionate claim in Romans. "Who shall separate us from the love of Christ? Shall tribulation, or distress, or persecution, or famine, or nakedness, or peril, or sword? . . . I am sure that neither death, nor life, nor angels, nor principalities, nor things present, nor things to come, nor powers, nor height, nor depth, nor anything else in all creation, will be able to separate us from the love of God in Christ Jesus our Lord" (Romans 8:35, 38 RSV).

The beauty of those words took my breath away. I would be all right because I was loved by God no matter what. That was my peace and my strength.

The pain and reality of the event did not miraculously vanish. I still would spend this night with the ache of uncertainty. At dawn I would still slide onto a stretcher and rattle down the corridor to the operating room. I would still walk through every hard place in the road ahead. God's presence does not lift us out of our difficulties. Rather He holds us up with the searing knowledge that we are loved in the midst of them. We become more than conquerors in our situations because we know intimately and truly, in the midnight of our lives, that we are loved beyond reason. Loved through and through.

Awaking from surgery, I heard words dropping softly around me. "Very sick . . . peritonitis . . . watch her closely." I saw a strange array of hissing, blipping machines about my bed. Sandy moved in and out of focus above me. Then his face bent near. "It was not a tumor," he said, sounding as if he were a great distance away. "You had a ruptured appendix. Now rest. You have a very high fever."

My eyes fluttered closed as I sank back into a hot and wavy blackness. "Nothing can separate us . . ." The words repeated in my head again and again, filling me with peace. God dwelled in the thick darkness with me. The underpinnings of my journey anchored me through the storm.

What I learned was this. The journey into God's love helps us move into the future with a new assurance—all will be well, no matter what.

This does not mean that everything will go our way and we will be immune from reality. It means that where it counts—on the inside where we are fed and loved by God—all will be well. There we find an "all-right-ness" that transcends our wants and wishes.

Through our "being with" God, we will come to know a love that sustains in suffering, evil and fear. A love that holds us together inside despite what swirls around us. One that imbues our lives with the most difficult peace of all—peace in suffering. The more we find ourselves loved, the more we are set free. Free to face what is before us, free to find joy, hope and meaning in spite of it.

This is a miracle of grace and grit. Coming to say with joyous conviction, "Nothing can harm me. Nothing at all. I am loved by God!"

Such are the joyful surprises of God's love. Today, in the blue wing chair with the pink tree beyond the window, I know I have barely cracked the door upon them. Each new day the journey begins anew.

Notes

Chapter 1. *A Sound at the Door*

1. Robert Johnson, *She* (King of Prussia, PA: Religious Publishing Co., 1976), p. 73.

2. C. S. Lewis, *The Four Loves* (New York: Harcourt Brace Jovanovich, 1960), p. 181.

3. Darold Treffert, "Five Dangerous Ideas Our Children Have About Life," *Family Weekly* (Sept. 19, 1976), pp. 26–27.

4. John Claypool, "The Preacher as Timely Nurturer," *Catalyst* 11, no. 12 (September 5, 1979). A recording and transcription of his Beecher Lectures. They have been edited and published as *The Preaching Event* (Waco, Texas: Word Books, 1979).

5. Charlotte Elliott, "Just As I Am."

Chapter 2. *Who's That Knocking?*

1. Basil Pennington, *Called* (Minneapolis: The Seabury Press, 1983), p. 3.

2. Attributed to Mahatma Gandhi on a book jacket, which I have not been able to find again.

3. Helmut Thielicke, quoted by Calvin Miller, "Keeping an Ear to the Ground of Being," *The Student*, May 1977, p. 11.

Chapter 3. *Am I Lovable?*

1. William C. Miller, *Dealing with Stress: A Challenge for Educators* (Bloomington, IN: Phi Delta Kappa Educational Foundation, 1979), p. 8.
2. Richard Foster, *The Freedom of Simplicity* (San Francisco: Harper & Row, 1981), pp. 80, 81.
3. Dietrich Bonhoeffer, *Letters and Papers from Prison*, ed. Eberhard Bethge (New York: Macmillan, 1953), p. 55.

Chapter 4. *What's at the Center?*

1. Thomas Merton, *The Seven Storey Mountain* (New York: Harcourt Brace Jovanovich, 1948), p. 372.
2. Brother Lawrence, *The Practice of the Presence of God*. There are many editions of this work, but the one I have used was published by Fleming H. Revell (Old Tappan, NJ) in 1958.
3. Thomas Kelly, *A Testament of Devotion* (New York: Harper Bros., 1941), p. 29.
4. Louis Dupre, *The Deeper Self* (New York: Crossroad, 1981), p. 24.

Chapter 5. *Deciding to Open the Door*

1. Henri Nouwen, *The Genessee Diary* (Garden City, NY: Doubleday Image Books, 1981), p. 175.
2. John Claypool, *Opening Blind Eyes* (Nashville: Abingdon, 1983), p. 61, attributes this point to Elizabeth O'Connor. It occurs in her *Our Many Selves* (New York: Harper & Row, 1971), p. 23.
3. John of the Cross. I have been unable to find the source for this thought.
4. Lawrence, *The Practice of the Presence of God*, p. 13.

Chapter 6. *"I Will Speak Tenderly to Her"*

1. Evelyn Underhill, *The Fruits of the Spirit*, in *Treasures from*

the Spiritual Classics, comp. Roger L. Roberts (Wilton, Conn.: Morehouse Barlow Co., 1981), p. 28.

2. Richard Foster, *Celebration of Discipline* (San Francisco: Harper & Row, 1978), p. 95.

3. Carlo Corretto, *Letters from the Desert,* trans. Rose Mary Hancock (Maryknoll, NY: Orbis Books, 1972), p. xvii.

4. Anne Morrow Lindbergh, *Gifts from the Sea* (New York: Vintage Books, 1965), p. 42.

5. Lawrence, *The Practice of the Presence of God,* p. 44.

Chapter 7. Love Songs from God

1. Henri Nouwen, *Clowning in Rome* (Garden City, NY: Doubleday, 1979), p. 28.

2. Malcolm Muggeridge, *Something Beautiful for God* (New York: Harper & Row, 1971), p. 66.

3. Quoted in Constance FitzGerald, "Contemplative Life as Charismatic Presence," *Spiritual Life* 29, no. 1 (Spring 1983): 26.

4. Robert Frost. I have been unable to find this reference.

5. Dag Hammerskjold, *Markings,* trans. Leif Sjoberg and W. H. Auden (New York: Ballentine Books, 1964), p. 3.

6. Samuel Shoemaker, quoted in Tim Hansel, *You Gotta Keep Dancing* (Elgin, IL: David C. Cook, 1985), p. 51.

Chapter 8. I Am a Word of Love from God

1. Underhill, *The Fruits of the Spirit,* p. 6.

2. Sean Caulfield, *The Experience of Praying* (New York: Paulist Press, 1980), p. 36.

3. Beatrice Bruteau, "Activating Human Energy for the Grand Option," *Cistercian Studies* 19, no. 2 (1984): 155.

4. Thomas Merton, *New Seeds of Contemplation* (New York: New Directions, 1961), p. 37.

5. Maggie Ross, *The Fire of Your Life* (New York: Paulist Press, 1983), p. 139.

6. Caulfield, *The Experience of Praying,* p. 38.

7. Thomas Merton, *Conjectures of a Guilty Bystander* (Garden City, New York: Doubleday Image Books, 1965), p. 156.

8. Underhill, *The Fruits of the Spirit,* p. 49.

Chapter 9.   *God Lives on Oak Street*

1. Madeleine L'Engle, *Walking on Water* (Wheaton, IL: Harold Shaw, 1980), p. 50.

2. Paul Tournier, *The Adventure of Living*, trans. Edwin Hudson (New York: Harper & Row, 1965), p. 204.

3. Nicholas of Cusa, *Of Learned Ignorance*, quoted in Roger Corless, *I Am Food* (New York: Crossroad, 1984), p. 94.

4. Glenn E. Hinson, *A Serious Call to a Contemplative Life-Style* (Philadelphia: Westminster Press, 1974), p. 42.

5. Evelyn Underhill, I am unable to find the source for this observation.

Chapter 10.   *Putting Out the Welcome Mat*

1. William of Thierry, *On Contemplating God, Prayer, Meditations*, trans. Sister Penelope, CSMV, Vol. 1, The Works of William Thierry (Shannon: Irish University Press, 1971), p. 103.

2. William Blake, "Jerusalem: The Emanation of the Giant Albion," in *The Poetry and Prose of William Blake*, ed. David V. Erdman (Garden City, NY: Doubleday & Co., 1965), p. 229.

3. Martin Buber, *The Way of Man According to the Teachings of Hasidism* (London: Routledge & Kegan Paul, 1950), pp. 45, 46.

4. *Maranatha* (1 Corinthians 16:22, KJV), or *marana tha* is an Aramaic phrase meaning "Come, Lord," or "The Lord comes." See RSV footnote to that verse.

5. Thomas Merton, *What Is Contemplation?* (Springfield, IL: Templegate Publishers, 1950), p. 41.

6. L'Engle, *Walking on Water*, p. 189.

Chapter 11.   *Surprised by God Everywhere*

1. Karl Rahner, *Everyday Faith* (New York: Herder & Herder, 1968), p. 203.

2. Emilie Griffin, *Clinging* (San Francisco: Harper & Row, 1984), p. 64.

3. Tilden Edwards, *Living Simply Through the Day* (New York: Paulist Press, 1977), p. 137. See also Dorothy Soelle, "Faith, Theology and Liberation," *Christianity and Crisis* 36, #10 (June 7, 1976): 140.

4. Ernest Campbell, a sermon delivered December 2, 1973, printed by Riverside Church, New York, NY.

5. Gabriel Marcel quoted in Matthew Fox, *On Becoming a Musical Mystical Bear* (New York: Paulist Press, 1972), p. 29.

6. Pierre Teilhard de Chardin, *The Divine Milieu,* (New York: Harper & Row, 1960), p. 131.

7. Thomas Merton, quoted by Henri Nouwen, *Clowning in Rome,* p. 89.

8. Simone Weil, *Waiting on God,* in *The Fire and the Cloud,* ed. David A. Fleming (New York: Paulist Press, 1978), p. 318.

9. Teilhard de Chardin, *The Divine Milieu,* p. 136.

10. I grew up hearing this little rhyme from my father. It appears in books of quotations in slightly different forms. In Burton Stevenson, *The Home Book of Quotations,* 10th ed. (New York: Dodd, Mead, 1967), it is attributed to Frederick Langbridge as follows:

> Two men look out through the same bars:
> One sees mud, and one the stars.

11. Henry David Thoreau, *Selected Journals of Henry David Thoreau,* ed. Carl Bode (New York: New American Library, 1967), p. 114.

12. George Fox, quoted in Douglas Steere, *Together in Solitude* (New York: Crossroad, 1982), p. 28.

Chapter 12. *Making a Home for God*

1. Teresa of Avila, *The Collected Works of St. Teresa of Avila,* trans. Kieran Kavanaugh and Otillio Rodriguez (Washington: ICS Publications, 1980), 2:283.

2. "Henri Nouwen," *The Wittenburg Door* (December 1985/January 1986, no. 88), p. 13.

3. Lawrence, *The Practice of the Presence of God,* p. 46.

4. Annie Dillard, *Pilgrim at Tinker Creek* (New York: Bantam Books, 1974), p. 35.

5. Leslie Weatherhead, *The Significance of Silence* (New York: Abingdon-Cokesbury, 1945), pp. 154–55.

6. Henri Nouwen, *Gracias* (San Francisco: Harper & Row, 1983), pp. 17–18.

7. Karl Menninger, *Whatever Became of Sin?* (New York: Hawthorne Books, 1973).

8. Lawrence LeShan, *How to Meditate* (New York: Bantam Books, 1974), p. 33.

Chapter 13. *Living with God in the Scriptures*

1. Quoted in Marie-Francois Herbaux, "Formation in Lectio Divina," *Cistercian Studies* 17, no. 2 (1982): 136.

2. Dietrich Bonhoeffer, *The Way to Freedom*, trans. Edward H. Robertson and John Bowden (New York: Harper & Row, 1966), p. 59.

3. A. W. Tozer, *The Pursuit of God* (Harrisburg, PA: Christian Publications, Inc., 1948), p. 82.

4. Arthur Green and Barry Holtz, eds. and trans., *Your Word Is Fire* (New York: Paulist Press, 1977), p. 46.

5. Abraham Heschel, *God in Search of Man* (1955; reprint, New York: Farrar, Strauss & Giroux, 1983), p. 252.

6. Morton Kelsey, *Transcend* (New York: Crossroad, 1981), pp. 82, 83.

7. Carlyle Marney, *He Became Like Us* (Nashville: Abingdon Press, 1964), pp. 46–47.

Chapter 14. *Focusing on God Through Prayer*

1. Dietrich Bonhoeffer, quoted in Richard Foster, "Meditation Is Nothing New," *His,* October 1983, p. 28.

2. Edward Thornton, "Lord, Teach Us to Pray," *Review and Expositor* 76, no. 2 (Spring 1979): 225.

3. Gabriele Lusser Rico, *Writing the Natural Way* (Los Angeles: J. P. Tarcher, Inc., 1983), p. 65.

4. Harry Emerson Fosdick, *The Meaning of Prayer* (1915; reprint, Nashville: Abingdon Press, 1983), p. 32.

5. Peter of Celles, quoted in Thomas Merton, *Contemplative Prayer* (Garden City, NY: Doubleday Image Books, 1969), p. 59.

6. John Killinger, *Bread for the Wilderness, Wine for the Journey* (Waco, TX: Word Books, 1976), p. 65.

7. Thomas Keating, in an undated interview.

8. Joseph Goldstein, *The Experience of Insight* (Santa Cruz, CA:

Unity Press, 1976) p. 2, quoted in J. Willis Robert, "Meditation to Fit the Person: Psychology and the Meditative Way," *Journal of Religion and Health* 18, no. 2 (1979): 23–24.

9. Thomas Merton, quoted in Basil Pennington, *Centering Prayer* (Garden City, NY: Image Books, 1982), p. 56.

10. Karen Burton Mains, *Karen, Karen!* (Wheaton, IL: Tyndale, 1979), p. 190.

11. Fosdick, *The Meaning of Prayer,* p. 129.

12. Teresa of Avila, quoted by Dr. Bill Harris in a sermon delivered March 2, 1983, at Anderson College, Anderson, SC.

13. Quoted in LeShan, *How to Meditate,* p. 15.

14. Pennington, *Centering Prayer,* pp. 70–73, 76.

15. Charles Cunningham, *The Mystery of the Ordinary* (San Francisco: Harper & Row, 1982), p. 110.

16. Teresa of Avila, *The Collected Works,* 2:448.

17. Killinger, *Bread for the Wilderness . . .,* p. 32.

18. A popular song of 1910, with words by Frank Dumont and music by R. P. Lilly, published by Witmark, has the last two lines of its chrous the same as the first two lines of this ditty, but the rest of the words are different.

19. Quoted in Pennington, *Centering Prayer,* p. 56.

20. Scott Peck, "The Use of Religion in Psychotherapy," an address delivered at the 18th annual Pastoral Care Institute Conference on Religion and Psychology, September 17, 1984, Columbia, SC.

Chapter 15. *Keeping a Running Conversation with God*

1. Lawrence, *The Practice of the Presence of God,* p. 33.

2. Origen, quoted in Matthew Fox, *On Becoming a Musical, Mystical Bear,* p. 17.

3. O. Hallesby, *Prayer,* trans. C. J. Carlsen (Minneapolis: Augsburg, 1931), p. 146.

4. Quoted in Clarence Enzler, *In the Presence of God* (Denville, NJ: Dimension Books, 1973), p. 105.

5. Douglas Steere, "Introduction," in Thomas Kelly, *A Testament of Devotion* (Nashville: The Upper Room, 1955), quoted in *Alive Now!* September/October 1980, p. 30.

6. Frank Laubach, *Laubach's Prayer Diary* (Westwood, NJ: Fleming H. Revell, 1964), p. 5.

7. Meister Eckhart, *Meister Eckhart*, trans. C. de B. Evans (London: John M. Watkins, 1956), 1:59.

8. Paul Jones, *Province Beyond the River* (New York: Paulist Press, 1981), p. 20.

9. Francis de Sales, quoted in Enzler, *In the Presence of God*, p. 23.

10. Frank Laubach, *Learning the Vocabulary of God* (Nashville: The Upper Room, 1956), p. 5.

11. Henri Nouwen, *Clowning in Rome*, p. 68.

12. Ibid., pp. 70–71.

13. Evelyn Underhill, *Ruysbroeck* (London: Bell & Sons, 1915), p. 184.

14. Teilhard de Chardin, *The Divine Milieu*, p. 31.

15. Lawrence, *The Practice of the Presence of God*, p. 46.

16. *The Way of a Pilgrim*, trans. Helen Bacovcin (Garden City, NY: Doubleday Image Books, 1978), p. 41.

17. Edwards, *Living Simply Through the Day*, p. 92.

18. Quoted in Nouwen, *The Genessee Diary*, p. 178.

Chapter 16. *Meeting God in Others*

1. Thomas Merton, *New Seeds of Contemplation* (New York: New Directions, 1961), p. 64.

2. Evelyn Underhill, *Worship* (Harper & Bros., 1937), p. 168.

3. B. B. McKinney, "Let Others See Jesus in You," copyright 1924 by Robert H. Coleman (#423 in *The Broadman Hymnal*).

4. Frederick Buechner, *The Hungering Dark* (New York: Seabury Press, 1969), p. 23.

5. Merton, *New Seeds of Contemplation*, p. 66.

6. Scott Peck, "The Use of Religion in Psychotherapy."

7. John Youngblut, "Becoming a Contemplative Where You Are," a lecture delivered in October 1984 at St. John's United Methodist Church, Anderson, SC.

8. Bruce Larson, *There's a Lot More to Health Than Not Being Sick* (Waco, TX: Word Books, 1981), p. 63.

9. Underhill, *Worship*, p. 167.

10. Laubach, *Laubach's Prayer Diary*, p. 35.

11. Martin Buber, *Tales of the Hasidim, the Later Masters* (New York: Schocken Books, 1948), p. 135.

Epilogue

1. John Claypool, "Ministry and Expectations," a sermon preached on November 4, 1979, printed by Northminster Baptist Church, Jackson, MS. See also his *Opening Blind Eyes*, pp. 97ff.

2. L'Engle, *Walking on Water*, p. 156.